Theory of International Politics

Theory of International Politics

P. N. Chaturvedi

KUNAL BOOKS

New Delhi-110002 , India

KUNAL BOOKS
4596/1A, First Floor,
11, Daryaganj, New Delhi-110002
Phones: 9811043697, 011-30125412
E-mail: *Kunalbooks@gmail.com*

Theory of International Politics

First Published 2010

ISBN - 978-81-910085-1-7

Published in India by Prem Singh Bisht for Kunal Books, and printed at **Deepak Offset Press**, Delhi.

PREFACE

International politics, like all politics, is a struggle for power. Whatever the ultimate aims of international politics, power is always the immediate aim. States-men and peoples may ultimately seek freedom, secu-rity, prosperity, or power itself. They may define their goals in terms of a religious, philosophic, eco-nomic, or social ideal. They may hope that this ideal will materialize through its own inner force, through divine intervention, or through the natural develop-ment of human affairs. They may also try to further its realisation through non-political means, such as technical co-operation with other nations or inter-national organisations. But whenever they strive to realize their goal by means of international politics, they do so by striving for power. Political power is a psychological relation be-tween those who exercise it and those over whom it is exercised. It gives the former control over cer-tain actions of the latter through the influence which the former exert over the latter's minds. That influence derives from three sources: the ex-pectation of benefits, the fear of disadvantages, the respect or love for men or institutions. It may be exerted through orders, threats, persuasion, the authority or charisma of a man or of an office, or a combination of any of these.

While it is generally recognized that the inter-play of these factors, in ever changing combina-tions, forms the basis of all domestic politics, the importance of these factors for international poli-tics is less obvious, but no less real. There has been a tendency to reduce political power to the actual application of force or at least to equate it with successful threats of force and with persuasion, to the neglect of charisma. That neglect ac-counts in good measure for the neglect of prestige as an independent element in international poli-tics.

Theories of international politics deal with events at both the sub- and supra-national levels. Reductionist theories explain "the behavior of parts"-they seek to explain international outcomes solely through the behavior of units, leaving aside the effect their environment may have. However, "it is not possible to understand world politics simply by looking inside of states." This is because every new observed phenomenon would require the addition of new unit-level variables, which leads to the highly subjective addition and wild proliferation of variables. Moreover, though the actors and nature of actors in international politics change significantly, patterns of international politics recur. "If the same effects follow from different causes, then constraints must be operating on the independent variables in ways that affect outcomes."

Constructivism is one of the basic theories of international politics. Its central tenet is that most or even all important elements of international politics are the product of specific social circumstances and historical processes, rather than being inevitable consequences of the nature of humans or the nature of politics. This willingness to see international relations as socially constructed sets constructivism apart from traditional approaches to realism and liberalism/idealism. Significant authors include Alexander Wendt, John Ruggie, and Martha Finnemore.

P. N. Chaturvedi

Contents

	Preface	*v*
1.	Introduction	1
2.	Perspectives in the Study of International Politics	35
3.	Analytical Tools and Procedures	59
4.	International Politics and the One-party Regime	105
5.	Competing Visions of International Political Order	131
6.	Shifting the Politics of International Development	167
7.	Mass Politics in India	189
8.	Movement in the Key Concepts	217
9.	Politicizing Secularism	253
	Bibliography	273
	Index	277

1

Introduction

The science of international politics as a separate branch of academic learning is still in its infancy. The first chair of international politics was founded in 1919 at the University of Wales. That its first two occupants, Professors Zimmern and Webster, were distinguished historians is not an accident. For the subject matter of what we call today international politics has traditionally been regarded as a branch of historical studies, either of modern history in general or of diplomatic history in particular. Its recognition as a separate academic discipline coincided with, and was stimulated by, the establishment of the League of Nations, which was widely expected to transform international relations, to do away with international politics altogether, and thus to create the conditions for permanent peace.

In the letter offering a chair of international politics to the University of Wales, its purpose was described as "the study of those related problems of law and politics, of ethics and economics, which are raised by the project of a League of Nations, and for the encouragement of a truer understanding of civilisations other than out own." In its earliest stage, which is roughly delimited by the two World Wars, the science of international politics has indeed remained faithful to the purposes thus formulated. It has been eclectic in taking fragments from all kinds of sciences, social, humanistic, and natural, without being able to create of them a new and different whole.

It has been legalistic in conceiving international relations to move on two different levels: the legal one where states were told how to act and the diplomatic one where their actions were judged in view of their conformity or lack of conformity to the rules of international law. Finally, it has been moralistic in being more interested in the reform of international relations than in their understanding or at least in being unable to separate these two tasks in theory and practice. The first of the following selections brings the historic tradition to bear upon the problem of international politics and of politics in general. The second selection represents the school of thought predominant in the interwar period. The third selection exemplifies the methodological awakening which since the end of the Second World War has stimulated the development of a real science of international politics.

THE ART OF GUESSING IN POLITICS

Sir Herbert A. L. Fisher (1865-1940) was Professor of History at Oxford University, Member of Parliament, and British Delegate to the League of Nations. In this lecture, given a few days before the First World War came to an end, the great historian puts up, as it were, a warning sign for the new science of international politics which was just about to gain academic recognition. He shows the clairvoyance with which certain political events were foreseen by statesmen, scholars, and poets, and the complete surprise by which other political developments caught even the most experienced observers. The historic examples, taken from all periods of history, are most instructive in that they warn us against overconfidence in anybody's judgment where politics and especially international affairs are concerned.

The emphasis upon imagination and upon the limited usefulness of quantitative methods, upon the distorting effects of emotional involvement and upon the increase in the unreliability of forecasts in proportion to the vastness of the problem considered, is as timely today as it was more than thirty years ago.

POLITICAL PROPHECIES

The great perturbation of human affairs which the world has experienced during the past four years has given rise in every region of society to a vague expectation of change. In whatever direction we turn, whether we listen to the voices of the crowd in our own streets or to the murmurs which float in upon us from India or Arabia, from the Siberian Plains, or the sunlit coasts of the Pacific, we hear the same multitudinous hum of vague expectancy. The great war will usher in a new era, create a new society, replace old ideals by new ideals, establish the human family on a new basis, draw the lines of states upon a plan dictated by reasoned foresight, and once and for all eliminate the poisons which infect the body politic of Europe and those other parts of the habitable world which have fallen under European influence and control.

Unless statesmanship and morality are alike bankrupt, the tragedy of such a war as this must not recur. Schemes are drawn up for a regenerate Europe, for a purified and pacified world. Belief in progress is too deep-rooted to admit of our seeing in this European cataclysm nothing but a great retrogression, only by long and painful struggles to be retrieved. The greater the obvious calamity, the more determined are we to read into it a presage of benefits commensurate with the unchallenged and palpable evil. Never have the prophets been more active. Never since the great age of Messianic expectation has the human race been so much absorbed with the dark prospect of the future.

The phantom host from Archangel who marched through England on its way to Belgium during the autumn of 1914 reminds us of a fact, long known to the historians of religion, that beliefs are more often proportionate to desire than to evidence, and that if we only wish for a thing to happen with sufficient intensity, we may easily persuade ourselves that the object of our desire will be, or even has been fulfilled. It follows that, if we wish to estimate the aptitude of the present age for framing a correct forecast of the future, allowance must be made for this source of error. Sentiment obscures the judgement, passion clouds the vision. We refuse to admit that any prospect which seems to us to be odious and incompatible with a benignant scheme of the universe can in fact be possible.

In the same gallant spirit of optimism, with hopes hardly more exuberant and measureless, Condorcet, the condemned prisoner of the Jacobin tyranny, composed his grand design for the future of a perfected humanity. The materials for exact political forecast have been vastly improved since the French Revolution. We know more about the world in which we live, and are in a better position to gauge the forces which move it. Our statistics are more complete, our knowledge of the past is fuller; we have acquired, through the influence of the public press and of democratic institutions, a more perfected and better schooled habit of political calculation.

Certain vital factors affecting the growth and prosperity of nations, which were hardly appreciated by statesmen and publicists a hundred years ago, are now the common property of political observation. We can clearly predict, with a tolerable degree of accuracy, the life of a mine, and in time our geological surveys should enable us to forecast the development of all the mineral resources of a nation. We are, indeed, learning to estimate national power, not in terms of acres and square miles, but of iron ore and potash, of rubber and petroleum, of water-power and coal, of canals and textiles.

We cast the horoscope of states, peoples, and races by a study of comparative birth-rates, death-rates, emigration rates, and by such means essay to detect some of the larger features of the coming world, such as the growing urgency of the Yellow

Races, or the diminishing share of the Roman Catholic Church in the conduct of the world's affairs. But although our arms have gained in precision, the factors to be assessed have increased in number and complexity. In place of the isolated rivalries of the past, we are now faced with struggles in which the whole habitable globe is either directly or indirectly involved.

The problems have become so vast, their solution depends upon a forecast of so many improbable and concurrent factors, upon so vast a complexes of doubtful contingencies, that statesmanship, which should be all prescience, has become three parts guesswork. What statesman in 1914 could have predicted that the European War would last four years, that it would lead to the capture of Jerusalem or Bagdad by British armies, bring about the collapse of the Russian Tsardom, throw Finland into the arms of Germany, and cast the weight of the American Republic into the scale against the Central Powers?

For all our instruments of precision, our statistics, our historical and economic knowledge, our trained and experienced statesmen, we did not foresee any one of these events. I do not say that these occurrences ought not and should not have been predicted. Good modern historians, had they brought their knowledge up to date, which they very seldom permit themselves to do, might have regarded each one of these occurrences in the light of a probability. The fact, however, remains that none of these things were predicted, and that the whole course of the military and political evolution of the world during the last few years has been full of surprise even for those who are paid to be prescient.

To the mind of the ancients the experience of such great and unexpected changes in the disposition of the world, as those which are familiar to our own generation, suggested the play of a capricious Fortune or Providence, of whom little else could be predicated save a delight in confounding the anticipations of mankind. In recounting the last agonies of the Macedonian Empire, Polybius reminds his readers that the fall of the Macedonians was foretold by Demetrius of Phalerum a hundred and fifty years before, in a prophecy so remarkable as to deserve the name of inspiration. It is clear, however, that there is nothing in this prediction which we should now regard as evidence of distinguished prescience.

While recounting the conquest of Persia by Alexander the Great, Demetrius was naturally moved to comment upon the sudden obliteration of a powerful empire by a people, only fifty years earlier, unimportant and obscure. Who would have predicted such a revolution? It was clearly one of Fortune's favourite paradoxes, and not the last of them, for it was only to be expected that the same inscrutable Providence which had placed the Macedonians in the seat of pre-eminence would one day elect to withdraw its favours. In all this there is no profound philosophy. Demetrius does not attempt to assign a cause for the future downfall of the Macedonians, but is content to argue from his knowledge of the habits of Fortune that their empire was no more designed for immortality than the famous Persian polity which the sword of the Macedonian conqueror had humbled to the dust.

It is the more remarkable that Polybius should go out of his way to exalt this vague prediction, seeing that of all the historians of antiquity he is himself most noticeable for the true prophetic quality. Living in an age of astounding political revolutions, he has a keen eye for the large lines and decisive points of history. He sees the great fact of the rise of the Roman Empire in its true significance, assigns it to its true causes, and is prompt to realize that the Roman conquests have woven all the scattered threads of Mediterranean history into a single indissoluble whole. The duel between Rome and Carthage is presented in its genuine lineaments, at once as the collision between two incompatible types of polity and as the turning-point in the fate of the civilized world.

The son of the Achaean Lycortas and the friend of Scipio Aemilianus had no illusions as to the decadence of Greece and as to the enduring ascendancy of Rome. A long life consumed in war, politics, hunting, study, and travel had taught him the secret of the decline and fall of states. He notes the depopulation of the Greek cities, as a consequence of self-indulgence and a cause of decay, comments on the way in which the Macedonian conquests contributed to the spread of luxurious tastes among the simple Romans, and argues that some day in the revolution of things conquest will bring its own nemesis, and that the brilliant world state, the swift creation of which was the arresting fact of his own times, would be brought to the dust through the moral enervation of success.

For many centuries these passages of solemn warning must have seemed to the Roman readers of Polybius to be idle words. The Republic was succeeded by the Empire; the Eagles of the Empire were planted on the Tees and the Tigris, and the decline of this imposing polity, which, next to its rise, is the greatest event in world-history, was spread over so long a space of time and accompanied by means so gradual and complex, that the real significance of the vast changes which produced the mediaeval out of the ancient world was never distinctly apprehended by contemporaries. Ammianus Marcellinus, the soldier historian of the fourth century, comes nearest to the truth in the spirited narrative recording the decadence of Roman society and the formidable pressure of the barbarian tribes upon the fabric of the Empire. But though dimly conscious of impending fate, Ammianus never nerves himself to look into its stern and pitiless eyes.

The Roman Empire for him belongs to the eternal order of the Universe; and the same spirit of fatalism, running through all the political speculation of the middle Ages, prevented any just estimate of the measure and quality of the political transformations which were steadily breaking up the unity of the ancient world. Another great historical event, the falling away of the American colonies from their allegiance to England, had been considered probable by many acute observers for a generation before it actually occurred.

In France, where the wish was naturally father to the thought, Montesquieu gave it as his opinion as early as 1730 that England would be the first nation to be abandoned by her colonies, and similar predictions were subsequently made by D'Argenson, Turgot, and Vergennes. Montesquieu's argument was based upon the view that the colonist would not continue to tolerate the irksome fiscal restraints imposed by the mother country; but another and even stronger argument was supplied by a reflection as to the probable consequences of a British conquest of French Canada. In 1748 the Swedish traveller Kahn was told, not only by native Americans but by English emigrants, that within thirty or fifty years the English colonies in America might constitute a separate Republic entirely independent of England, and was persuaded that the neighbourhood of the French colony was the chief power making for the maintenance of a union which had long ceased to be grounded on any foundation of friendly sentiment.

And as the Seven Years' War proceeded it was an opinion common in France, and not altogether unrepresented in England, that the loss of Canada to the French would usher in the defection of the American colonies from Great Britain. The French Revolution presents a case of an event confidently and frequently predicted, but ill-measured and ill-judged when it actually occurred. It is, however, worthy of remark that the sense of impending revolution was more acute during the despotic anarchy of Louis XV's reign than in the years immediately preceding the catastrophe.

In the earlier period even a foreigner like Lord Chesterfield was impressed by the presence of all the symptoms of approaching change and revolution, and D'Argenson's Journals between 1740 and 1756 are full of the same apprehension; but as the long uneasy reign of Louis XV came to a natural end, and the ancient monarchy of France was found to have safely survived its period of disorder and humiliation and to be refurnished with a stock of good intentions, the presentiment of impending evil died away. Mr. Lecky points out that neither Franklin nor Frederick the Great, both of whom had special reasons or special opportunities for watching French affairs, had any glimpse of the approaching downfall of the monarchy, and it is a curious fact that in the voluminous correspondence of Madame Roland, who from the very first played an energetic part in French revolutionary politics, there is not a single allusion to current or future politics before the storm burst in 1789.

In general, the Revolution was judged in its initial stages with a lighthearted optimism, shared even by the gravest of German metaphysicians. The most profound diagnosis was supplied by Burke, whose warm and splendid imagination, upon this as upon other occasions, threw shafts of golden light into the obscurity of the future. Political philosophers are not famous for divination, seeing that even Aristotle, for all his opportunities at the court of Alexander, failed to detect the future of the Nation State, but Burke belongs to that small group of political thinkers among whom must be reckoned Polybius, De Tocqueville, Treitschke, and Seeley, whose minds are quickened to the large impending issues of the future.

We do not remember him so much for his detailed predictions, though he predicted the loss of the American colonies through the fiscal policy of the British Government, as from the fact that he was the first Englishman to envisage in its true promise and potency the growing polity of the North American States, the first to bring the peoples of India in a living shape to the minds of the distant mother nation who had drifted into the position of governing them, and the first to grasp the tremendous depth and devastating range of the French Revolution. Burke's estimate of the French Revolution is open to many criticisms, but in three respects he proved himself to be the best kind of political prophet, travelling to the right conclusions by a well-laid course of reasoning from the facts before him.

He was right in holding that a movement, springing not from a miscellany of opportunist calculations but from a coherent body of political doctrine having all the quality of religious faith, could not be confined to France alone, that it would spread through Europe like a flame, and that all the conservative elements in European society were concerned to resist it. He was right again in his view that the civil constitution of the clergy would constitute an irreparable breach between the new society and the old, and that the destruction of the privileges and independence of the Gallican Church would lead the way to a more highly centralized State. Finally, he was right in predicting that all this tumult and turmoil would end in a military despotism.

In all these respects Burke was led to the right conclusion by the employment of a sound method, and when we consider that these declarations were made in the autumn of 1790, before the fall of the monarchy, before the outbreak of war, and before the rise of the Jacobins, they must be acknowledged to be among the most remarkable documents of human prescience in the sphere of political speculation. Pitt's false prophecy that the end of the Papacy was in sight must be set off against the astonishing prediction (if indeed it be authentic) that Napoleon would meet with his ultimate check through a national rising in Spain. Napoleon's oracle, ' Europe will be either Cossack or Republican,' has not yet been realized, but another vaticination was more successful: he divined that France would soon tire of the Bourbons, and that, in spite of Waterloo, there was still a chance for his dynasty.

These are the predictions of statesmen. For the higher gifts of divination which depend upon an insight into the fundamental moral forces and aspects of the world, Wordsworth was superior to either Pitt or Napoleon. From the first he divined in the Spanish rising the presence of a fresh power in Europe, calculated to frustrate the designs of French Imperialism. His picture of the degraded condition of the boy operative in a cotton-mill might have been cited without irrelevance in all the denunciations of the half-time system from the date of the publication of *The Excursion* in 1814 until the abolition of the system by the passage of the Education Act in the present year.

The evils of industrialism, the establishment of a national system of compulsory education, the dangers of the illustrated press, are all foretold in the books of his prophetical statesmanship. On such matters he felt deeply, and therefore without extravagance, which is always shallow. Nobody with a decent mind desires to see the scenery of his home spoiled by the intrusion of railroads or factory chimneys, and Wordsworth in 1844 wrote a well known sonnet against the projected Kendal and Windermere railway- but that commonplace objection was not the only word which Wordsworth had to say on railways. In an earlier sonnet, composed during a tour in the summer of 1833, he had foreseen that the spread of industrialism would not be fatal to poetry, but that poetry would absorb industrialism and turn it to its own spiritual uses:

Nor shall your presence, howso'er it mar The loveliness of Nature, prove a bar To the Mind's gaining that prophetic sense Of Future change, that point of vision, whence May be discovered what in soul ye are.

The larger and more impressive tendencies of modern history have been too unmistakable to escape the notice of competent observers, though even the most sagacious have erred in their estimate as to the time at which or the mode in which a particular change was to be accomplished. In so far as it is based upon an intellectual process at all, a political prediction is nothing more than an historical generalisation, varying in exactitude with the knowledge and acumen of the prophet. From his insight into the nature and historical antecedents of the German people Heine was well advised in warning the French in 1834 that they must not be deceived by mild-eyed philosophies, but that one fine day the old heathen gods of Germany would rise from their graves, and Thor with his giant hammer set to work upon Gothic cathedrals. A feeling of national pride, stimulated by the stirring achievements of his race, led an Elizabethan poet to predict in the year 1602 the spread of the English language over the world:

Who in time knows whither we may vent The treasure of our tongue? To what strange shores This gain of our best glory shall invent To enrich the unknowing nations with our stores? What worlds in the yet unformed occident May come refined with accents that are ours?

Yet Bacon thought that his Essays would survive rather in their Latin than in their English garb, and, long after Bacon and Daniel were laid in their graves, Gibbon, doubting the appeal of his own language, wrote an early work on the History of Switzerland in French, as the tongue likely to secure for it the greatest circulation among polite readers. The incident is also memorable as the occasion of a striking prediction. Hume, to whom the manuscript was submitted, recommended the author to use his native English in words which show a real intellectual grasp of the future.

'Let the French,' he wrote, 'triumph in the present diffusion of their tongue. Our solid and increasing establishments in America, where we need less dread the inundation of Barbarians, promise a superior stability and duration to the English language.' Advice of uncommon sagacity which the recipient of the letter was wise enough to follow. In making predictions as to the future of his own country a prophet is helped by a great mass of instinctive, as well as of acquired, knowledge which is not available when he attempts to generalize as to the future course of foreign States.

The knowledge possessed by the inhabitants of any one country as to the social and political conditions of any other country is almost always so imperfect and superficial that popular generalisations upon foreign peoples and foreign policies go, for the most part, wildly astray. In the later part of the eighteenth century it was the accepted view upon the continent of Europe that England was a decadent power, a sort of 'insular Poland'-selfish, corrupt, torn by factions, without nerve or consistency, fast tottering to a bankrupt's grave.

'It is very easy,' wrote Rousseau in 1760, 'to see those twenty years hence England will be ruined, and furthermore will have lost her liberty,' a view not confined to men of letters but widely held in Courts and Cabinets. Thus Joseph II of Austria declared that England was fallen wholly and for ever, that she had become a second-class power like Sweden and Norway, and was probably destined to fall under the sway of Russia; and judgements equally unfavourable were passed upon us by Catharine II of Russia and by Frederick II of Prussia. Indeed there was upon the Continent during the years preceding the wars of the Revolution and the Empire an undervaluation of British power and resources as serious and misleading as that which prevailed in Germany in the first decade of the twentieth century.

In each case enormous policies, affecting the whole future of the world, were based on insufficient knowledge and false estimates of the future. Of the governing tendencies of the modern world by far the most important is the spread of democracy, and the literature which has grown up round democratic institutions is as voluminous as the importance of the subject demands. Yet it is no exaggeration to say that many leading features of modern democracy were wholly unforeseen by the men who first undertook to enlighten the world upon the subject. The political writers at the end of the eighteenth and the beginning of the nineteenth centuries wrote and thought of democracy in terms coloured, if not dictated, by memories of classical antiquity.

Even the founders of the American constitution, who were not theorists but practical statesmen, failed to foresee some of the most important features of American social life and constitutional development. They laboured under the delusion that because simplicity and equality had been the marks of the ancient Republic, and were certainly features of the social conditions then prevailing in the colonies, these qualities would permanently belong to the gigantic State which it was their office to create. They foresaw neither the large fortunes nor the huge and dominating Trusts which have given the ply to American institutions, and in general they were precluded, by reason of the fact that all previous experience of democracies had been confined to small States, from apprehending the way in which the problem of popular rule would work itself out in the immense framework of the American Republic.

The political boss, the Nominating Convention, and all the unseen arts of management without which the new machine could not be effectually worked, were quite beyond the apprehension of the members of the Philadelphia Convention, and if Alexander Hamilton could have lived to see the day when it could be truthfully said that 'the man who designates the delegates to the Nominating Convention is really the most powerful man in the United States, and that everybody but a President in his second year is at his mercy,' he would have been the first to confess that the fabric of the Federal Constitution had undergone a profound change which no one of his contemporaries did in fact predict or could have been expected to infer from the available evidence before him.

Among the early observers of the democratic institutions of the New World, De Tocqueville is fullest of the prophetic spirit. In 1833 he saw the main characteristics of democratic civilisation with all the clairvoyance of temperamental dislike. Many of the defects which he noted as present in American society, and regarded to be incidental to democratic civilisation in general, have been mitigated by the sobering influences of history, though it would be rash to say that they are not still perceptible both in America and in other democratic countries.

He may have overrated the extent to which subservience to public opinion, jealousy of personal eminence, blind acquiescence in vulgar standards, are to be counted as permanent qualities in democratic society, and but that every such society is especially susceptible to these charges is probably true. Mill, whose sympathies were on the side of democracy, thought that if De Tocqueville had lived to know what the New England States had become thirty years after, he would have acknowledged that much of the unfavourable part of his anticipations had not been realized. However this may be, De Tocqueville certainly estimated aright the true proportions of the colour problem, and in effect predicted the American Civil War.

It is also part of his claim to greatness to have explained to Europe that democracy was a form of civilisation rather than a form of government, and that the world was entering on a democratic age. The full significance of the survival in Prussia of a mediaeval polity, based on the divine right of kings, served by a feudal aristocracy and capable of employing all the arts and sciences of modern life to serve its ends, had not dawned upon him. He was too wise, however, to claim oracular powers, and upon his own confession the history of his own country was full of unexpected disenchantments. 'I set myself,' he wrote after the revolution of 1848, 'to retrace in my memory the history of the last sixty years, and I smiled bitterly as I thought of the illusions which accompanied each stage of this long revolution, the theories on which these illusions were nourished, the learned dreams of our historians, and all the ingenious and erroneous systems with the aid of which men had tried to explain a present which was not yet clearly seen and to predict a future which was not seen at all.'

Another error not confined to any one country or to any one school of political thought, has been the common assumption that democracy inevitably desires democratic legislation. Up till the Franchise Act of 1917, all the Reform Bills in this country have been violently attacked and energetically advocated upon this erroneous assumption. Yet, though eighty-six years have passed since the first Reform Act, there is still a great fund of conservative policy in the country. The House of Lords is in being, the Anglican Church holds its own, and the Tory party has enjoyed its fair share of office. Experience has shown that few speculations are so uncertain as those concerning the probable consequences of an extension of the franchise, nor was there any more remarkable feature of the franchise debates of 1917 than the abandonment by tacit consent of this ancient field of contentious augury and gratuitous error.

Nor has History been kind to those thinkers who, standing in the main line of the English liberal tradition, too hastily assumed that the world was passing out of a military into an industrial stage. The first apostles of Free Trade judged aright the economic consequences likely to flow from the adoption of their policy, but were disposed to exaggerate the influence of economic exchange as a factor making for peace. Closer intercourse, while it is a condition of friendship, is also a cause of friction, and the first result of the Commercial Treaty of 1860 between England and France was the outburst of a storm of indignation against this country in the forests and factories of our present Ally. It was reasonable to hope with Michel Chevalier that the development of the railway system in Europe would 'remove hereditary animosities and firmly cement nation to nation in a lasting peace.' But has this prediction been fulfilled?

A few years after it was uttered Von Moltke and Roon were giving the world the first demonstration of the scientific use of railway power in modern war. The union of the German States under the hegemony of Prussia had been foretold so often that many sagacious minds were doubtful whether, in fact, it could ever be realized. Lord Robert Cecil, who, as Lord Salisbury, was destined to rule in our Foreign Office for many years, contended in a *Quarterly* article on the Danish duchies, written in 1864, that Germany would never be united. Such a view was by no means foolish or fantastic. For centuries the most prominent fact in European politics had been the disunion of Germany and the rivalry of her warring States.

One short-lived movement towards union had been crushed in 1815; another, more recent and more determined, had broken down in a calamitous failure in 1849. It was not, therefore, unreasonable to imagine that the obstacles, which had prevailed for several centuries, would be sufficiently strong to avert union even four years before union was, in fact, accomplished, and, indeed, it is probable that anything short of the very surprisingly rapid success of the Prussian army in the campaign against Austria would have involved the whole Prussian project in uncertainty.

Posterity should not be too hard on statesmen if, in order to meet the urgent necessities of the moment, they consent to arrangements which, later on, under altered conditions, are found to be prejudicial. All political decisions are taken under great pressure, and if a treaty serves its turn for ten or twenty years, the wisdom of its framers is sufficiently confirmed. In view of the great period of rivalry between the British and German Empires which has opened out since 1890, it seems to argue a strange lack of foresight in British statesmen that they should have promoted the cession of Rhenish Provinces to Prussia in 1815 and of Heligoland in 1890.

Yet each transaction is defensible in the light of the general system of foreign policy which this country was pursuing at the time, the first when we reflect upon the danger which Europe had experienced from the ambition of Napoleon and upon the assumed necessity of erecting a powerful bulwark against the repetition of any French scheme of aggrandizement, and the second (though here the defence is far weaker) when it is recalled that it was then the established policy of Lord Salisbury's Government to maintain cordial relations with the German Empire, that the growth of a powerful German Navy was not suspected, and that a set-off to the cession of Heligoland was supplied by the acquisition of Zanzibar.

It is, however, remarkable how little the military strength of Prussia was appreciated at its true value in the decade preceding the Franco-Prussian War. 'The Prussians,' wrote Lord Palmerston in 1863, 'are brave and make good soldiers, but all military men who have seen the Prussian Army at its annual reviews of late years have unequivocably declared their opinion that the French would walk over it and get without difficulty to Berlin.' A year later Disraeli, who was even more fundamentally misinformed, declared, 'Prussia is a country without any bottom, and in my opinion could not maintain a war for six weeks.'

When two years later, war did break out between Prussia and Austria; it was the universal expectation, even in the best instructed circles of Germany, that the war would be long and sanguinary. Mohl, the Wórttemberg jurist, expected it to last for a generation; Hohenlohe, the Bavarian statesman, looked forward to protracted campaigns. Even the rapid victory of the needle gun in Bohemia did not unseal the eyes of Europe. When the war of 1870 broke out, Delane wrote to W. H. Russell: 'Nothing shall ever persuade me except the event that the Prussians will withstand the French, and I would lay my last shilling upon Casquette against Pumpernickel.' Such was the wisdom of the editor of the leading newspaper of the world.

The acquisition of Alsace-Lorraine by Prussia in 1871 was at the time regarded by Bismarck with just misgiving; but he allowed himself to be overborne by the soldiers. The consequences of this unprincipled act of spoliation were, however, foreseen, even in Germany, more particularly by Karl Marx, who predicted at the time that France would be thrown into the arms of Russia, and that the robbery would bring upon Germany a racial war against the united power of the Slavs and the Latins. Never has a prophecy been more exactly fulfilled.

That war is full of surprises is a maxim as old as Thucydides, and there has never been a war which has not brought confusion to the prophets. Many years before the great storm broke, in August 1914, Europe had been uneasily conscious of gathering clouds, and a whole literature had grown up about the impending conflict. Yet the attitude which Great Britain and Italy would adopt upon the outbreak of hostilities between the German Powers and the Dual Alliance was quite uncertain, and few people before 1898 predicted that Turkey would be ranged on the side of the Central Powers.

Moreover, the entry of America into the War, by far the most important occurrence of our age, was, so far as I am aware, entirely unforeseen by any of those numerous thinkers who concerned themselves with speculations as to the immediate political future of the world. It was as unforeseen in America as it was in Europe and this on many grounds of political tradition and racial mixture: but the unforeseen has come to pass. On the other hand, some leading military and economic features of the world struggle were divined as early as 1898 by a sagacious Polish banker, who applied a trained economic intelligence to the task of interpreting such lessons as might be extracted from the latest improvements in the military art.

The principal data before Camille Bloch were the magazine rifle, the range-finder, smokeless powder, and the increased power and accuracy of the artillery arm. From a study of these data Bloch was led to conclude that a war waged upon a large scale between such international combinations as the Triple and the Dual Alliance would lead to a stalemate. Owing to the destructiveness of modern warfare the next war would be a war of entrenchments, in which the spade would be as indispensable to the soldier as the rifle. 'Battles,' he said, 'will last for days, and at the end it is very doubtful whether any decisive victory would be gained.'

The war of the future would be a long war, for there was no chance of armies running short of munitions. Of necessity 'it would partake of the character of a siege operation, and would be brought to an end not by a military decision, in the old sense of the term, but by famine.' 'The future of war,' he declared, 'is not fighting but famine, not the slaying of men but the bankruptcy of nations.' Even the victorious power would be fatally injured by the destruction of resources and the break-up of society. On the assumption that the five continental countries, comprising respectively the Triple and Dual Alliance, were engaged, he calculated that two and a half million men would be fighting, and that the total cost distributed among the combatant nations would be four million sovereigns a day.

All this furnishes an excellent example of the limits within which it is reasonable to hope that a careful and dispassionate study of economic and technical data may enable accurate predictions to be made as to the course and character of future wars. Bloch had not all the technical data before him, with which we are all now familiar, nor had he the imagination to forecast them. He knew neither aeroplane nor machine gun, neither tank nor submarine, neither gas nor gas-mask, but he had seen enough to realize that modern military science had created engines of destructiveness so greatly in excess of all previous records as to create a new problem, and he was entitled to argue that any future developments of the military art would only aggravate the general tendency which he had set himself to explore.

In the event his forecast of the future course of the present war was more correct than that of the German Higher Command; but it might easily have been otherwise, and, as an exhaustive statement of the possibilities of the case, his ingenious volumes are clearly defective in that they omit to consider the possibility of a sudden collapse of one of the combatant nations either owing to military mismanagement or to failure of the popular nerve. On the economic side, again, Bloch failed to pay adequate regard to the stimulus which war imparts to industrial inventiveness, organisation, and economy. In common with all other political reasoners, he failed to predict the part which women might be made to play in modern war and in the industries on which modern war is nourished, and in a hundred other particulars history has refused to substantiate his predictions.

Nevertheless, to him belongs the credit of pointing out for the first time a fact of surpassing importance, the significance of which we have only just begun to realize, that as the destructiveness of armaments increases, the rate of destruction diminishes until the cost of a slain enemy reaches a figure which is not only uneconomic but ruinous. In a graphic way he said that war was impossible, by which he meant, not that war would not be waged in future, but that the old-fashioned, chivalrous, swift, and decisive war, the *frisch-frφhlicher Krieg* of the egregious Crown Prince, was henceforward an affair of the *ancien rıgime,* an historic curiosity.

Narrow the problem of war to one or other of its technical aspects, and the chances of an accurate prediction are increased. The forecast of the Blue Water School that this island could not be successfully invaded from the sea is a triumphant exemplification of accurate reasoning within a limited sphere governed by considerations capable of accurate measurement. So, too, was Admiral Sir Percy Scott's forecast of the part which the submarine was destined to play in naval warfare.

As soon, however, as the question is extended beyond the possibilities contained in this or that application of military or naval power to a survey of the future of war in general, with all the moral and psychological imponderables, the possibilities of error become infinitely greater. In this sphere the imaginative historian is more likely to hit the mark than the encyclopaedic statistician. Travelling through the clouds, he may, nevertheless, find the goal. Renan, writing in September 1870, under the shadow of a great military disaster, argued that in the next war, which would be a war of races and therefore of extermination, England would be found on the side of France. The reason which he advanced was a poet's reason.

We were steadily becoming, like France, more Celtic and less Germanic in our general outlook upon life. 'France,' he writes, 'is one of the conditions of English prosperity. England is every day becoming more Celtic and less Germanic in virtue of that great law which ordains that the primitive race of a country eventually asserts its supremacy over all the invasions. In the great struggle of races England is with us. The alliance of France and England is founded for centuries. Whether we think of the United States, of Constantinople, or of India, England will see that she has need of France and of a strong France.'

These are remarkable words. Renan had a clear sense of the mediaeval character of Prussian militarism and of the danger which it opposed to the democratic countries of the West. At the same time he had been impressed by the quality of contemporaneous English literature, and more particularly by the Free Trade philosophy which had led to the commercial treaty between England and France in 1860. He felt instinctively that in all this there was something utterly alien to the Prussian spirit, and that the collision of ideals would lead one day to the clash of arms. The opposition between English ways and Prussian, which was so present to the minds of Bismarck and Treitschke, seemed to Renan, who knew so much less but divined so much more, to be one of the great facts which would dominate the future of Europe.

So, while Moltke's guns were booming, he foretold the ultimate opposition of the British and the German Empires, and at the same time, with the prescience of genius, discerned the unsound quality of the new German Imperialism. I cannot deny myself the pleasure of a quotation from the *Nouvelle Lettre ΰ Strauss,* written in 1871, with the exquisite measure and delicacy of which Renan was a master: 'Excess of patriotism injures those works of universal significance which are grounded in the words of St. Paul: *Non est Iudaeus neque Graecus.*

It is just because your great men eighty years ago were not too patriotic that they opened out that large way wherein we are their disciples. I fear that your ultra-patriotic generation, repelling as it does everything which is not purely Germanic, is preparing for itself a more restricted audience. Jesus and the founders of Christianity were not Germans. Your Goethe recognized that he owed something to the corrupt France of Voltaire and Diderot. Let us leave these narrow fanaticisms to the lower regions of opinion. Permit me to say it, you have declined.'

Two forms of oracle we shall always do well to examine with special care, those which proceed from the advocate and the pessimist. When has a measure been defended without confident asseveration of golden consequences which have never ensued, or attacked without predictions of evil which experience has refused to endorse? No one was more closely concerned with the inner history of working-class radicalism during the first decade of the nineteenth century than Francis Place, the Westminster tailor. Yet he prophesied that the repeal of the combination law of 1800 would put an end to Trades Unions.

Anxiety to secure support for the removal of an odious statute, coupled with a dislike of Trades Unions as obstacles to individual liberty, led him to express a belief calculated, indeed, to assuage the anxieties of his opponents, but destined to be completely overthrown by the realities of subsequent history. ... In general it is wise for the fighting politician, even if he be eminent in letters, to eschew predictions with respect to causes which he has at heart, unless he is careful to adopt language of the vaguest and most general description.

Ten years ago it was confidently asserted by one of our most brilliant living Englishmen that Australians could never be reconciled to paying for a war undertaken for the defence of

Belgian neutrality. At the time when the words were written the chances seemed a thousand to one against a disproof of such a proposition being afforded within a generation. Yet the very thing, which was cited in disparagement of Seeley's outlook on contemporary history, has, in fact, been brought to pass.

If the verdicts of our best men are very fallible, even when they are dealing with the prospects of a civilisation which they know, how much more fallible are our estimates of the mysterious East? If we exclude the prescient anticipations of Brinkling and Oliphant, what western statesman or publicist can claim to have foretold in the sixties the rise of Japan? How few, even with the evidence supplied by the Chinese students who frequented the universities of America, predicted the establishment of a Republic in China?

It is equally safe to distrust the pessimist. The prophet who foretells the degeneracy of his race may be doing a useful service in his day, but he is almost always convicted by the searchlight of to-morrow. A Cambridge pedant once published a lament over the degeneracy of England, but the sheets were hardly dry from the press before the conquests of Wolfe and Clive laid the foundations of the British Empire. The jeremiads of Robert Lowe and Thomas Carlyle are pretty reading, but after all we have 'shot Niagara' and are still a flourishing people, not altogether devoid of valour, faith, endurance, charity, and other estimable qualities of hand and heart: nor, so far as we can see, is the race of heroes entirely extinct upon this planet.

THE ENCYCLOPEDIC SCIENCE OF INTERNATIONAL RELATIONS

Sir Alfred Zimmern was Professor of International Relations at Oxford from 1930-44 and Deputy Director of the League of Nations International Institute of Intellectual Co-operation from 1926-30. It is safe to say that Professor Zimmern was the most influential representative of our field during the interwar period. His opinions concerning the nature of the science of international relations, as they were expressed at the numerous study conferences held under the auspices of the International Institute of Intellectual Co-operation, were rarely questioned by his colleagues. The following statement can therefore be regarded as representative of the conception of our subject matter, as it prevailed in the interwar period.

Three of its characteristics stand out: its extreme vagueness, which envelops virtually all fields of human knowledge; its unconcern with methodological problems, which not only deprives it of the ability to distinguish between what belongs rightfully to the subject matter and what does not, but also blurs the vital difference between mere unprovable opinion and objective truth; finally, its aimless humanitarianism, which is more interested in "international understanding," that is, the spreading of good will among individuals of different nationalities, than in the understanding of the facts of international life, that is, a real science of international affairs.

What is "International Relations," conceived as a branch of study? It is described in the *Examination Statutes and Regulations* of the University of Oxford as a subject which "includes the study of the relations both between governments and between peoples, and of the principles underlying their development." This phrase was drafted with characteristic British vagueness. The word "includes" is vague, since it leaves open the possibility for extension outside the specified field. The word "peoples" is vague, since it may refer solely to the citizens or subjects of the governments referred to in the line above, or also to the other unspecified social groups existing within or across the dividing lines of States and their governments. And the word principles" is vague, since it may simply mean a scientific generalisation or may contain a normative implication.

Let us stretch the definition to its widest limits and see how far it carries us. We are committed by it to the study of the relations between social groups in general and, arising out of this, to the study, firstly, of the uniformities observable in this field - call them laws, principles, tendencies, forces, or what you will; secondly, of the rules of conduct that come into play in connection with them; I do not say "arise out of them," for rules of conduct cannot be deduced from the uniformities of science; they can only arise from the application of a criterion of a different order, residing within the individual consciousness.

Thus considered, the study of international relations extends from the natural sciences at one end to moral philosophy, or even further, at the other. One cannot rule out of it the factors of physical geography which determine the life and mutual relations of social groups, or those factors of biological or, more specifically, of medical science which affect the growth or diminution or physical improvement or deterioration of populations; or even such a law of physics as that which gives large ships a natural economic advantage over small ones because a ship's carrying power varies as the cube of her dimensions, whilst the resistance offered by the water increases only a little faster than the square of her dimensions.

Nor, at the opposite end, can we rule out such considerations of moral philosophy or religious principle as *led Francesco de Vitoria* to lay it down that Christian duty and Natural Law were not bounded by latitude and longitude and that "the whole earth is in some sort one republic." So regarded, the study of international relations would be practically identical with the study of Sociology in its widest extent. The only difference would be one of emphasis. Sociology lays the stress on the unity of human society, whereas International Relations lays it upon the diversity of the various human groups and the necessity for studying their interaction. It would also be practically identical with the study of history, if History is regarded, as Professor Toynbee in his recent study has pleaded that it should be regarded, as the record of the rise and fall, growth, development and interaction of civilisations.

The difference here would be that History lays the stress on the movement of societies and the changes to which they are subjected, whereas International Relations tends to study them in their interaction at any given moment. But, it will be said, these are barren and abstract definitions, very unhelpful to the cause of our Conference. If any practical conclusion is to be drawn from them, it can only be that one should admit into our body institutions studying any branch of human and even perhaps of natural science....

On such questions, for instance, as migration or the growth of population, biologists would enable us to see connections of cause and effect where students of politics in the narrower sense might be inclined to see nothing but the play of policy or even of accident. Thus, in the interests of the Conference itself we might well inscribe on our banner the words: *Nihil humani alienum a nobis putamus.* Having thus surveyed the field which we can legitimately claim as our own, let us consider how much of it we can effectively occupy in the present stage of the development of our study. Here we cannot but be guided by the experience of our Conference the composition of which, looked at - as we can now look at it - over a period of years, seems to testify to the working of a kind of unconscious logic.

The Conference, in its present form, with the wide variety of institutions represented in it and of the qualifications of the scholars who have taken part in its deliberations, would appear to have accepted the broad definition suggested above but to have limited it to the study of *contemporary international relations.* It has been hospitable to every branch of social and humane study, from geography to philosophy, but the subjects chosen for discussion have been problems of the world of to-day. It has, in fact, changed one word only in the comprehensive programme laid down for it above -*Nihil hodierni alienum a nobis putamus* might well have been inscribed on the title-pages of our published volumes and other proceedings. And if, as is suggested, the next subject of discussion is chosen from the field of the social studies, in the narrower sense of the term, this spirit of comprehensiveness will be even more in evidence.

We can now perhaps turn back to consider the effect of our broad definition and of the not very much less broad practice of the Conference itself upon the problem of university organisation. From the academic point of view, International Relations, as we have just been regarding it, are clearly not a subject in the ordinary sense of the word. It does not provide a single coherent body of teaching material. It is impossible to compress its elements within a textbook or within the limits of an examination syllabus. It is not a single subject but a bundle of subjects; if our Italian colleagues will allow me to use the expression, it is a *fascio*. Of what is this bundle composed? Of law, economics, political science, geography, and so on - but not of the whole range of each of these subjects.

Large tracts of them have not come directly within our purview at all. If our legal, economic, geographical and political science colleagues respectively had found themselves in a specialist Congress instead of in our midst, they would have handled their material very differently. Thus, we are not simply dealing with a group of subjects indiscriminately thrown together but with a group of subjects viewed from a common angle. Viewed from that angle, one part of them is in the light, the rest remaining, as it were, in the shadow.

The different subjects converge, so to speak, to a common point, a point from which the contemporary world of public affairs can be observed. Prehistoric geography, for instance, is in the shadow, the political geography of the present-day world is in the light. The mathematical analysis of the abstract economist is in the shadow, the play of economic tendencies in 1935 is in the light. The social contract theory is in the shadow, the analysis of the working of the Geneva institutions is in the light. The relations between the Civil and the Canon Law are in the shadow; the relations between municipal and international law are in the light. And so with the other special sciences with which we have come into contact.

What is the bearing of this on the problem of academic organisation? Surely it is that International Relations is not a new branch of study the claims of which require to be championed as against the competition of older subjects, but that it is a point of view which is accessible to the teachers of those older subjects themselves. Many of them have, in fact, been teaching the subject in the past without knowing it. One distinguished example must suffice. When Ernest Renan, who was neither a lawyer, nor a political scientist, nor an economist, nor a geographer, delivered a lecture at the Sorbonne on March 11th, 1882 On *Qu'est-ce qu'une Nation,* was he not making a contribution to the study of international relations?

By all means let Chairs of International Relations be founded, so long as they are not occupied by men who claim a monopoly of the subject. By all means let Departments of International Relations be established, by a grouping together of kindred studies, if this is found to be convenient for teaching or examination purposes. But let it never be forgotten that no academic regulations can set frontiers to our study, which, like the wind, bloweth where it listeth, and, like the birds, can pick up seeds of wisdom in the most unexpected quarters.

But if we can lay down no hard and fast rules for the academic organisation of our common study, something can nevertheless be said about the type of student best adapted for it. To penetrate to the understanding of the contemporary world, in all the complexity and simultaneity of its manifestations, is a gift not lightly bestowed. It requires a special quality of mind, and indeed of the whole personality, which is sometimes inborn, sometimes the result of training, but in any case unusual, even in academic circles. At its best it is a species of modern humanism, with a rich background of culture nurtured by philosophic reflection and the prolonged observation of men and cities. ...

The greatest danger which confronts our subject is to regard it as a subject for beginners. The greatest danger which confronts our students is that they should approach the material of our subject in what our French colleagues call *l'esprit primaire.* It is this spirit, more perhaps than any other single cause, which has blocked the path of international understanding during the last fifteen years, both in the field of ideas and in the field of political action. The attempt has been made to simplify international relations, to clothe them in language intelligible to the man in the street, to enshrine them in attractive formulae, to reduce them to watchwords, even to enshroud them in a bewitching mysticism.

Against all such tendencies, we teachers should set ourselves with all our forces. Our subject is not easy; it is very difficult. International relations are not simple; they are very complex. To simplify them is to destroy their essence, to eliminate the whole substance of their problems. Our task as teachers is to keep the eyes of our students fixed upon the world, in all the variety and simultaneity of its problems, to help them to understand even better what, if the philosophers will forgive me, I would call the altogether ness of public affairs, that problem of the One in the Many, the Many in the One, which has been in the minds of the great political thinkers ever since the Greek age and must be more than ever before our minds in the first generation of the League of Nations.

And it is equally our task to inspire our students with the courage to face this great and difficult task like men - to fortify their wills, to invigorate their powers, to call up the utmost resources of their personality. It is perhaps because we have not been bold enough in this way, because we have not had the courage of our own intellectual convictions that the appeal to heroism has been left to those whose doctrines are in reality soft and easy narcotics rather than energizers. In a book written nearly a hundred years ago, a great English educational thinker, Cardinal Newman, describes in a few sentences the contrast which I have been trying to suggest between what I called the primary approach and the educated approach to world affairs. The passage, familiar though it will be to some, may perhaps fitly conclude this brief introduction to a large subject:

> We sometimes fall in with persons who have seen much of the world, but who generalize nothing, and have no observation, in the true sense of the word. They abound in information in detail, curious and entertaining, about men and things; and, having lived under the influence of no very clear or settled principles, religious or political, they speak of everyone and everything only as so many phenomena, which are complete in themselves and lead to nothing, not discussing them, or teaching any truth, or instructing the hearer, but simply talking.
>
> The case is the same still more strikingly where the persons in question are beyond dispute men of inferior powers and deficient education. Perhaps they have been much in foreign countries, and they receive, in a passive, otiose, unfruitful way, the various facts which are forced upon them there. Seafaring men, for example, range from one end of the earth to the other; but the multiplicity of external objects which they have encountered forms no symmetrical and consistent picture upon their imagination; they see the tapestry of human life, as it were on the wrong side, and it tells no story.
>
> They sleep, and they rise up, and they find themselves, now in Europe, now in Asia; they see visions of great cities and wild regions; they are in the marts of commerce, or amid the islands of the South; they gaze on Pompey's Pillar, or on the Andes; and nothing which meets them carries them forward or backward, to any idea beyond itself. Nothing has a drift or

relation; nothing has a history or a promise. Such is mere acquisition, and, repeat, no one would dream of calling it philosophy. Every thing stands by itself, and comes and goes in its turn, like the shifting scenes of a show, which leave the spectator where he was.

Perhaps you are near such a man on a particular occasion, and expect him to be shocked or perplexed at something which occurs; but one thing is much the same to him as another, or if he is perplexed, it is not knowing what to say, whether it is right to admire, or to ridicule, or to disapprove, while conscious that some expression of opinion is expected from him; for in fact he has no standard of judgment at all, and no landmarks to guide him to a conclusion. With this picture of the seafarer of his day, and of some of the "Current Events" students of our own, Newman contrasts what he calls "the illuminative reason" which "puts the mind above the influences of chance and necessity, above anxiety, suspense, unsettlement and superstition, which is the lot of the many."

Such an intellect, he says, "which has been disciplined to the perfection of its powers, which knows, and thinks while it knows, which has learned to leaven the dense mass of facts and events with the elastic force of reason, such an intellect cannot be partial, cannot be exclusive, cannot be impetuous, cannot be at a loss, cannot but be patient, collected, and majestically calm, because it discerns the end in every beginning, the origin in every end, the law in every interruption, the limit in each delay; because it ever knows where it stands, and how its path lies from one point to another. ..."

THE METHODOLOGICAL FOUNDATION

In the paper from which the following excerpts are taken, we have what is to our knowledge the first rigorous examination of the methodological prerequisites of a science of international politics. The paper is also remarkable for its emphasis of international politics as the core of the study of international relations, an emphasis which is now widely accepted but was in 1933 a rather daring dissent from the prevailing opinion. The contrast between this chapter and Professor Zimmern's contribution to the problem reveals in the most striking fashion two fundamentally different approaches to the science of international politics. While Professor Spykman's pioneering effort has found little direct recognition, the general trend of the development since the end of the Second World War follows clearly the lines drawn by him. This is obvious from the recent systematic attempts to give the science of international politics a firm conceptual framework and from the recent contributions to the methodology of that science to be found, for instance, in the journal *World Politics*.

2

Perspectives in the Study of International Politics

A subject called international relations began to appear in the curricula of American colleges and universities before World War I. These courses were taught chiefly by scholars trained in history and in international law, and reflected strongly the approaches and perspectives of those ancient and respected disciplines. After World War I, international studies put out new branches. Formation of the League of Nations inspired the introduction of courses on international organisation. The term international relations acquired new dimensions, some of them nonpolitical. Largely for this reason, some teachers and writers began to use the term international politics to denote the interactions and relations of organized national communities, especially those transactions which involved some element of opposition or resistance or struggle or conflict.

During the 1930's, scholars who specialized in international politics moved progressively away from the approaches and perspectives of diplomatic history and international law. Writing on international political subjects became more analytical, topical, and schematic. In this, international political analysts were following a trail blazed by some of the great pioneers in the development of social science. Broadly speaking, the trend was towards more formal modes of analysis, more explicit concepts, a growing collection of models and theories, and technical vocabularies.

Most of the recent writings on international politics reflect the influence of these newer tools and approaches. This book is no exception. The reader will find some technical vocabulary, numerous conceptual schemes, analytical models and theories-all introduced for just one purpose: to stimulate insights and to promote understanding of the activities called international politics. Those who attempt to use the newer tools of political analysis occasionally run into resistance. This comes, in part, from those who believe that intuition is inherently superior to more formal approaches and theories, which are sometimes contemptuously dismissed as mere "methodology."

Resistance comes also from disillusioned souls who expected much from the newer tools and approaches, and have become disappointed and even cynical because of the comparatively meager results thus far achieved. These two kinds of criticism can perhaps be illustrated by a homely analogy. The first set of critics can be likened to the carpenter who goes on using familiar tools after new (and possibly more efficient) tools are invented. The second are like the carpenter who builds a house with the new tools, dislikes the finished structure-and throws away the tools.

Every complex human activity develops special concepts and theories, and technical vocabularies to express them. In order to comprehend any specialized activity one has to learn its technical terms and theories. Take baseball, for instance. This game has a formidable vocabulary, words used with highly specialized meanings: diamond, outfield, the grass, mound, strike, ball, double play, sacrifice, fielder's choice, triple, and many others. Baseball also has inspired elaborate theorizing regarding the conditions or odds favouring one strategy in preference to some other: for example, when to walk a hitter deliberately; when to sacrifice to advance a base runner; when to attempt a play at the plate; and a great many other strategies.

The spectator rarely learns as much about the game as the professional who devotes most of his time to it. Nevertheless, most knowledgeable people would probably agree that it is impossible to understand baseball without learning most of its jargon (technical vocabulary), some of its theory, and something about the reasoning that may underlie choice of strategy. Much the same can be said of international politics. In order to understand the moves and countermoves upon the international stage, and the operational results that flow therefrom, one needs to know the vocabulary of statecraft, something of the kinds of intellectual operations that are involved, and the concepts and theories, both old and new, that may be utilized in political analysis and interpretation.

This opening chapter is designed to bring these matters into focus at the outset. We hope that it will be read by everyone who reads the book at all. If this is done, we believe that it will help one to read more effectively, and thereby get ahead with the business of identifying and forming judgments about the conditions and events which are shaping the destinies of nations, our own included, in these days of revolutionary change.

LANGUAGE, THE BASIC TOOL

The most basic tool of political analysis and communication is language. Discussions of international politics, as of political affairs in general, are carried on almost exclusively in the verbal language of everyday speech. This is sometimes called the literary language, to distinguish it from the mathematical language of numbers. We say that the literary language is almost exclusively the language of politics because there have been attempts, increasingly numerous in recent years, to describe and explain political events and relationships in the language of numbers. One could cite many books and articles on political subjects in which liberal use is made of statistics, formulas, and equations.

Political scientists are divided regarding the fruitfulness of such efforts, and seem likely to continue so. In any case, the language of mathematics or any other nonverbal notation will not soon displace the everyday verbal language as the chief medium of political discourse and communication. However, before considering some of the characteristics of the verbal language, one should note well that simple mathematical ideas can be expressed in words as well as in numbers and other nonverbal symbols.

One such idea is relative size or relative frequency of occurrence. When one says that A is greater than B, or that there are more of A than of B, or that A occurs more frequently than B, one is thinking mathematically, albeit at a very elementary level. This mode of thinking contrasts with "either ... or," "yes ... no" modes of thinking. Instead of contrasting blacks and whites, one compares shades of gray, so to speak. This comparative mode rejects absolutism. In the words of Harold Lasswell, the "either ... or" mode tends to "rigidify thinking" and to reduce complex relationships to a simplicity rarely confirmed in the world of affairs.

Comparing relative size, or frequency of occurrence, or other aspects of a problem has many uses in international political analysis. For example, instead of asserting that China's international behaviour is aggressive and India's nonaggressive, it may be more enlightening to say that China's behaviour is *more* aggressive than India's in such-and-such respects. Instead of asserting that China is or is not a "Great Power," it may be more informative to say that, with respect to certain specified aspects of power, China has more or less, or is stronger or weaker, than India.

Relative size, relative frequency, etc., are very elementary mathematical ideas. But they are none the less useful. Indeed, this mode of thinking is generally more fruitful in political analysis than the "either ... or," "yes ... no" mode, for it evokes comparisons that reveal significant differences between states in policies, power and influence, and in the changes occurring in these phenomena through time.

The verbal language is more closely linked than the mathematical language to particular national cultures or groups of cultures. Broadly speaking, $E = mc$ (one of the basic descriptive statements of modern physics) conveys the same meaning to a Russian as to an American scientist. But this clearly is not the case with the verbal language, as anyone learns when he translates from one language to another. For example, the notion of causation -A determines (or influences or affects, etc.) B -is much more sharply delineated in English and other Western languages than in many Asian and African languages. Even where the language is ostensibly the same, as in Britain and America, for example, words and phrases may carry quite different connotations, in some instances fundamentally different ideas. Linguistic frontiers present one of the most refractory obstacles to effective diplomacy or other transnational communication.

Even within a single cultural milieu, the language of everyday speech is a most imprecise medium. Imprecision springs from numerous sources. One of these is poetic license, of which more will be said in a moment. Another source of imprecision is multiple meaning. Hundreds of words in common use stand for two, or often as many as five to ten, different referents. With regard to a single referent, moreover, a word may be overlain with multiple connotations or different shades of meaning.

Connotations of many key terms in political discourse trigger off prejudices that obstruct rational thinking and frustrate communication. The vocabulary of political discourse includes a large assortment of terms which normally denote only the vaguest abstractions. These and other properties of words render it difficult to carry out precise analyses or to formulate precise hypotheses and theories in the language of everyday speech. Nevertheless, we repeat, the verbal language is the basic tool with which the political analyst and interpreter of events has to make do.

A pernicious source of imprecision is poetic license. The poet Shelley began a famous poem about a skylark with the familiar lines

Hail to thee, blithe Spirit!

Bird thou never wert.

Judged by the standard canons of meaning, this statement is patently nonsense. In everyday speech a skylark is a bird, whether Shelley says so or not. But in the context of the poem, the contradiction is not offensive, though contradiction there indisputably is. The man of letters justifies playing fast and loose with words, since for him words are like colors in a painting or sounds of different pitch and timbre in music. Using words to evoke moods, regardless of accepted meanings, is inherent in the art of poesy, and is appropriately called poetic license.

However, poetic license does not end with poetry. It has invaded other fields in which verbal precision is of the essence of fruitful discourse. Writers who purport to speak scientifically, or at least precisely, about social behaviour and relationships also play fast and loose with the verbal language. Consider, for example, the following sentence from a highly regarded work of serious scholarship: "The mountains ... have pushed the Japanese out upon the seas. ... Sea routes have beckoned the Japanese abroad."

We shall return to this passage when we come to examine the nature of man's relations to his environment. Here we are concerned simply with its figurative use of language, usage which amounts to a sort of poetic license. Such rhetoric, prevalent in books and articles on social subjects, is a fanciful and inexact mode of expression. Poetic license may infuse otherwise dreary prose with some sense of struggle and drama, but its rhetoric is likely to be an obstacle to precise description and explanation. It is as inappropriate in social science as it is appropriate in poesy.

Multiple meanings of words may or may not produce confusion. It depends in considerable degree on the audience. Take the word power, for example. This is a technical term of political discourse. Yet the word carries several distinct meanings outside the boundaries of political discourse altogether. There is a mathematical concept of power: "the product arising from the continued multiplication of a number into itself." In the vocabularies of physics and engineering, power denotes "the rate of transfer of energy, as in work done by an engine." Then there is an optical concept of power: "the degree to which an optical instrument magnifies."

Probably most of the readers of this book will suffer no confusion from these nonpolitical meanings of the word power. But what of the two distinct meanings of power which one encounters within the frame of political discourse? One speaks of the power of Congress, and of the power of the United States. The first means legal authority to act; the second, actual capacity to affect human behaviour-two distinct and different referents. To confuse matters still more, power in the political as distinct from the legal sense, carries various shades of meaning. To some readers of this book, we imagine, power will connote effective military force conceived in terms of prospective ability to win wars.

To others, power may convey the idea of ability to override opposition by means of threats as well as actual warfare. In some contexts, power seems to connote only physical coercion; in others, non coercive influence as well. Since power is a key term in the vocabulary of international politics, and since it carries different connotations or shades of meaning, its use presents constant risk of imperfect communication. It will be desirable, of course, to define such words very carefully. But so sloppy are prevailing linguistic habits in America, even among well-educated people, that there can be no assurance whatever that the most careful and precise definitions will be heeded when the term recurs in discourse.

The probability of imprecision increases whenever the term triggers prejudice or other emotional responses. Take the word communism, for example. A teacher of government wrote on the blackboard the following formula: "From each according to capacity; to each according to need." He asked his students to comment on this formula as a basis of public policy. Initial responses were generally favourable. Students pointed out that this seemed to be the basis of free education, free highways, various welfare services, graduated income taxation, and other accepted policies. Then someone said: "It sounds like communism to me!" Whereupon everyone who had supported the formula hastily retracted. The emotional connotation of communism was sufficient to block further rational thinking on the subject.

Communism is also a good example of the vagueness which plagues so many terms in the vocabulary of international politics. Communism, democracy, freedom, security, aggression, justice and many other political terms not only mean different things to different people, but also to most people what is connoted is vague and imprecise. If the reader has any doubt about this, let him invite his friends to define the terms listed above. Vague reference is clearly another obstacle to precise thinking about political events. It would be difficult to overstress the importance of explicit definitions, especially for technical terms. Since the meaning of a word has to be described by recourse to other words, there are manifestly limits to the precision that can be achieved.

This is especially the case with words in everyday use (power is a good example) which acquire technical meanings in the context of special subjects. But words are the basic tools of political analysis and communication. For better or for worse we are stuck with the verbal language. The most anyone can do is to be as explicit and precise as possible in the choice and definition of these verbal tools. Every sector of human activity, as already emphasized, has technical words and idioms. To the uninitiated, technical language is apt to be confusing, often meaningless. Technical terms which a person does not understand are simply jargon so far as he is concerned.

The average American sports fan has no difficulty understanding a broadcast of a baseball game. But let him switch to a British broadcast of a cricket match, and listen to him complain of the incomprehensible jargon (incomprehensible to him) in which the broadcast is phrased. The average American male is apt to react similarly to instructions for knitting a sweater or for making a cake. Used in appropriate context, technical terms constitute a sort of shorthand, designed to speed up communication. One technical term may express a concept that would otherwise require a sentence or even a paragraph or more. Take cathexis, for example. This is a term borrowed by sociologists and some political scientists from the vocabulary of psychoanalysis.

Cathexis can be defined as "concentration of desire upon some object or idea"-eight words to do the work of eight letters. Or consider empathy, another term in common use in sociopolitical discourse. Empathy can be defined as "imaginative projection of one's consciousness into another being"; or more simply, as "imagining sympathetically how things appear to the other fellow"-one short word in place of eight or nine. There has been a mushroom growth of technical vocabularies in all the social sciences. In general this seems to reflect attempts to attain greater precision and economy in expression of concepts and theories.

One of the requisites for effective reading and communication in any special field is to learn its technical vocabulary. This is no less true of international politics than of economics or biology or knitting. We shall endeavour throughout this book to use few unfamiliar terms. We shall make do as far as possible with terms in common use. But it will be necessary to define these terms with care, especially since many of them are used loosely and imprecisely in ordinary discourse.

KINDS OF INTELLECTUAL OPERATIONS

Words are employed to communicate various kinds of intellectual operations. One of the requisites of clear thinking is to be able to distinguish between the intellectual operations represented by (1) descriptive statements, (2) explanatory statements, (3) predictive statements, (4) engineering statements, and (5) normative statements. Any newspaper provides exhibits of all five types: after reading this section, let the reader go through one or two news stories and editorials, identifying the different kinds of statements exemplified therein.

Clear-cut understanding of these different patterns of thought is useful in any subject. It is especially important in international politics. This is a realm in which prejudices are rampant and passions run high. It is a realm in which dispassionate contemplative thought is too rarely encountered and immensely difficult to achieve. Hence the importance of differentiating at the outset between description, explanation, prediction, prescription, and polemical argument and disputation. Descriptive statements are designed to communicate an image of an object, a state of mind, a sequence of events, a layout in space, or some other state of affairs. A descriptive statement answers such questions as what is it? What is it like? Where is it? What happened? When did it happen?

Any newspaper provides scores of descriptive statements. For example, on September 14, 1959, *The New York Times* told its readers: "The Soviet Union hit the moon with a space rocket early this morning." On the same front page was a news story which began: "Washington was engaged this weekend in the most painstaking preparations ever made for the reception of an official visitor to the United States. The preparations are for Premier Nikita S. Khrushchev. ..."

Description always involves selection. A great deal more could be said about any subject than is ever said. Whether the story is about a space rocket hitting the moon or the Soviet Premier's visit to the United States or the state of the Atlantic Alliance or the economic development of China, a particular description includes only a limited selection of the infinite number of things that could be said about the subject. What is said in a particular description depends, of course, on the context in which the description is given. Frequently, by his selection of "facts" the speaker gets into a descriptive statement a certain explanatory slant. That is to say, he conveys a certain meaning that is not inherent in the "facts" per se.

Explanatory statements are statements designed to interpret or give meaning to an object, a state of mind, a sequence of events, a layout in space, or state of affairs. An explanatory statement typically answers the question: Why? In the context of human affairs, explanatory statements more specifically answer the questions: How was it possible for a given event or state of affairs to occur? Or, with reference to a choice or decision: How did it come about that the given choice or decision was taken? In answering these questions, one usually asserts correlations or other meaningful connections between the condition or event to be accounted for and collateral or antecedent conditions and events.

Explanatory statements are not quite as easy to identify in newspaper or other discourse. Such statements generally do not take the simple form of "*x* happened because ..." or "*A* chose *x* because ...". Here are a couple of samples from the same issue of the newspaper quoted above:

Professor A. C. B. Lovell, director of the Jodrell Bank radio telescope [in Britain] called the [Soviet moon] shot "a brilliant demonstration of the advanced stage of Russian science and technology."

In a feature article on Soviet art and literature, it was stated:

Only occasional echoes of the battles on the artistic front are heard in the West because the Soviet censorship often refuses to pass dispatches that touch on vital aspects of the controversies.

Explanation is a complex idea, with many ramifications. Whole books have been written about it. The subject as a whole is far beyond the compass of this discussion. But two or three points should be noted here. Explanatory statements invariably refer to past events, or to past or currently existing states of affairs. In the idiom of logic, the process of explanation consists typically of locating the necessary or the necessary and-sufficient antecedent conditions of the event or state of affairs to be explained.

Without going into technical detail, one may define a necessary condition as something in the absence of which the given event or state of affairs could not have occurred. Thus, an engine with a trust capable of pushing a rocket beyond the effective counter pull of the earth's gravitation is a necessary condition of travel into outer space. Or, to take another example, access to iron ores and various other raw materials is a necessary condition of the existence of a steel industry.

In general, one can define a sufficient condition as anything, the presence of which renders it highly probable that the event or state of affairs will occur. Thus, assuming the requisite necessary conditions to be present (available goods and services), a favourable Congressional vote was the sufficient condition for the inauguration of the famous European aid program popularly known as the Marshall Plan. The necessary and sufficient conditions of an event or state of affairs are established by the application of suitable explanatory propositions (also called explanatory hypotheses or "laws").

More will be said about these explanatory propositions when we come to consider the relationships between environmental factors and policy decisions and the operational results of decisions, later in this chapter. For the moment, we leave the subject of explanation by saying that "meaning" is given to an event or state of affairs by the application of some hypothesis or theory which may be (but usually in practice is not) set forth explicitly. Predictive statements assert that a given event or state of affairs will occur at some future time.

A predictive statement may, of course, be simply a blind guess or the result of drawing numbers from a hat or throwing dice. We are concerned here not with that kind of prediction, but rather with predictions which are derived by extrapolating past and present trends, or by applying explanatory propositions to assumed sets of future conditions. Predictive statements of this type are derived from the formula: If conditions are so-and-so, then such-and-such will occur.

Excellent illustrations of this predictive process are the population projections constructed by demographers. Such a projection, for example, might deal with American population growth during the next twenty-five years. The first step would be to construct a sort of matrix of assumed environmental conditions. Thus, for example, the demographer might assume that there will be no general war during the given period; that there will be no radical change in the economic standard of living; that the average American family size will remain about as at present; that the birth and death rates will show such-and-such trends; etc. Within some such matrix: of assumed conditions, the demographer applies the formula: If conditions are so-and-so, then such-and-such will occur.

All rational policy making, and all rational study of trends in the policies and capabilities of nations, involve this kind of reasoning. Its essential ingredients are explanatory propositions that serve as logical premises which, when applied to assumed future conditions, yield predictive. Thus prediction resembles explanation in its logical structure. It differs from explanation in that the predicted event or state of affairs, and at least some of the necessary and/or sufficient conditions have not yet occurred. There is much argument these days as to the limits of fruitful prediction in the realm of human behaviour. Prediction also presents some special difficulties for the political analyst. We shall return to these later.

Description, explanation, and prediction may all enter into the intellectual operations which we call scientific. A government report defines science as "systematic knowledge and methods of discovering new knowledge, especially knowledge arranged in a logical structure or theory which is constantly under test and revision." The American physicist, Henry DeWolf Smyth, divides scientific knowledge into three categories: that which we know to be so or will occur: that which we believe to be so or will occur; and that which we guess to be so or will occur.

It is evident that a great deal more is known about certain phenomena (for example, radiation) than about others (for example, how the Cold War appears to Russian peasants). But a common feature of all scientific investigation and analysis, the feature which distinguishes scientific statements from engineering and normative statements, is the quest for knowledge without regard to the practical uses to which such knowledge may be put.

Engineering statements represent intellectual operations that are performed for the purpose of affecting a course of events. Engineering may be regarded as an aspect of technology, about which a great deal will be said in this book. To quote again from the report cited just above: "By technology we mean a systematic body of methods for the achievement of human purposes in any field." As Smyth puts it: "Science seeks knowledge; technology seeks utility."

One ordinarily thinks of engineering and technology as applied physical science. But the intellectual operations involved in building a bridge are not very different from the kind of intellectual operations involved in planning and executing a foreign policy. Both are designed to manipulate conditions and events so as to accomplish a desired purpose. Engineering or manipulative or policy-oriented operations contrast with descriptive, explanatory and simple predictive operations, which are essentially contemplative than manipulative. Explanatory statements deal with events that have already occurred, and hence (by definition) cannot be manipulative or policy-oriented. Predictive statements which relate simply to the future implications of assumed conditions are likewise free from overtones of engineering or policy making.

A particular form of predictive statement however, is manipulative or policy-or-oriented-indeed, is the very essence of engineering and policymaking. We refer to the form of prediction which answers the question: If x is to occur, what must be done? Or, alternatively, what must be done in order to get *x*? In more general terms: What course of action will accomplish a given purpose? Applied to our immediate subject, we have such questions as what can the United States do to combat Chinese in fluence in Southeast Asia? How can NATO be strengthened? How can we change the prevailing image of the United States in India?

In each question, the purpose to be achieved is given. The problem is simply one of selecting an effective means to the given end. In solving this kind of problem, one makes in effect a prediction that if so-and-so is done, the desired end will be accomplished. The problem and its solution are logically analogous to any engineering problem. For example, given the end-to build a bridge across the Hudson River-the problem is to determine what type (or alternative types) of structure will do the job effectively with the resources available. The political scientist and the civil engineer alike solve their engineering problems by applying suitable propositions with regard to the properties of their respective materials and the consequences of utilizing these in certain ways.

Engineering-type analysis can also yield negative predictions. The civil engineer's knowledge of materials and processes may enable him to tell the sponsors that their projected bridge cannot be built with any materials and structures known, or with the funds available, or for other reasons. Or like the builders of the medieval cathedrals, he may not know whether his materials and methods will suffice, and can only proceed with a large element of faith and guesswork. Similarly, an expert public-relations consultant to the Department of State might have to report that no instrumentalities and techniques which the United States government commands would accomplish very much towards counteracting Chinese influence in Southeast Asia. Or, alternatively, that nothing much can be accomplished with the appropriations available. Or, that he believes certain methods are likely to be effective, though he really doesn't know.

There is a great deal more uncertainty in political than in physical engineering these days. It is comparatively rare for a policy maker and his staff to justifiably say with confidence: we know what will happen if we adopt such-and-such a strategy. The intellectual approach and operations involved are essentially similar; the degree of faith and guesswork is generally much greater. The engineer-be his problem political or mechanical-may or may not approve of the purposes for which his expert knowledge is demanded. There is no intrinsic reason why a physicist-turned-engineer should not do first-rate work on nuclear-weapons development, even though he totally disapproves of his government's policy of building such weapons. Comparably, an economist and a political scientist who are against all foreign aid should nevertheless be able to give sound technical advice to the government on how to formulate and administer a foreign-aid program.

Discrepancies between the expert's personal values and preferences (his notions of what is good and right and proper) and the exercise of his expertise are everyday occurrences in the relations of lawyer and client. Such discrepancies are also prevalent in any bureaucratic (hierarchical) organisation in which subordinates are expected to work loyally for the boss whether they like his policies or not. What is involved here is the problem of multiple roles. On the one hand, the expert is the embodiment of specialized knowledge, the use of which on assigned tasks may or may not fit in with his scheme of values. On the other hand, he is a citizen, a member of the community with more or less positive convictions as to what is good, right, and proper. If the two roles conflict, and if he cannot keep them separate, he becomes at best an inefficient worker and at worst a menace to the organisation which he serves.

This brings us finally to normative statements. These are statements which express a preference in terms of right or wrong, good or bad, desirable or undesirable, proper or improper. Here is a first-rate example, culled from The Observer, the distinguished London newspaper. What purports to be a straight news story, in 1957, on the psychological impact of the first Soviet space satellites, opens with the headline: "Sputnikitis will do Americans good." Why? Because from these events "must spring a multitude of changes, a surprising number of which will be all to the good." Clear-cut normative statements expressing moral preferences of a British journalist and his paper! Then follows some prophecy, non normative in itself: "Americans will never again enjoy quite the same sort of luxurious defense politics, nor for a very long time disrespect their international opponents quite so wholeheartedly."

Every policy-oriented prediction-that is, every engineering statement as defined a few paragraphs back-proceeds from some value or preference or image of a future state of affairs desired by someone. But an engineering statement is not thereby a normative statement. If the formula runs "In order to get *x,* do *y,*" it is an engineering statement-a prediction that if one does *y, x* will occur. If however, the formula runs "*x* is good; therefore y should be done if *y* will produce *x,*" then the statement becomes normative.

Every society, every social group, every individual exhibits conceptions of what is good, right, and proper. Many people profess to believe that their values are universally valid. This is an unproved and unprovable position. Disputation about whose values are best rarely leads to any fruitful result. Consider, for example, a proposition to which most Americans unquestionably subscribe: that democracy is better than communism. This proposition means no more and no less than that the person saying so prefers democracy to communism.

In the context of political action, normative statements frequently take the form of policy prescriptions: The United States should (or should not) recognize Red China; nuclear weapons should (or should not) be outlawed; the United States should (or should not) encourage the practice of birth control in India; etc. In such statements the value or norm may be implicit rather than explicit; but policy prescriptions are normative none the less. Such statements, we repeat, express moral preferences; that is to say, the ethical norms which the speaker desires to see prevail. It is fruitless to brand such statements as right or wrong, good or bad, in accordance with any universal standard. They are right or wrong, good or bad, only in the sense that they conform to or deviate from the standard set by a given individual or social group or community as a whole.

One can estimate the engineering (that is, operational or practical) consequences of any policy prescription. One can find out something, for example, as to what may be the operational consequences of opening up diplomatic relations with Red China. Also, one who commands the necessary votes or the "big battalions" or sufficiently persuasive public relations experts or other effective instruments, may be able to make his values (that is, his preferences) prevail. But might does not make right in any ultimate moral sense; and that holds also for persuasion, bribery, intimidation, pressure, and all the other ways of influencing human behaviour.

Popular discussion of international affairs-in newspapers and over the air-tends to be strongly ethnocentric in all countries. Even books and articles that purport to be scholarly frequently embody more or less disguised pleas for national viewpoints or policies. Dispassionate contemplative analysis of the behaviour of nations has become a scarce commodity these days.

Not only public discussion but virtually all government-sponsored reporting and research are heavily loaded with national viewpoints and values. A typical example was furnished in 1959 by the Draper Committee. President Eisenhower appointed this committee of distinguished citizens to investigate the extent to which military and economic aid to foreign countries could buttress the security of the United States. Judging from the published reports, the Draper Committee and its research staff never deviated in the slightest from the assumption that the purpose of Soviet economic aid is to enslave recipient nations, whereas the purpose of American aid is to liberate them. This position stands in marked contrast to that of the Soviet government. Just as frequently and just as emphatically, Soviet spokesmen have asserted precisely the opposite: that it is the Soviet Union that liberates and the United States that seeks to enslave.

A considerable number of educators and others appear to believe that such partisanship is unavoidable. According to this view, a person can never divest his discourse of values. Discussion of international affairs, runs the argument, may be critical, but it can never be dispassionate. It will always be partisan. Hence the sensible course is to accept the inevitable: make all teaching and discussion of international subjects frankly and openly partisan, value-loaded, and policy-oriented. Some in our midst would go still further. They would argue that we are caught up in a life-and-death struggle with evil and implacable enemies.

Under these conditions they see no place whatever for dispassionate or contemplative "ivory tower" analysis of international conditions and events. The function of education and public discussion, they appear to contend, should be to close the ranks and consolidate support behind whatever policies and strategies our government happens to be following at the moment. This attitude carries a dangerous implication. It is common knowledge that people feel intensely for or against a particular administration or a particular ideology or a particular policy or a particular nation or foreign lands and peoples in general. But it is less generally recognized that people may pay a heavy price for their partisanship.

Too much preoccupation with parochial values and norms distorts one's perception of conditions and events as well as one's judgments regarding meaning and implications. This is the point of Falstaff's remark, "The wish was father to the thought." To the extent that the wish prevails over the thought, one limits his capacity to describe and to explain, to predict and to evaluate, what is happening in the real world. To recognize this is not to imply that anyone can divest himself of ethical norms, in particular those which prevail strongly in the local and national communities of which he is a member.

Nor are we suggesting that one should even try to do so. Shared ideals, values, and preferences are an essential ingredient of the social cement which binds people together in communities, and without which a sense of community could scarcely exist at all. Our point is rather that one should be alert to the tendency of values and norms to dominate judgment. It is a primary function of formal education to teach to distinguish between the different kinds of intellectual operations outlined above. Only when they are distinguished does it become possible to come to grips with the problems which stir so deeply the emotions of nearly everyone in these troubled and swiftly changing times.

ACTOR AND OBSERVER

We come next to two concepts nearly always implicit in descriptive, explanatory, predictive, and polemical discourse. These are the concepts of actor and observer. The concept of actor is derived from the vocabulary of the theater. In that context an actor is a person who represents a character, or acts a part in a play. In the broader theater of public affairs, an actor may be defined as the persons or group whose behaviour is being described, explained, or predicted. In political discourse, as in the vocabulary of the theater, the concept of actor is always associated with the concept of role: the position or status which the actor occupies in the political system under discussion. Thus, in order to discuss political actions meaningfully, it is necessary to identify the political system (international, national, local, or other), the unit of action (nation-state, head of government, legislative body, citizen pressure group, or other), and that unit's role in the system (foreign policy making, or other).

It is customary to treat nation-states as the acting units in the system which we call international politics. It is also customary to attribute personality and other human traits to these corporate entities. Here it is sufficient to emphasize that the ultimate acting units of all social systems are human persons. Diplomacy, transnational propaganda, subversive activities, foreign-aid programmes, technical assistance to underdeveloped countries, and military operations are initiated and carried out not by intangible abstractions but always by human persons acting in describable roles defined by law and practice. When one speaks of action by the state, he is necessarily (though perhaps not consciously) speaking of action by human persons authorized to perform in certain ways as agents of the national political community.

Political events and situations can be viewed from either of two points of observation. One is the viewpoint of the political actor in the situation. The other is the viewpoint of someone who (from the side lines, as it were) observes, analyzes, describes, explains, or predicts the actor's behaviour and evaluates his performance.

The man on the side lines is in a position a little like that of the drama critic who watches the play from a seat on the aisle. In the universe of public affairs, non actor reporting and evaluating is performed by numerous categories of persons: journalists, teachers, research specialists, as well as just interested citizens. Persons who perform this function are variously called reporters, commentators, analysts, observer-analysts, or simply observers. The term *observer* has the merit of emphasizing the distinction between actor and non actor. The academic study of international politics falls exclusively within the category of side-line observation. Scholars write about international politics. Teachers lecture and conduct classroom discussions about international politics. Students read about international politics. Hence the importance of appreciating the characteristics and limitations of the role of observer.

An observer can examine political decisions and situations from two perspectives. He can attempt to see things as these are seen by the political actor under observation. This is variously called "probing the mind" of the actor, reconstructing the actor's "image of the situation," "putting oneself into the actor's position," etc. Or the observer can proceed from his own independent viewpoint.

How to infer another person's motivation, knowledge, and mode of thinking and acting has occupied jurists and philosophers of history from time immemorial. The conclusions of jurists are represented in the complicated rules governing what is and what is not admissible as evidence in court. Historiographers have laid down somewhat different rules of evidence to govern verbal reconstructions of the behaviour of historical personages. Investigation of these issues leads one ultimately into a morass of controversy regarding "reality" and "knowledge."

It is unnecessary for us to delve deeply into these philosophical controversies. It will suffice if (when reading any description, explanation, or prediction of a government's purposes and strategies, or of the interactions of two or more governments through time, or of other operational results of political decisions) one keeps clearly in mind that he is reading someone's version of reality; that this someone may be either one of the actors in the situation, or (more probably) a sideline observer; that the discourse always reflects in some degree the perspective of the particular narrator; and that his perspective and image of reality depend not only on his access to events and reports of events but also on his own cultural background through which all perception and thinking are filtered.

3

Analytical Tools and Procedures

When making a systematic study of any subject, one employs various analytical tools and procedures, including: (1) the process of analysis, (2) concepts, (3) conceptual schemes, (4) models, (5) hypotheses and theories, (6) assumptions and premises, (7) facts and factors, (8) constants and variables.

ANALYSIS

In its more limited sense, the process of analysis consists of separating or resolving something into its constituent parts or elements. So defined, analysis precedes systematic description, explanation, and prediction. Analysis normally precedes synthesis in building bridges, drafting government policies, or performing any other engineering operation. Analysis may or may not precede expressions of moral preference.

The term analysis is also used to denote all the intellectual operations performed in connection with a given problem. In this broader sense, we shall repeatedly use such expressions as foreign policy analysis, capabilities analysis, international system analysis, etc.

CONCEPTS

A concept is simply the name given to a class of objects, activities, qualities or other phenomena. Since the subject of international politics is concerned only with empirical phenomena-that is, phenomena locatable in space-every concept in this book has some empirical referent. Empirical concepts divide into two general classes: those which refer to so-called "concrete structures," and those which refer to so-called "analytic" qualities, properties, or aspects of concrete structures. Concrete structures are physically separable; analytic aspects are not.

A table is a concrete structure; its shape, height, and weight are analytic aspects of it. The United States is a concrete structure; democratic form of government is an analytic aspect. The British Isles is a concrete structure; insularity is an analytic aspect. The clearer and more precise the reference, the more useful will a concept is for most purposes. This is emphatically so with respect to engineering statements which prescribe what must be done if a desired result is to be achieved. Sometimes, however, the purpose of discourse is not to enlighten but to confuse and muddy an issue, to inflame passions, to sway people by appeals to the "heart." For such purposes, it may be more effective to avoid sharply defined referents. Blurred reference is characteristic of much popular use of such terms as democracy, communism, peace-loving, war-mongering, aggression, security, intervention, national honor, national interest, limited war, and the like.

CONCEPTUAL SCHEMES

Concepts may be systematically arranged in sets of various kinds for various purposes. Such a set is called a conceptual scheme. A conceptual scheme can be likened to a collection of filing boxes, into which one sorts elements or aspects of a process or a state of affairs. Conceptual schemes, built in accordance with an ordered set of principles and relationships, are called taxonomies.

Another canon of classification is that parallel categories should exhaust all cases covered by the classifying principle employed. Since the five aspects of climate, in the example just above, do not quite exhaust the observable properties, one includes a residual category labeled "other aspects." Still another, and very important, canon of classification is that parallel categories should be mutually exclusive. That is to say, data should fit into no more than one category. This is very difficult, indeed almost impossible, to achieve with conceptual schemes built around terms in common use in discussions of international politics.

Suppose, for example, one desires to classify the different kinds of functions performed in the conduct of foreign affairs. Here are some of the terms in common use: diplomacy, negotiation, declaration, material aid, technical assistance, economic warfare, public relations, psychological warfare, subversion, sabotage, intervention, cold war, hot war, limited war, total war, etc. These terms have evolved over the years without much rhyme or reason. The more or less firmly established meanings and connotations of almost every one of them overlap those of one or more of the others. In short, the terminology of international action is a hodgepodge of imprecise and overlapping concepts. It is no exaggeration to characterize this as a state of semantic chaos which poses a formidable problem at the very threshold of any serious political analysis.

Any conceptual scheme has built into it a set of reasons for the particular categories selected. Such reasons may or may not be made explicit. But some rationale underlies every conceptual scheme. For example, any taxonomy of the "elements" or "foundations" of national power is virtually certain to include a category labeled "geographical position," or "geographical location," or some equivalent term. Why? Certainly not because location has any intrinsic or inherent political quality or value! Inclusion of this category will be found in every case to depend upon some such proposition as: A state's geographical position affects significantly its ability to influence in desired ways the behaviour of other nations, because ... From this point the proposition may take various forms.

But the point to emphasize here is that every conceptual scheme, every classification, rests upon some set of justifying propositions. Thus the very process of constructing a conceptual scheme carries the builder some way along the road towards a "theory" of his subject. Conceptual schemes are invaluable analytical tools. They reveal relationships and evoke insights and explanatory hypotheses. These deal with such phenomena as (1) targets of political action, (2) kinds of instrumentalities employed in the practice of statecraft, (3) ways in which such instrumentalities are utilized, (4) kinds of effects produced by different techniques, (5) factors that enter into deliberations and calculations of policy makers, (6) sources of national strength and weakness, (7) composition and characteristics of the Society of Nations ... etc.

MODELS

The term model, like power, has many shades of meaning. Everyone is familiar with the scale models which are reduced replicas of ships or other objects. It is common knowledge that such scale models are not exact replicas, but simplified designs intended to display and emphasize only selected features of the original. A familiar example of scale model, widely used and indispensable in the study of international affairs is the geographical globe, which presents a simplified design of the intricate configuration of lands and seas which cover the earth. Political boundaries, likewise simplified, may be sketched in on a globe; so may mountain ranges, railroads, and other physical features of the landscape.

Flat maps represent another kind of model in common use, also invaluable in the study of international politics. As is well known, it is mathematically impossible to transfer any design from a sphere to a plane without distortion. Shapes may be distorted, as may areas or directions or some combination of these properties. The simplifications and distortions which characterize all models of the earth's surface affect our conceptions of reality. At the same time, no one seriously proposes that globes and maps should be banned from classrooms or maps from newspapers. It is recognized that these models are valuable tools for acquiring knowledge about the earth and about human activities related to the earth.

Nor do most people feel uncomfortable in the presence of charts and graphs of various kinds-to depict business trends, flow of commerce, growth of population, and a great many other phenomena. These charts and graphs are models, symbolic devices for focusing attention on particular aspects of reality. When we read popular accounts of scientific achievements, we accept without hesitation various pictorial devices for illustrating the structure of atoms and molecules, and other facts about the physical universe. Though most of us do not understand them well, we likewise accept the mathematical equations by which scientists describe this universe more precisely. All these devices, we repeat, are models.

Military strategy is another field in which men have proliferated models. The so-called war game, worked out with diagrams and other symbols, is a model designed to simulate operations as these might occur in the event of real war. Simulated behaviour of one kind or another forms the basis of research into many other kinds of human activity. In addition to maps, charts, graphs, equations and other devices already noted, the term model has also come to denote any orderly set of interrelated concepts and propositions designed to show how some institution or process functions. This kind of model may be quite useful in the study of international politics. We have (1) decision-making models, designed to illuminate the processes by which statesmen decide what is to be undertaken, (2) capability models, designed to help identify the factors which set limits to what a government can accomplish, and (3) international system models, designed to cast light on the patterns of interaction in the Society of Nations.

More will be said about these specific kinds of models later on. Here it will suffice to observe that all explanations and all predictions that involve something more than a throw of the dice are based on images regarding the ways things are arranged and how they function in the real world. Such images, even though never set down in ink or print, are models. They are models in the sense that a map is a model, or a diagram of a molecule is a model. That is to say, certain aspects of reality are abstracted from the totality and form the basis of a simplified picture or description of how things work, how people behave, what will happen, etc.

People often deny that they think in terms of models. Such denials are no more than quibbles over the meaning of words. Laboratory experiments as well as everyday experience show that people do make assumptions about their universe, and that they do form pictures in the mind, so to speak. However described and labeled, such images constitute a person's set of working models, to which he relates his choices and decisions and without which he could scarcely survive a single day in our complicated modern world.

HYPOTHESES, THEORIES, ASSUMPTIONS, PREMISES

Let us suppose that we are waiting at a traffic light to cross a busy street. The light turns green, and we step confidently from the curb. In stepping into the street, one is proceeding on the basis of a prediction (rarely verbalized) that adverse traffic will obey the signal. In effect, such a prediction is simply an inference (generally instantaneous and subconscious or nearly so) from a "picture in the mind" (generalized model) of how a "typical" motor car driver behaves when he comes to a red traffic light. The pedestrian rarely has any specific knowledge about the drivers of oncoming cars. He usually knows nothing about their individual driving habits. But he does have a "picture in the mind" of how drivers normally behave in the given locality; and he predicts driving behaviour on the expectation of probable conformity to that hypothetical norm.

Such a model, we repeat, is not a description or image of any specific person's behaviour. It carries no built-in guarantee that the image of typical behaviour fits any particular person. No behavioural model or any other model can possibly anticipate individual deviations from the hypothetical norm. Models are generally derived from observation of events. However derived, a model is useful to the extent that it helps one to understand or to predict events in the real world. If it does so, the model is said to be confirmed. The process of confirmation or disconfirmation involves the formulation of hypotheses, theories, assumptions, and premises.

Let us return to our street-crossing example. Suppose that we are newly arrived visitors from a country with different traffic rules and driving patterns. We watch the flow of traffic and the alternation of green and red signals. On the basis of what we see, we formulate a working hypothesis: green means go; red means stop; and vehicles almost invariably obey the rules. This working hypothesis is a generalized description of patterned activities-in this case, response of vehicle drivers to traffic signals. As further observation demonstrates that cars do in fact obey the rules, and that it is safe to cross the street when the red signal stops adverse traffic, the hypothesis is said to be confirmed. Then, and then only, strictly speaking, does a hypothesis become a theory.

In practice, this distinction is not rigorously observed. Propositions advanced without confirmation or proofs are often called theories. Conversely, propositions, such as the one made Darwin famous, are often called hypotheses-thus, the Darwinian hypothesis-long after experts have accepted the hypothesis as confirmed. In due course, a theory hardens into a firm expectation that future cases will provide further confirmation. When this stage is reached, a theory comes to be regarded sometimes as manifest common sense. It is then frequently referred to as an assumption. This usage is not free from risk of ambiguity because the word assumption is also used to denote elementary rules or axioms which are used in building hypotheses, and accepted as self-evident without confirmation-as, for example, the Euclidean axiom that a straight line is the shortest distance between two points.

At any stage in the evolution from trial hypothesis to firm expectation, the proposition-in our example, that drivers obey traffic signals-may constitute the major premise (also called explanatory hypothesis, or "law") from which future events are predicted by logical deduction. Some historians, geographers, political scientists and other students of human affairs have contended that every human being is unique. From this premise they argue that human behaviour is unpredictable. But such persons, we have noticed, do not hesitate to cross a busy street when the light turns green. In stepping from the curb, they are acting upon a premise that is just the opposite of their contention of the uniqueness of human behaviour.

Generally, such inconsistency is more apparent than real. No one will argue that any two human beings, or social groups, inanimate objects, or other "concrete structures" are exactly alike in all respects. Nor will anyone deny that units of the same class or type-whether human beings or ships or anything else-have qualities, properties, traits, characteristics, or aspects in common. Indeed, it is by the discovery of common properties that one derives concepts, gives names to them, and arranges them in various kinds of conceptual schemes.

Smith and Jones are unlike in many respects; but they are both human beings, they cannot survive without oxygen to breathe, they are United States citizens, they are presidents of corporations, they dislike socialism, and they have countless other traits in common. Britain and Japan are unlike in many respects; but their homelands are islands, they are relatively poor in indigenous mineral bodies, they are heavily dependent on foreign trade, and have many other aspects in common. Hypotheses, theories, assumptions and logical premises are derived, in the main, by abstracting and generalizing selected common aspects, properties, traits, etc., not by searching fruitlessly for identical total entities.

No model and no hypothesis or theory, we repeat, embodies all the phenomena which, in the real world, constitute the concrete units under consideration. The essence of a model, as of explanatory propositions, is the selection of one factor or some limited set of factors which are deemed to be strategic (that is, highly significant) for the state of affairs or events to be explained. In a sense it is redundant to call these tools limited-variable models, hypotheses, and theories. We do so here simply to emphasize that this is a character of all models, hypotheses, and theories.

The fact that no model or explanatory proposition takes into account all possibly relevant factors does not make these intellectual tools less useful. On the contrary, the abstraction of similar limited aspects from different concrete units that are unique in their respective totalities and the derivation of general descriptions from such abstractions form one of the most powerful techniques by which modern man reduces his complicated universe to some kind of intelligible and increasingly manageable order.

If repeated observations show that where factor a is present, there event x occurs, we then have empirical justification for concluding that a is the cause-or more precisely, the sufficient condition-of x. That is to say, we conclude that the presence of a justifies a prediction that x will probably occur. In many instances it may prove to be impossible to locate the sufficient condition of x. But it may still be possible in such instances, to identify several strategic (that is, immediate and important) necessary conditions. And it may be feasible, looking towards the future, to predict the conditions that must prevail in order to make possible the occurrence of x.

Consider, for example, a geopolitical hypothesis: that the relative power and influence of states varies in proportion to their relative utilisation and control of inanimate energy. This hypothesis rests upon a limited set of variables-coal, oil, hydroelectric power, etc.-and holds, in its extreme form, that these factors are the sufficient condition of differences in the power and influence of nations. This is equivalent to saying: Where a, there x.

But, the critic may ask, what about other sources of political power and influence, such as manpower, skills, economic equipment, social organisation, etc.? Consideration of such factors may lead one to the conclusion that control of inanimate energy does not by itself explain satisfactorily the differences that are observed in the international influence of nations, even though this set of factors certainly helps to explain such differences. This conclusion shifts "inanimate energy" to the category of necessary but not sufficient conditions. In doing so, one modifies the original hypothesis.

Instead of saying that where energy is abundant, power is great, the hypothesis now says that ability to control and utilize energy is one of the necessary conditions of international influence. This amounts to saying that where energy is not abundant, influence is unlikely to be great. By now it should be apparent that we are using the term *theory* in a narrower sense than is usual in political discourse. Examination of the socalled classics of political science- Aristotle's *Politics*, Machiavelli's *Prince*, Montesquieu's *Spirit of the Laws*, Hobbes' *Leviathan*-reveals two kinds of discourse subsumed under the label political theory. One consists of ethical arguments regarding various kinds of rule. The other consists of generalized descriptions and explanations of institutions and processes of political rule.

Typical of the first are the criteria by which men have weighed their preferences for various forms of government, and the arguments by which they have defended particular forms, or, alternatively, incited other men to revolt. It might clarify the study of government and politics a good deal, if such discussions of political norms and values were called political philosophy. This would leave the term political theory to denote generalized descriptions and explanations of how political institutions and processes work. It is in this latter sense that we are using the terms hypothesis and theory throughout this book.

FACTS AND FACTORS

Hypotheses and theories are derived from facts, and facts are utilized to test hypotheses. The dictionary tells us that a fact is "something declared to have happened, or to have existed." To this definition one should add that, in practice, facts are phenomena as observed and reported by someone. Facts may be imprecise impressions of untrained observers, or very precise observations of trained specialists. Facts may come unsorted; or they may come in tidy packages, such as statistical tables, maps, etc.

Such prepackaging is useful, indeed essential, especially when one has to cope with enormous masses of data. But, the packages prepared by economists, sociologists, and other specialists may sometimes fail to fit the needs of the political analyst. Public opinion polls may not ask the questions we want answered. National economic statistics may not tell us what we want to know about military outlays and foreign aid.

A fact becomes a factor, to quote the dictionary again, when it is identified as "one of several circumstances, influences, elements or causes which produce a result." The definition is silent as to how one is to identify such factors. The question is easy to answer in general terms, though often very difficult in specific cases. In general, identification of factors is achieved by applying explanatory propositions as discussed earlier in the chapter.

The link between facts and theories may be denied. How often one hears: "I have no theory; I simply let the facts speak for themselves." Facts never speak for themselves! Even the purest description or chronicle of events involves an element of interpretation. No one can report everything. What one observes and records, what he retains and discards, how he arranges the data which he calls facts, all reflect an exercise of judgment as to what is relevant and significant. By the very act of selecting and ordering data and by the verbal or other symbols employed in presenting these, even the purest empiricist indulges in explanation and interpretation, protests to the contrary notwithstanding. As a famous economist is said to have observed: "The most vicious theorists are those who claim to let the facts speak for themselves."

CONSTANTS AND VARIABLES

Phenomena may vary in space or through time or both. Variation in space means uneven or irregular distribution. Spatial variation is nearly always a significant dimension of international politics. Such variation is the basis of all geopolitical hypotheses, in which the relations of nations are explained or predicted on the basis of the irregular layout of lands and seas, the irregular conformation of the land's surface, the uneven distribution of mineral bodies and other natural resources, regional variations of climate, uneven distribution of population, and still other spatial variations.

Whether phenomena observed to be unevenly distributed in space are also significantly variable through time depends on the rate or amount of change during the period involved in the problem in hand. Suppose, for example, the problem is to compare the relative abilities of the United States and the Soviet Union to supply tractors to Nigeria during the next two months. In this problem, uneven distribution in space would certainly be relevant, whereas variations of the spatial variables through time would probably be rather inconsequential. In plain English, what would matter would be stocks of tractors on hand or in production in the two countries. If, however, the time span in the problem is lengthened to two years, the time factor might become much more important.

That is to say, one would have to calculate trends in the productive capacities of Soviet and American industries as well as relative capacities at a given time. Variations through time, and especially different rates of variation in different places, are especially important when one attempts to project longer-term trends and patterns of international politics. Population, technology, economic development, weapons systems, military forces in being, transnational ideologies, the morale and discipline of national populations under stress, and many other clusters of phenomena change significantly through time at different rates in different countries and regions. This fact of differential change was emphasized in the Introduction. It is probably the most significant aspect of international politics in our time.

HEREDITY AND ENVIRONMENT

All human activities take place within limits of variation set by human heredity and environment. This is a truism of behavioural and ecological science. But the implications and mechanisms involved are not self evident. Since both hereditary and environmental concepts and theories have important bearings on political actions and outcomes, it will be well to give a little attention to these matters at the outset.

First, some definitions. By heredity we mean all the structures of the human organism which can be transmitted genetically from one generation to the next; by environment, all phenomena locatable in space which set limits to the activities of the human organism, excepting the limits set by heredity. This concept of environment includes both phenomena physically external to and separable from the person under consideration and his image of reality as internalized by the sensory processes of perception. Additional terms are needed to denote these two aspects of environment, to which we shall return after a further note on heredity.

Human activities involve both sets of limits, genetic and environmental. For example, neither heredity nor environment alone can provide a complete explanation of man's inability to fly through the air without mechanical assistance. A person jumps from a high window and flaps his arms-but he falls to the ground. One bystander says that gravity (an environmental factor) pulled him down. Another contradicts him, saying that human beings, unlike most birds, lack wings capable of sustaining flight (a hereditary factor). Both are right, but neither explanation is complete; it takes both to account for the event.

The theory of evolution rests upon the assumption that hereditary characters change (that is, undergo mutation) through time. With regard to human heredity, the rate of change has been so gradual as to justify students of politics treating heredity as a constant within the time-spans involved in such studies. However, the release of huge quantities of radioactive materials into the atmosphere opens up the possibility of more frequent and radical human mutations in the future. All this is still very speculative and controversial. No politically significant mutations resulting from radioactive fallout are known to have occurred to date; and, so far as we are aware, no precise predictions of such mutations have received widespread support from experts in the biological sciences.

Hence one is probably on sound ground in still treating heredity as a constant through time in the context of international politics. Heredity, however, presents other facets of interest to the student of international politics. One is the widespread belief that there are significant inheritable differences in intellectual ability, in capacity to function in different climates, and in other characteristics, among the various "races" of mankind. The policies of Nazi Germany were overtly predicated upon an assumption that ethnic groups classified as "Nordics" possess superior genetic endowment. Many people in many countries have shared this or comparable belief in the hereditary superiority of one race over another.

That such racist beliefs have affected the motivations and decisions of statesmen and their constituents is well known. That such beliefs-quite apart from any evidence confirming them-have had a bearing on legal rules, social taboos, or other restrictions affecting the utilisation of human resources, and hence on the relative capabilities of nations, is also well known. Whether the various races of mankind do in fact embody genetic differences which, if taken into account, would help significantly to explain or to predict distributions of political power and influence in the Society of Nations is a question on which all evidence known to us is negative or at least inconclusive. Hence, in the present state of knowledge, one has to conclude that there is no scientific basis for treating genetic variations among races as having any calculable international significance whatever.

There still remain to be considered the undeniable differences (not among races but) among individuals, either of the same or of different races. We refer in particular to the personal qualities of great and not so great individuals who play roles upon the international stage: Churchill, Roosevelt, Hitler, De Gaulle, Stalin, Khrushchev, Mao Tse-tung, Nehru, Castro, and scores and hundred of others. It is generally agreed that heredity is related to the qualities of leadership. But there is no agreement whatever as to the relative importance of heredity and environment in the making of leaders. As things stand today, the bearing of heredity on leadership constitutes one of the unpredictable intangibles in political analysis and interpretation.

ENVIRONMENTAL CONCEPTS AND THEORIES

Turning to the other set of limitations-those derived from environment-certain distinctions must be observed if one is to avoid confused thinking about human behaviour and accomplishment. The general concept of environment was defined above as all empirical factors (excepting hereditary factors) that set limits to human activities. So defined, environment includes not only tangible objects, human as well as non human, at rest and in motion. Environment also includes institutions, laws, customs, and other social patterns as well. Defined in this way, environment is equivalent to the French word milieu.

In analyzing a particular outcome, performance, or state of affairs, it is generally possible to identify certain elements of the total environment that appear to be strategic (that is, very immediate and important). These specific elements constitute the operational environment of the actor in that situation. The operational environment (the factors which an outside observer judges to be relevant and significant in explaining an event or state of affairs) should be distinguished from the environment as it appears to the actor in the situation. His image of reality we shall call his psychological environment.

A person's psychological environment consists *not* of phenomena external to his physical being. On the contrary, his psychological environment consists of ideas derived from his perception of conditions and events interpreted in the light of his conscious memories and subconsciously stored knowledge. An individual's psychological environment may or may not correspond closely to his operational environment. The linguistic expert B. L. Whorf once characterized the psychological environment of a person ignorant of those aspects of the physical universe which one cannot perceive directly and can conceive only within a frame of scientific theories and inferences.

For such a person the earth is flat, the sun and moon are shining objects of small size that pop up daily above an eastern rim, move through the upper air, and sink below the western edge; obviously they spend the night somewhere underground. The sky is an inverted bowl made of some blue material. ... Bodies...fall because...there is nothing to hold them up. ... Cooling is not a removal of heat but an addition of "cold"; leaves are green...from the "greenness" in them. ... *

On the same issue, the British geographer K. G. T. Clark says:

An African with no experience of the world outside his native forest, transported by magic carpet to one of our own [brick] houses, would perceive what we also perceive, a prevailingly red object of a certain shape. But because his previous experience vastly differs from ours it is impossible he should perceive it as a house. Yet in physicochemical terms the house is the same whoever looks at it. In our two perceptions there is something in common, the objective element, and something different, the subjective element. Human geographers, and others who study phenomena embracing human action and its results, are up against complications due to the fact that the reaction of man to a given physical background is apt to be strongly colored by this subjective element in his apprehension of that background. The way we have ... been shaped in the past influences the reactions of the present.

The study of human behaviour tends to concentrate on human images and perspectives, sometimes to the virtual exclusion of the operational environment. For example, the British historian David Thomson says:

It is not a river itself that matters as a geographic feature; it is whether the inhabitants of both its banks think of it as a main artery of their common life, or as a "natural frontier" between them.

To similar effect, another British historian, R. C. Collingwood, says:

> The fact that certain people live ... on an island has in itself no effect on their history; what has an effect is the way they conceive that insular position.

To this the geographer O. H. K. Spate replies that "people cannot conceive of their insular position in any way unless they live on an island."

Spate's rejoinder is patently contrary to experience. From time immemorial, men have formed opinions and shaped their actions on the basis of inaccurate images of their environment. One thoroughly investigated demonstration of such a discrepancy and its consequences was the now all but-forgotten panic produced in 1938 by Orson Welles's vivid radio broadcast of an imaginary landing near Princeton, New Jersey, of invaders from Mars. A more recent example was the epidemic of reports of flying saucers and other unidentified objects in the sky during the later 1940's, when millions of people were very jittery about atomic bombs, rockets, and other new gadgets of the nuclear age. To contend that "people cannot conceive their insular position in any way unless they live on an island" is equivalent to saying that they cannot conceive of nonexistent invaders from outer space or that they cannot perceive nonexistent flying objects.

One can distinguish two kinds of psychological events in the above examples. On the one hand, individuals may perceive what does not exist or may fail to perceive what does exist. On the other hand, since what is perceived is interpreted in the light of past experience, individuals with different backgrounds may interpret quite differently the same perceived objects or events. It is possible, of course, to carry these points too far.

The fact that the human species has survived (so far) indicates that there must be considerable congruence between conditions and events as people conceive them to be and as these actually are in the real world. Man's increasing mastery over the physical universe seems to confirm this hypothesis and to suggest that congruence between image and reality is one of the conditions of technological advancement. One may also go a step further and speculate that individuals with similar cultural background tend to perceive and interpret conditions and events rather similarly. Otherwise it is difficult to imagine how social institutions could survive and continue to function even as well as they do on the whole.

The term real world, in the preceding paragraph, poses a philosophical issue about which men have argued since the days of Plato, and probably long before. That issue is whether there *is* any reality apart from someone's perception of it. We do not propose to re-argue this issue. We simply assume that there is a real world, distinct from someone's image thereof, though knowable only through the processes of perception from which are derived concepts and theories about reality. The distinction between image and reality is a fruitful one, and we shall continue to use it.

Perhaps the reader is asking: What has all this to do with international politics? The answer is: A great deal. In the study of international politics, one is concerned with both the attitudes and decisions of statesmen and their constituents, and also the outcomes or operational results of decisions. In general, only the concept of psychological environment is relevant in the analysis of attitudes and decisions; and only the concept of operational environment in the analysis of outcomes and operational results. Environmental factors are related very differently to these two aspects of action.

In the explanation and prediction of attitudes and decisions, one is dealing not with a set of conditions external to and separable from the environed individual. One is concerned rather with some kind of psychological interaction between the individual's felt needs and his stored knowledge, on the one hand, and the signals or messages conveyed to him via his sensory organs, on the other. That is to say, what matters in shaping human attitudes and decisions (and in explaining these) is not how the real world actually is, but rather how it is perceived or imagined to be by the individuals under consideration. This elementary proposition, self-evident though it clearly is, is constantly neglected in discussions of foreign policy and the interactions of nations.

When the task is to explain a decision made in the past, it may be possible to reconstruct more or less plausibly the intellectual operations that actually took place. This procedure breaks down if the necessary historical evidence has been destroyed or is for other reasons unavailable. The procedure will not work at all, of course, when the task is to predict decisions not yet taken. Under these conditions, the alternative to pure guessing is to draw inferences on the basis of the actor's probable conformity to a set of hypothetical norms.

Such behavioural models are almost never so labeled. They usually appear as assumptions (oftener implicit than explicit) which a writer makes with regard to the person or group whose attitudes and decisions are under examination. In general, such assumptions relate mainly to the actor's purposes and motivation, to the accuracy and completeness of his information, and to his mode of utilizing such information in formulating alternatives and taking decisions.

Careful reading will usually yield clues as to a writer's behavioural assumptions. One may discover, for example, that he assumes one set of statesmen to be predominantly acquisitive and power-hungry, but another set to be altruistic and self-abnegating. With regard to the extent of an actor's information (that is, his knowledge of the environment in which he is operating), one may discover writers assuming anything from perfect knowledge to total ignorance. Assumptions relating to a decision maker's mode of utilizing information turn mainly on the issue of rationality, as rationality is conceived by the person making the analysis.

One further assumption is almost always present. The observer (the person doing the explaining) tacitly assumes that his own image of the situation corresponds closely to that of the actor (the person or group whose activities are being explained or predicted). Given this final assumption, the observer proceeds to explain the actor's past choices and to predict his probable future choices, simply by imagining how a "rational" person (such as the observer himself) would behave in the circumstances.

What we have just been describing are the rock-bottom elements of what is commonly called behavioural analysis, or the behavioural approach. It is essentially a probabilistic form of reasoning. Its essence is reasoning from assumptions regarding what would be normally expectable behaviour in the context under consideration. Thus, starting with a given past decision and the set of environmental facts which the observer deems to have been relevant, he reasons backward to an explanation of the decision. Starting with a set of environmental facts and assumptions regarding the actor's purposes, knowledge, and intellectual habits, he reasons forward to a prediction of the probable future decision.

These intellectual operations may or may not be self-evident. In a sense, what we have described is a little like the scaffolding which the workman takes down when the house is finished. But it is generally possible to infer from the context of a conversation or piece of writing how the conclusions were reached. We believe that the probabilistic model outlined above will be found to fit rather closely a good deal of political discourse in general, and discussions of international politics in particular.

When, as often happens, the speaker or writer tacitly assumes that his own national perspective and values are shared by actors of other nationality, and when, as is still oftener the case, this assumption fails to fit observable facts, the reasoning outlined above can lead to dangerously untenable conclusions. When this occurs, the root of the trouble generally will be found to lie in failure to recognize that differences in national perspectives and values may be highly consequential and hence significant in the explanation or prediction of national reactions to conditions and events.

There seems to be growing awareness of the significance of these basic behavioural differences among nations. This awareness is reflected in increasing use, on the part of those who study international politics, of ideas and theories developed by those anthropologists, sociologists, psychologists and other specialists who have probed more deeply into social patterns which differentiate each national culture from all others. Thus far we have been examining the relations of environmental factors to attitudes and decisions. We turn now to the quite different kind of relationship between environment and outcomes or operational results of decisions.

The basic proposition here is that environmental factors can affect outcomes, results, and accomplishments, regardless of whether the actors in the situation perceived and took these factors into account. In the analysis of outcomes and results, the issue of choice and decision is bypassed completely. The task is rather to identify the factors which significantly affected the outcome of whatever was attempted. In this type of analysis, the operational environment is conceived as a sort of channel or matrix, within which the undertaking runs its course, a matrix which affects the course of the action and the outcome of a given decision or strategy of action.

These environmental limits may vary from time to time and from place to place. The limits implicit in one set of factors (for example, Atlantic winds and currents) may vary with changes in other factors (for example, changes in ship design and mode of propulsion). Thus the westerly winds which handicapped westward crossings in the days of sail, became relatively insignificant limitations in the later era of steamships. Though the limits vary, some set of limits is present at any given place and time and affects the outcome of any attempted course of action.

A particular set of limits may circumscribe broadly or narrowly; that is to say, the environment may leave room for much, little, or no range of fruitful choice. Under conditions of primitive technology, the limits are generally very restrictive. As men attain more efficient tools and skills, accumulate capital, and perfect their social organisation, the limits are pushed back, and the range of fruitful choice widens. Before men learned how to build mechanical flying machines, gravitation imposed an absolute limit on human flight. Today the size of a particular person's bank account or the state of his credit may just as effectively prevent him from riding in airplanes.

Or he may have enough money to do so, but prefer to spend it on "the horses." In the second and third cases, the limitation is one of preference when available resources are insufficient to cover all desires. An exciting aspect of history is mankind's progressive mastery over his physical environment. Broadly speaking, each new scientific hypothesis formulated, each new tool invented, each new skill acquired, each new application of nonhuman energy to get something done, has enlarged somebody's range of effective choice. Yet, as the late Isaiah Bowman once put it: "For all his independence and ingenuity," man "can never wholly escape from his environment. He cannot move mountains without floating a bond issue."

He "conforms to many defective layouts because it would cost him too much to alter them," even where he clearly has the technical knowledge and necessary equipment to do so. That is to say, with advances in technology and accumulation of capital, the question: Can it be done tends increasingly to give way to the question: Is it worth the cost? How does one go about identifying opportunities and limitations latent in the environment, with reference to a particular activity? Mainly by applying general explanatory propositions - the major premises of formal logic.

> Proposition 1. Until well into the nineteenth century, the design of square-rigged sailing ships was such that they could not sail close to the wind-that is, with the wind blowing at an angle much forward of a right angle to the keel of the ship.
>
> Proposition 2. Redesign of sailing ships to enable them to sail closer to the wind reduced somewhat the limiting effects of headwinds and adverse currents.
>
> Proposition 3. The development of internally powered ships reduced these limitations to a level where they no longer affected significantly the westbound courses of ships crossing the Atlantic.

In environmental theory, limitations on performance may be operative irrespective of human knowledge and decisions. In the example just cited, Atlantic winds and currents limited certain movements of pre-nineteenth-century ships irrespective of the desires and decisions of shipmasters. But explanatory propositions to account for outcomes and performances do not exist apart from human observation and thought. Such propositions are formulated by someone; they are strictly man-made in every respect-creative acts of imagination. Generally, though not necessarily, such propositions are derived from observed events.

There is no certainty that any two observers will formulate identical hypotheses or regard the same hypothesis as relevant and sufficient in a given case. However, in any given society and historical period, there is likely to be considerable agreement as to how things work and why. It is never inevitable that a given person or group will discover the limits of fruitful choice before reaching a decision. Nor is there any ground for assuming, as a general rule, that prior discovery of the limits would necessarily affect the decision taken. For reasons better known to psychiatrists, people often persist in courses which they recognize to be futile, even self-destructive.

In the explanation of outcomes and performances, some decision, some project or undertaking is always taken as given, not as an event to be explained. Similarly, in estimating future possibilities. The function of this kind of analysis is to identify and evaluate the environmental factors as well as the qualities of the acting units themselves which set limits to what can happen subsequent to a given decision, or undertaking. This frame of reference is technically called environmental possibilism. It is, broadly speaking, an important part of the intellectual framework within which the international capabilities of states are calculated.

ENVIRONMENTAL INFLUENCES RECONSIDERED

In the light of the foregoing brief discussion of the relationships of environmental factors to attitudes and decisions, on the one hand, and to outcomes and results of decisions, on the other, it remains to examine critically the deterministic or near-deterministic rhetoric in which these relationships are frequently phrased.

How is one to construe such rhetoric? Manifestly mountains do not push; sparse resources do not drive; sea routes do not beckon; steel furnaces do not lead inevitably to anything or anywhere. One possible hypothesis is that speakers who employ such rhetoric are expressing a naive teleology. Indeed, one can find plenty of instances in which a literal interpretation of a passage allows no other alternative. Take, for example, the following sentences in a standard treatise on resources and industrial development:

Nature...does infinitely more than merely set the outer limits within which human arts and wants can operate. She makes suggestions and man is wise enough to listen. At times this suggestive power of nature is very evident, as in cases when she lures man by rich rewards or blocks his road with discouraging threats. More often nature speaks with a less audible voice. In ways hardly noticed by man she affects the development of human arts and wants. It is human willingness to respond to even these suggestions of nature that marks man as *homo sapiens*. ... * [Italics added.]

Another possible hypothesis is that deterministic and near-deterministic statements, especially those imputing purposeful activities on the part of a personified Nature, are simply examples of the sort of poetic license described earlier in this chapter: a figurative and fanciful mode of expression employed to infuse prose with a synthetic atmosphere of high drama.

Quite often, it would appear, such rhetoric is neither teleology nor poetic license, but a sort of verbal shorthand. Take the verb influence. This is easily the most overworked verb in the environmentalist's vocabulary. The essence of dictionary definitions of influence is "some activity on the part of a person or thing that produces without apparent force an effect on another person or thing." Thus, for example, a police officer blows his whistle and traffic stops. There is no physical contact between the affecting agent and the affected unit. The effect is produced without apparent force.

By a sort of analogical extension, a writer slips into the habit of speaking of geographical location or climate or mountains or a new machine or some other nonhuman human factor of environment as influencing people to do so-and-so. Construed in context, such statements as those quoted above may be merely equivalent to saying that the influenced person or group took cognizance of the environmental facts in question; that he (or they) evaluated it with reference to their felt needs and desires; and that he (or they) then acted in the light of the conclusions thus reached.

Depending on the verb employed-determine, lead inevitably, drive, beckon, influence, or some other-such rhetoric can be construed as expressing the speaker's estimate of the odds that the environed person or group would recognize and heed the limitations and opportunities latent in the environment. Thus when one reads that the "sea routes beckoned the Japanese abroad," perhaps all that the passage means or was intended to mean is that substantial numbers of Japanese persons, at a certain stage of Japanese history, envisaged more attractive opportunities in seafaring than in farming or other pursuits ashore.

This conclusion suggests that environmentalistic rhetoric, when employed to explain attitudes and decisions, may reflect the kind of probabilistic reasoning. What was there called the "model of typical behaviour" included, it will be recalled, assumptions as to purpose, knowledge, and mode of relating knowledge to purpose in making decisions. Such a behavioural model carries a built-in assumption that people are capable of choosing among alternatives. But that is not equivalent to saying that all choices, which by definition are possible choices, are equally probable choices. The essence of probabilistic thinking about behaviour is that some choices are regarded as more probable than others.

The function of the model is to enable one to arrange a set of possible choices in order of estimated degrees of probable occurrence. By reference to the assumptions of normally expectable behaviour, the analyst eliminates as very improbable or less improbable those choices which would represent greater or lesser deviations from the hypothetical norm. Though this kind of reasoning appears to be implicit, if not explicit, in most predictions of behaviour, one should always keep in mind its limitations. First, it is manifestly better suited to predicting the odds of occurrence in a large aggregate of units, than to pinpointing the choice of a specific unit. Second, no behavioural model can be any more valid than the historical experience from which it is derived.

With respect to the first point, a market analyst, for example, may be able to predict within a more or less calculable range of error how many persons per thousand in a given country will buy new automobiles next year. But if he should attempt to identify specific purchasers of next year's automobiles, the incidence of error would increase enormously. That is to say, the statistical methods employed in handling large aggregates of data might prove quite unfruitful when one comes to predicting the behaviour of particular members of the aggregate. Yet it is the decisions of specific units-heads of state, cabinets, foreign offices, etc.-with which the student of international politics is usually concerned.

This is not to contend that probabilistic reasoning based upon assumptions of normally expectable behaviour, is fruitless. It is the best, often indeed the only, analytical tool one has for this purpose. But it is a tool of limited utility at the present level of knowledge regarding the springs of human behaviour. The second limitation relates to the validity of generalizing from historical experience. Assumptions as to what is normally expectable behaviour in any context are derived ultimately from historical evidence. The process, it would appear, is more or less as previously described in the street-crossing example. The relevance of past experience, however, may vary. It all depends on the rate and scale of change through time.

If the kind of behaviour at issue exhibits relatively stable patterns through a given time span, precedents are manifestly more trustworthy guides than in periods of rapid and radical change. This principle is exemplified in numerous unconfirmed predictions in the late 1940's and 1950's, that one or another international crisis-Berlin blockade, Korean attack, etc.-was the opening move of World War III. In each case the predicted general war failed to occur. Study of these episodes suggests a possible recurring source of error.

The prophets of World War III were manifestly reasoning from patterns of the pre-1914 and pre-1939 periods. Yet the enormous increase in the destructiveness of weapons, together with the concentration of super weapons in American and Russian hands during that period, created a situation without any precedent. Under those conditions, statesmen repeatedly exhibited a caution unknown in earlier periods. They might bluster and threaten; they might hurl insulting epithets that would have started the armies marching in the past; but they showed extreme reluctance to pass the point of no return. In consequence the outcomes of pre-1945 crises offered much less reliable guidance to the probable course of post-1945 crises than might otherwise have been the case.

Though nearly all historical experience has lost some predictive value in our era of revolutionary change, such experience is clearly more relevant in some fields than in others. The point is simply that the rapid and differential changes which characterize almost every sector of our environment today add a baffling uncertainty to the task of predicting future decisions and interactions upon the international stage.

Finally, one should be alert to possible significant differences in the way people behave as individuals and as members of complex decision-making groups or organisations. Such differences have become more clearly understood and more widely appreciated in recent years, with the development of knowledge and theories regarding communications and the operations of complex organisations. Broadly speaking, significant differences between individual and organisational behaviour may extend to motivations and purposes, to the amount and accuracy of information available to the decision maker, and to the mode of framing alternative strategies and choosing among them.

CONCEPTS AND THEORIES OF STRATEGY

Recent development of concepts and theories of strategy has added a new set of analytical tools for the study of international politics. Strategy used to be an essentially military concept. In one of the older dictionaries it is defined as "the science or art of employing the armed strength of a belligerent to secure the objects of a war." Since World War II a much broader concept of strategy has taken form. Today the term is applied to operational plans in all sorts of situations involving the interaction of adverse parties: labor disputes, legislative processes, law enforcement, and a great many others. In the context of international politics, strategy has come to denote the operational plans in accord with which governments manipulate all kinds of instrumentalities-nonmilitary as well as military-in their efforts to accomplish desired objectives vis-ΰ-vis other nations, including allies and neutrals as well as potential or declared enemies.

This broadening of the concept of international political strategy has coincided with the development of so-called game theory. This development dates from the publication in 1944 of a book, by John von Neumann (professor of mathematics at the Institute for Advanced Study) and Oskar Morgenstern, entitled *The Theory of Games and Economic Behavior*. This pioneering work and others dealing with game theory have inspired numerous attempts to apply this kind of analysis to the Cold War and other phenomena of international politics.

It may be doubted whether formal game theory has much to contribute at this stage to the analysis or solution of international problems. But the notion of international politics as a game with describable rules, moves, stakes, and payoffs has certainly stimulated interest in strategy. In America, heightened interest in international strategy has tended to focus on the problem of deterrence: how to prevent potential enemies, the Soviet Union in particular, from attacking the United States or our allies.

This consuming preoccupation with deterrence arises, of course, from the mutually destructive potentialities of nuclear weapons systems. There is a very widespread belief that military war, fought with nuclear weapons, would likely ruin the victor as well as the vanquished. This belief has stimulated a great deal of new thinking about international strategy. One result is a revival of the idea-widely current within political communities, and formerly applied in the sphere of diplomacy and war-that most situations exhibiting conflict of purpose or interest are *ipso facto* situations with potentialities for bargaining. Another product of recent thinking about international strategy is the idea that satisfactory solutions are generally those in which each side gains enough to make acceptance of a compromise solution seem preferable to the mutually suicidal risks inherent in full-scale war.

When one begins to think about international conflict, strategy, and deterrence in such terms, the question arises whether students of international politics may not derive fruitful insights from analogous bargaining and deterrence situations in other spheres of human behaviour. This question, among others, is dealt with by Thomas C. Schelling, in a book entitled *The Strategy of Conflict*. This book should be read in *toto*, but the following short selection from it will suffice perhaps to indicate the perspective which concepts and theories of strategy can give to the study of international politics.

We can be interested in [the strategy of conflict] ... for at least three reasons. We may be involved in a conflict ourselves; we are all, in fact, participants in international conflict, and we want to "win" in some proper sense. We may wish to understand how participants actually do conduct themselves in conflict situations; an understanding of "correct" play may give us a bench mark for the study of actual behaviour. We may wish to control or influence the behaviour of others in conflict, and we want, therefore, to know how the variables that are subject to our control can affect behaviour. ...

But, in taking conflict for granted, and working with an image of participants who try to "win," a theory of strategy does not deny that there are common as well as conflicting interests among the participants. In fact, the richness of the subject arises from the fact that, in international affairs, there is mutual dependence as well as opposition. Pure conflict, in which the interests of two antagonists are completely opposed, is a special case; it would arise in a war of complete extermination, otherwise not even in war.

For this reason, "winning" in a conflict does not have a strictly competitive meaning; it is not winning relative to one's adversary. It means gaining relative to one's own value system; and this may be done by bargaining, by mutual accommodation, and by the avoidance of mutually damaging behaviour. If war to the finish becomes inevitable, there is nothing left but pure conflict; but if there is any possibility of avoiding a mutually damaging war, of conducting warfare in a way that minimizes damage, or of coercing an adversary by threatening war rather than waging it, the possibility of mutual accommodation is as important and dramatic as the element of conflict. Concepts like deterrence, limited war, and disarmament, as well as negotiation, are concerned with the common interest and mutual dependence that can exist between participants in a conflict. ...

To study the strategy of conflict is to take the view that most conflict situations are essentially bargaining situations. They are situations in which the ability of one participant to gain his ends is dependent to an important degree on the choices or decisions that the other participant will make. The bargaining may be explicit, as when one offers a concession; or it may be by tacit maneuver, as when one occupies or evacuates strategic territory. It may, as in the ordinary haggling of the market-place, take the status quo as its zero point and seek arrangements that yield positive gains to both sides; or it may involve threats of damage, including mutual damage, as in a strike, boycott, or price war, or in extortion.

Viewing conflict behaviour as a bargaining process is useful in keeping us from becoming exclusively preoccupied either with the conflict or with the common interest. To characterize the maneuvers and actions of limited war as a bargaining process is to emphasize that, in addition to the divergence of interest over the variables in dispute; there is a powerful common interest in reaching an outcome that is not enormously destructive of values to both sides. A "successful" strike is not one that destroys the employer financially; it may even be one that never takes place. Something similar can be true of war. ...

Deterrence has been an important concept in criminal law for a long time. ... It has figured prominently enough for one to suppose the existence of a theory that would take into account the kinds and sizes of penalties available to be imposed on a convicted criminal, the potential criminal's value system, the profitability of crime, the law-enforcement system's ability to apprehend criminals and to get them convicted, the criminal's awareness of the law and of the probability of apprehension and conviction, the extent to which different types of crime are motivated by rational calculation, the resoluteness of society to be neither niggardly nor soft-hearted in the expensive and disagreeable application of the penalty and how well this resoluteness (or lack of it) is known to the criminal, the likelihood of mistakes in the system, the possibilities for third parties to exploit the system for personal gain, the role of communication between organized society and the criminal, the organisation of criminals to defeat the system, and so on.

It is not only criminals, however, but our own children that have to be deterred. Some aspects of deterrence stand out vividly in child discipline: the importance of rationality and self-discipline on the part of the person to be deterred, of his ability to comprehend the threat if he hears it and to hear it through the din and noise, of the threatener's determination to fulfill the threat if need be-and, more important, of the threatened party's conviction that the threat will be carried out. Clearer perhaps in child discipline than in criminal deterrence is the important possibility that the threatened punishment will hurt the threatener as much as it will the one threatened, perhaps more. There is an analogy between a parent's threat to a child and the threat that a wealthy paternalistic nation makes to the weak and disorganized government of a poor nation in, say, extending foreign aid and demanding "sound" economic policies or cooperative military policies in return.

And the analogy reminds us that, even in international affairs, deterrence is as relevant to relations between friends as between potential enemies. (The threat to withdraw to a "peripheral strategy" if France failed to ratify the European Defense Community Treaty [in 1954] was subject to many of the same disabilities as a threat of retaliation [in case of Soviet attack on the West]. The deterrence concept requires that there be both conflict and common interest between the parties involved; it is as inapplicable to a situation of pure and complete antagonism of interest as it is to the case of pure and complete common interest. Between these extremes, deterring an ally and deterring an enemy differ only by degrees. ...

The deterrence idea also crops up casually in everyday affairs. Auto- mobile drivers have an evident common interest in avoiding collision and a conflict of interest over who shall go first and who shall slam on his brakes and let the other through. Collision being about as mutual as anything can be, and often the only thing that one can threaten, the maneuvers by which one conveys a threat of mutual damage to another driver aggressing on one's right of way are an instructive example of the kind of threat that is conveyed not by words but by actions, and of the threat in which the pledge to fulfill is made not by verbal announcement but by losing the power to do otherwise.

Finally, there is the important area of the underworld. Gang war and international war have a lot in common. Nations and outlaws both lack enforceable legal systems to help them govern their affairs. Both engage in the ultimate in violence. Both have an interest in avoiding violence, but the threat of violence is continually on call. It is interesting that racketeers, as well as gangs of delinquents, engage in limited war, disarmament and disengagement, surprise attack, retaliation and threat of retaliation; they worry about "appeasement" and loss of face; and they make alliances and agreements with the same disability that nations are subject to-the inability to appeal to higher authority in the interest of contract enforcement.

There are consequently a number of other areas available for study that may yield insight into the one that concerns us, the international area. Often a principle that in our own field of interest is hidden in a mass of detail, or has too complicated a structure, or that we cannot see because of a predisposition, is easier to perceive in another field where it enjoys simplicity and vividness or where we are not blinded by our predispositions. It may be easier to articulate the peculiar difficulty of constraining a Mossadeq by the use of threats when one is fresh from a vain attempt at using threats to keep a small child from hurting a dog or a small dog from hurting a child.

None of these other areas of conflict seems to have been mastered by a well-developed theory that can, with modification, be used in the analysis of international affairs. ...

What would "theory" in this field of strategy consist of? What questions would it try to answer? What ideas would it try to unify, clarify, or communicate more effectively? To begin with, it should define the essentials of the situation and of the behaviour in question. Deterrence- to continue with deterrence as a typical strategic concept-is concerned with influencing the choices that another party will make, and doing it by influencing his expectations of how we will behave. It involves confronting him with evidence for believing that our behaviour will be determined by his behaviour.

But what configuration of value systems for the two participants- of the "payoffs," in the language of game theory- makes a deterrent threat credible? How do we measure the mixture of conflict and common interest required to generate a "deterrence" situation? What communication is required, and what means of authenticating the evidence communicated? What kind of "rationality" is required of the party to be deterred- a knowledge of his own value system, an ability to perceive alternatives and to calculate with probabilities, an ability to demonstrate (or an inability to conceal) his own rationality?

What is the need for trust, or enforcement of promises? Specifically, in addition to threatening damage, need one also guarantee to withhold the damage if compliance is forthcoming; or does this depend on the configuration of "payoffs" involved? What "legal system," communication system, or information structure is needed to make the necessary promises enforceable?

Can one threaten that he will "probably" fulfill a threat; or must he threaten that he certainly will? What is the meaning of a threat that one will "probably" fulfill when it is clear that, if he retained any choice, he'd have no incentive to fulfill it after the act? More generally, what are the devices by which one gets committed to fulfillment that he would otherwise be known to shrink from, considering that if a commitment makes the threat credible enough to be effective it need not be carried out? What is the difference, if any, between a threat that deters action and one that compels action, and a threat designed to safeguard a second party from his own mistakes? Are there any logical differences among deterrent, disciplinary, and extortionate threats? ...

This brief sample of questions may suggest that there is scope for the creation of "theory." There is something here that looks like a mixture of game theory, organisation theory, communication theory, theory of evidence, theory of choice, and theory of collective decision. It is faithful to our definition of "strategy": it takes conflict for granted, but also assumes common interest between the adversaries; it assumes a "rational" value-maximizing mode of behaviour; and it focuses on the fact that each participant's "best" choice of action depends on what he expects the other to do, and that "strategic behaviour" is concerned with influencing another's choice by working on his expectation of how one's own behaviour is related to his.

There are two points worth stressing. One is that, though "strategy of conflict" sounds cold-blooded, the theory is not concerned with the efficient application of violence or anything of the sort; it is not essentially a theory of aggression or of resistance or of war. Threats of war, yes, or threats of anything else; but it is the employment of threats, or of threats and promises, or more generally of the conditioning of one's own behaviour on the behaviour of others, that the theory is about.

Second, such a theory is nondiscriminatory as between the conflict and the common interest, as between its applicability to potential enemies and its applicability to potential friends. The theory degenerates at one extreme if there is no scope for mutual accommodation, no common interest at all even in avoiding mutual disaster; it degenerates at the other extreme if there is no conflict at all and no problem in identifying and reaching common goals. But in the area between those two extremes the theory is noncommittal about the mixture of conflict and common interest; we can equally well call it the theory of precarious partnership or the theory of incomplete antagonism. ...

Both of these points-the neutrality of the theory with respect to the degree of conflict involved, and the definition of "strategy" as concerned with constraining an adversary through his expectation of the consequences of his actions-suggest that we might call our subject the theory of interdependent decision. Threats and responses to threats, reprisals and counter-reprisals, limited war, arms races, brinkmanship, surprise attack, trusting and cheating can be viewed as either hot-headed or cool-headed activities.

In suggesting that they can usefully be viewed, in the development of theory, as cool-headed activities, it is not asserted that they are in fact entirely cool-headed. Rather it is asserted that the assumption of rational behaviour is a productive one in the generation of systematic theory. If behaviour were actually cool-headed, valid and relevant theory would probably be easier to create than it actually is. If we view our results as a bench mark for further approximation to reality, not as a fully adequate theory, we should manage to protect ourselves from the worst results of a biased theory.

Furthermore, theory that is based on the assumption that the participants coolly and "rationally" calculate their advantages according to a consistent value system forces us to think more thoroughly about the meaning of "irrationality." Decision-makers are not simply distributed along a one-dimensional scale that stretches from complete rationality at one end to complete irrationality at the other. Rationality is a collection of attributes, and departures from complete rationality may be in many different directions.

Irrationality can imply a disorderly and inconsistent value system, faulty calculation, an inability to receive messages or to communicate efficiently; it can imply random or haphazard influences in the reaching of decisions or the transmission of them, or in the receipt or conveyance of information; and it sometimes merely reflects the collective nature of a decision among individuals who do not have identical value systems and whose organisational arrangements and communication systems do not cause them to act like a single entity.

As a matter of fact, many of the critical elements that go into a model of rational behaviour can be identified with particular types of rationality or irrationality. The value system, the communication system, the information system, the collective decision process, or a parameter representing the probability of error or loss of control, can be viewed as an effort to formalize the study of "irrationality." Hitler, the French Parliament, the commander of a bomber, the radar operators at Pearl Harbor, Khrushchev, and the American electorate may all suffer from some kinds of "irrationality," but by no means the same kinds. Some of them can be accounted for within a theory of rational behaviour. ...

The apparent restrictiveness of an assumption of "rational" behaviour-of a calculating, value-maximizing strategy of decision-is mitigated by two additional observations. One, which I can only allege at second hand, is that even among the emotionally unbalanced, among the certified "irrationals," there is often observed an intuitive appreciation of the principles of strategy, or at least of particular applications of them.

The second observation is related to the first. It is that an explicit theory of "rational" decision, and of the strategic consequences of such decisions, makes perfectly clear that it is not a universal advantage in situations of conflict to be inalienably and manifestly rational. ... It may be perfectly rational to wish oneself not altogether rational, or-if that language is philosophically objectionable-to wish for the power to suspend certain rational capabilities in particular situations. And one *can* suspend or destroy his own "rationality," at least to a limited extent; one can do this because the attributes that go to make up rationality are not inalienable, deeply personal, integral attributes of the human soul, but include such things as one's hearing aid, the reliability of the mails, the legal system, and the rationality of one's agents and partners.

In principle, one might evade extortion equally well by drugging his brain, conspicuously isolating himself geographically, getting his assets legally impounded, or breaking the hand that he uses in signing checks. In a theory of strategy, several of these defenses can be represented as impairments of rationality if we wish to represent them so. A theory that makes rationality an explicit postulate is able not only to modify the postulate and examine its meaning but to take some of the mystery out of it. As a matter of fact, the paradoxical role of "rationality" in these conflict situations is evidence of the likely help that a systematic theory could provide.

And the results reached by a theoretical analysis of strategic behaviour are often somewhat paradoxical; they often do contradict common sense or accepted rules. ... It is not invariably an advantage, in the face of a threat, to have a communication system in good order, to have complete information, or to be in full command of one's own actions or of one's own assets. Mossadeq and my small children have already been referred to; but the same tactic is illustrated by the burning of bridges behind oneself to persuade an adversary that one cannot be induced to retreat. ...

The well-known principle that one should pick good negotiators to represent him and then give them complete flexibility and authority-a principle commonly voiced by negotiators themselves-is by no means as self-evident as its proponents suggest; the power of a negotiator often rests on a manifest inability to make concessions and to meet demands. Similarly, while prudence suggests leaving open a way of escape when one threatens an adversary with mutually painful reprisal, any visible means of escape may make the threat less credible. The very notion that it may be a strategic advantage to relinquish certain options deliberately, or even to give up all control over one's future actions and make his responses automatic, seems to be a hard one to swallow.

Many of these examples involve some denial of the value of skill, resourcefulness, rationality, knowledge, control, or freedom of choice. They are all, in principle, valid in certain circumstances; but seeing through their strangeness and comprehending the logic behind them is often a good deal easier if one has formalized the problem, studied it in the abstract, and identified analogies in other contexts where the strangeness is less of an obstacle to comprehension.

Here perhaps we perceive a disadvantage peculiar to civilized modern students of international affairs, by contrast with, say, Machiavelli or the ancient Chinese. We tend to identify peace, stability, and the quiescence of conflict with notions like trust, good faith, and mutual respect. To the extent that this point of view actually encourages trust and respect it is good. But where trust and good faith do not exist and cannot be made to by our acting as though they did, we may wish to solicit advice from the underworld, or from ancient despotisms, on how to make agreements work when trust and good faith are lacking and there is no legal recourse for breach of contract.

The ancients exchanged hostages, drank wine from the same glass to demonstrate the absence of poison, met in public places to inhibit the massacre of one by the other, and even deliberately exchanged spies to facilitate transmittal of authentic information. It seems likely that a well-developed theory of strategy could throw light on the efficacy of some of those old devices, suggest the circumstances to which they apply, and discover modern equivalents that, though offensive to our taste, may be desperately needed in the regulation of conflict.

CONCEPTS AND THEORIES OF SOCIAL SYSTEMS

System is a familiar term in political discourse. People speak of the American political system, the Soviet system, democratic and communist systems, the historic European States System, the balance-of-power system, the bipolar system, the inter-American system, the United Nations system, and many, many others. Some concept of system underlies every branch of organized knowledge. One speaks of chemistry, physics, biology, psychology, economics, and other university disciplines as systems of concepts and theories. One speaks of the solar system, climatic systems, atoms and molecules as systems, plants and animals as biological systems. All sorts of man-made machines are conceived as mechanical systems. Sociologists analyze various kinds of social systems: state, family, church, Business Corporation, and others.

All concepts of system have a common core of meaning. This can be defined as a set of elements or components or units which are observed to exist or to function in accordance with a discernible pattern. Kenneth E. Boulding characterizes every such system as a structure or complex of individuals of the order immediately below it-atoms as an arrangement of protons and electrons, molecules of atoms, cells of molecules, plants, animals and man of cells, social organisations of men. The "behaviour" of each individual is "explained" by the structure and arrangement of the lower individuals of which it is composed or by certain principles of equilibrium or homeostasis according to which certain "states" of the individual are "preferred." Behavior is described in terms of the restoration of these preferred states when they are disturbed by change in the environment.

The term 'homeostasis,' in the passage above, is the familiar concept of the self-regulating mechanism. A thermostat built into a refrigerator or into a domestic heating system or other heat-exchanging mechanism, for example, keeps the temperature of a given air-space within a prescribed range of variation. The governor on a motor, to take another example, keeps the shaft from turning faster or slower than a prescribed range of variation. An autonomic mechanism built into the human organisation keeps the body's temperature normally within a narrow range close to 98°F. Failure of the self-regulating mechanism may destroy the machine or the organism, or at least impair its efficiency.

Boulding and others contend that social systems exhibit properties analogous to homeostasis. A family, a fraternal order, a political community, or other organized social group penalizes those of its members who deviate too widely from approved norms, standards, and values. Failure to check such deviation may destroy the group or transmute it into something quite different. This is roughly what happens when a political revolution occurs.

Somewhat similar is the concept of equilibrium or balanced power which has been associated with the Society of Nations for several hundred years. When one nation-state or group of states becomes too strong or too aggressive, other governments enter into alliances and increase their military budgets to restore the balance of power. This historic principle and practice has been recently described as a sort of international homeostasis.

Useful as this concept may be, we would put in a word of caution with regard to it. Concepts and theories which purport to explain political systems by means of analogies drawn from machines and biological organisms may yield fruitful insights. But such analogies present certain dangers. They impart to political discourse a certain deterministic flavor, a certain automatic self-regulating behaviour beyond the control of the human persons who comprise the system under consideration.

Neither a nation-state nor any international system is a self-regulating mechanism. Nor do political systems bear any striking resemblance to biological organisms. For reasons that should become more and more apparent as we proceed, analogies comparing political systems either to machines or to organisms are more apt to confuse and mislead than to clarify and enlighten. This is not to contend that system is an unfruitful concept. On the contrary! The point is rather that in describing social systems in general, and political systems in particular, one should be aware of the pitfalls latent in all analogies drawn from biology and mechanics.

There have been numerous international systems, recognized as such, in the past. One of the most thoroughly studied, though mainly from the standpoint of narrative history, was the European States System, and generally dated from about 1650. That system evolved from a regional to a worldwide system in the eighteenth and nineteenth centuries, and then went to pieces in the twentieth. Today, various less-than-global groupings have been characterized as international systems: the United Nations, East-West bipolarism, the Communist Camp, the Anti-Communist Coalition, the Organisation of American States, and others.

Students of international politics have begun quite recently to explore the possible extension and application of concepts and theories regarding political systems at the national and sub national levels. One line of inquiry has sought to discover fruitful analogies from the historic processes involved in the formation and breakup of nation-states and empires. The hypothesis underlying such investigations seems to be that similar processes may be at work both globally and regionally in the Society of Nations today.

Most analyses of political systems, both international and national, are carried on within a framework of concepts and theories which has recently become known as structural-functional requisite analysis. We shall not attempt to describe this type of analysis in detail. In essence it involves formulating hypotheses regarding the conditions and events which made it possible for a given system to come into existence, and upon which the system's continued operation and survival depend. Broadly speaking, structural and functional requisites are equivalent to the "necessary conditions" involved in explanations.

The essential principles of requisite analysis are not new, but they have special utility in a revolutionary age such as ours. They help one not only to form judgments as to the conditions and events which made a given system possible in the first place, and upon which its future depends. By comparing postulated requisites with observed changes in conditions-changes either in the units of the system or in their environment-one may be alerted to impending changes in the system itself. In a word, structural-functional requisite analysis may lead one to a better understanding of a system both in a state of equilibrium and in process of breakup or transformation.

The intellectual apparatus of any science or body of knowledge has to meet one test: Does it help people to think more clearly and more fruitfully about the real world: what that world is like and how it functions. Every technical term, every analytical procedure, every model and construct, every hypothesis and theory, stands or falls ultimately on the degree to which it meets this test. In utilizing some of the newer analytical tools, one need not belittle the older ones. Narrative history, for example, has yielded rich insights into the purposes, strategies, and accomplishments of the actors upon the international stage. But more formal and systematic modes of analysis and interpretation may prove especially helpful in projecting trends and in estimating future possibilities and probabilities in the rapidly changing international scene of today.

4

International Politics and the One-party Regime

The peace agreement signed on 4 October 1992 between the Mozambican government and the Mozambican National Resistance ended a 16-year civil war that has left an estimated 1 million people dead, devastated the country's economic and social infrastructures and compelled more than 1.7 million people - the largest registered refugee population in Africa - to seek refuge in neighboring countries. The majority, about 1.1 million in October 1992, have found asylum in Malawi, one of the most densely populated countries in Africa and among the world's poorest nations, as well as a long-time South African ally and Frelimo opponent. Since 1986, the Malawian government has implemented and remains committed to a policy that not only has received international attention and praise from the United Nations High Commissioner for Refugees and the U.S. State Department, but also has contrasted sharply with its human rights record and with the number of forced repatriations and mistreatment of refugees occurring in Europe, North America and Asia.

Malawi's response to the refugee crisis follows a common trend among African countries of asylum which, when confronted with political and economic problems and refugee movements of great magnitude, embrace an open door policy and ensure the protection of refugees. Malawi's refugee policy, while firmly rooted on the African continent, remains ill-understood and little-explained, save for the idea offered by both international agencies and African governments of the shared ethnic ties between refugees and hosts.

The objective of this chapter is to identify the variables which account for the nature and formulation of Malawian policy toward the arrival and settlement of Mozambican refugees from 1986 to 1993. Specifically, it will show that Malawian refugee policy was historically produced; reflected the natural and structural economic constraints of the country; and resulted from the one-party regime's desperate quest to ensure its survival in the midst of increasing domestic and international pressures for democratisation following the end of the Cold War and political change in South Africa.

MOZAMBICAN REFUGEES IN MALAWI

The recent history of Mozambican refugees in Malawi and the response of the Malawian government can be divided into two main periods: the 1970s to 1986, characterized by sporadic and temporary movements of Mozambicans finding refuge and assistance among local Malawians; and late 1986 to 1993, in which a massive influx of refugees led to the implementation of an international program of assistance. Thus, one can differentiate between these two periods by the nature of the influx and the identities of the actors involved.

Sporadic movements of Mozambicans across the Malawian border were reported regularly during the 1970s and the early 1980s in the Mulanje and Dedza districts. During this initial stage, assistance was provided mainly by the community in which the refugees self-settled. The local residents usually shared housing, food, water and land with the refugees, who were displaced by what were then perceived as temporary disturbances. If and when the refugees reported their status to the district police, they were given temporary shelter and food. At the time, there was no UNHCR presence in Malawi, and the Malawian government had not yet ratified the 1951 Convention relating to the Status of Refugees or its 1967 Protocol.

By the end of 1986, the number of Mozambican refugees had increased dramatically. Over a six-month period, more than 70,000 Mozambicans sought refuge in five districts inside Malawi, bringing their estimated total in the country to 100,000. This first large influx of refugees into Malawi resulted from a shift in Malawian policy *vis-a-vis* Renamo. The mass movement took place a few weeks after the leaders of Mozambique, Zambia and Zimbabwe visited President Kamuzu Banda of Malawi, charging that Renamo was operating from Malawian bases and threatening him with sanctions. Banda denied the charges, but soon after the visit large Renamo contingents, apparently flushed out of Malawi, overran large parts of the Mozambican province of Zambezia and created the first influx of refugees into Malawi.

This movement had two major implications. First, given the number of refugees, it resulted in the abandonment of a "local" strategy in favour of a national one. The government intervened, calling upon the Malawi Red Cross to coordinate and distribute relief supplies to the Mozambican refugees in consultation with district commissioners. Refugee camps were opened in all receiving districts and transport and communication networks leading to the areas of settlement were constructed or rehabilitated. Second, the 1986 refugee influx set the stage for international intervention.

Until then, Renamo fighters had found a safe haven as well as logistical, military and medical support in Malawi, a situation which ruled out the involvement of international agencies and the presence of international observers in the areas of settlement. Malawi's alignment in 1986 with the policy taken by its immediate neighbors, namely Zimbabwe, Zambia and

Mozambique, resulted in the dismantlement of most Renamo bases in Malawi, the subsequent departure of Renamo fighters from the Malawian territory and, ultimately, the participation of international agencies in the relief activities.

UNHCR and non-governmental organisations (NGOs) became more involved in Malawi in January 1987, when the Malawian government officially requested their intervention, at a time when a major offensive in northern Mozambique by combined Zimbabwean, Tanzanian and Mozambican troops had led to a second major flow of Mozambican refugees into Malawi. In February 1987, the government signed a memorandum of understanding with UNHCR, thereby officially requesting a UNHCR presence in Malawi.

Then, in November 1987, Malawi ratified the 1951 Convention, its 1967 Protocol and the Organisation of African Unity (OAU) Convention Governing the Specific Aspects of Refugee Problems in Africa. By that time, more than 300,000 Mozambicans had sought asylum in Malawi and their numbers continued to increase at the rate of 20,000 per month in 1988. The 1989 to 1992 period saw a relative stabilisation of the number of refugees at around 900,000 up until the end of July 1992, when the peace talks between Renamo and Frelimo allowed thousands of Mozambicans, facing starvation in Renamo-held areas because of a devastating drought, to find refuge in Malawi, mostly in Nsanje district.

Since the signature of the Mozambican peace accord in October 1992, however, no new refugee flows into Malawi have been reported. In fact, according to the UNHCR sub-office in Tete province, as of June 1993, over 260,000 refugees had returned from Malawi. Such instances of spontaneous repatriation, which have multiplied in the fall and winter of 1993, are occurring along with the implementation of a reconstruction and reintegration plan of action in Mozambique and signal the disintegration of the program of refugee assistance in Malawi. As outlined previously, Malawi's implementation of international refugee law began in November 1987, when the government signed the 1951 Convention, the 1967 Protocol and the OAU Convention.

These ratifications merely confirmed a well-established practice regarding the admission of Mozambican refugees, for even prior to 1987, the government was pursuing an "open door" policy, accepting the presence of all Mozambicans on the national territory. Before turning to an explanation of this approach, it should be emphasized that Malawian practices regarding the status of Mozambicans differ from the 1951 Convention definition of refugee on one fundamental point: According to the latter, refugee status is determined on an individual basis, whereas Mozambican access to safety, and later to refugee status in Malawi, is conducted on a group basis. All asylum-seekers from Mozambique are recognized as prima facie refugees by virtue of the continuing civil strife in that country.

Malawian refugee admission and status determination policies follow a usual pattern found among most African countries of asylum, a pattern formally established by the expansion of the High Commissioner's mandate through the development of the "good offices" function in the late 195Os and by the 1969 OAU Convention. The latter especially includes external aggression, foreign domination or events seriously disturbing public order, as causes of refugee movements. It therefore recognizes as refugees all persons compelled to escape violence, regardless of whether they personally are in danger of political persecution, and mandates a group-defined standard for determination.

This approach is conceptualized by Zolberg, Suhrke and Aguayo, who distinguish between three sociological types of refugees: the activists, defined as "dissenters and rebels whose actions contribute to the conflict and eventually force them to flee;" the targets, "individuals who through membership in a particular group, are singled out for violent action;" and the victims, who are "randomly caught in the cross-fire or are exposed to generalized social violence." The majority of Mozambican refugees fall within the last category (accounted for in the OAU Convention but ignored in the 1959 definition), since their flights and subsequent refugee status do not result from personal political activities but from their mere physical location in areas of conflicts.

The interpretation most commonly held by both the United Nations and the Malawian government of the open door policy and practices in Malawi is that of "traditional African hospitality," further explained by the fact that refugees and hosts share a common culture and language and belong to the same ethnic group. In the words of the District Commissioner of Nsanje in Malawi, the refugees are "neighbors and friends who belong to the same ethnic group and the same tribes as our own people. We can thus identify with their trouble." While the existence of such ties does not apply to all circumstances in Africa, it has explanatory strength, particularly when restated within an historical and political context: the partition of Africa in general, and the Southern African region in particular, into nation-states and the enduring cross-border relationships between the populations of neighboring states.

As A.I. Asiwaju reports, the boundaries resulting from the 1884 Berlin Conference were drawn:

Across well-established lines of communication including, in every case, a dormant or active sense of community based on traditions concerning common ancestry, usually very strong kinship ties, shared socio-political institutions and economic resources, common customs and practices and sometimes acceptance of a common political control.

The partition and subsequent creation of state boundaries resulted in an important movement of people and materials across boundaries which invariably functioned less as "barriers" than as "conduits" between the states on either side. The current movement of Mozambicans into Malawi does not constitute an historical anomaly: Peoples originating from what now constitutes Mozambique migrated into Malawi before, during and after colonialism in search of asylum, land or work. Phiri's study of the Chewa and Ngoni in Zambia, Malawi and Mozambique indicates that the political boundaries separating the three countries never served as boundaries of exclusion; instead, they have been used as sanctuary by the peoples living in the three countries to evade tax collections under colonial rule and political persecution after independence.

Similarly, research conducted in the Southern region of Malawi (the lower Shire valley) underlines the persistence and importance of cross-border movements between Malawi and Mozambique. During the nineteenth and twentieth centuries, the Sena and Lomwe, inhabiting the north-central region of what now constitutes Mozambique, fled famine and violence induced, first by the slave trade and later by the Portuguese colonial practices of land alienation and forced labor. They settled in the southern region of Malawi where they usually worked as farmers or wage laborers on the colonial tea and coffee plantations. The Lomwe now constitute the majority of the population in the region, having displaced and absorbed the Mang'anja people, the original inhabitants of southern Malawi.

One of the results of these incessant movements is the development of ethnic, family, and economic links that unite Mozambicans and Malawians living on either side of the border. Interviews with Mozambican refugees in several camps and self-settlement areas in Malawi show that most respondents had established labor or market ties in Malawi long before their flight. Many Mozambican male refugees surveyed informally by UNHCR or NGO representatives indicated that the first destination of their flight to Malawi had been the plantation areas where they, or their relatives, had worked on several occasions in the decades preceding the outburst of violence.

While not all Mozambican refugees could claim labor and commercial links with Malawi prior to their flight, the existence of such links certainly characterized most Mozambican border residents. The study of the relationships across Malawi's international boundaries relates in two important ways to the study of its refugee policy. First, it indicates the incapacity (or unwillingness) of the government to control the movements of peoples (be they refugees, migrants or simply relatives of residents on the other side) across the boundaries of the national territory. The Malawian government, as all governments in Africa, does not have the military, logistical and technical apparatus to contain the flow of persons moving into the territory.

Even South Africa, which has developed a very sophisticated and deadly apparatus of border controls (such as a 70-kilometer electrified border fence), has been unable to stop an estimated 200,000 Mozambican refugees and migrants from entering the country. Second, it shows that the open door policy of the Malawian government regarding the arrival of refugees constitutes a de jure recognition of an historically grounded fait accompli, i.e., the persistence of cultural and economic relationships between Malawians and Mozambicans that defy nation-state building and allegiance.

Yet, the role of these historical routes of communication, in founding what can be referred to as a locally based refugee determination process, should not be overestimated. While there are numerous instances in Malawi and in other parts of Africa of hosts sharing food, water, housing and even land with refugees, there are also cases of refugees being attacked, exploited or despised by the local populations. Fieldwork in Malawi showed, for instance, that Mozambicans, who initially had found asylum among the host populations in Malawian border villages, eventually were obliged to register in refugee camps because of a drought-induced decrease in local resources in 1992.

Informants in the district of Ntcheu reported that on several occasions, Mozambicans had been severely beaten by local inhabitants because the agricultural and business activities of the former were interfering with local interests. Research conducted in other parts of Africa underlines similar types of interactions indicating that hospitality is "a function of resource availability" and therefore of the activities and policies of the government of the country of asylum. The host government plays a central function in controlling both the economic and political impact of the presence of refugees through the policies of settlement, economic integration and repatriation that it follows.

Governments often move refugees away from the borders for reasons of security or for broader economic purposes. As the following analysis will show, Malawian settlement and integration policies have consisted of a *laissez-faire* approach coupled at times with interventionism, reflecting the natural constraints of the country and the nature of the Malawian economic system, which is dominated by the plantation sector and presidential interests. While forced repatriation does not characterize current Malawian policy towards Mozambicans, it does describe the past. For instance, on multiple occasions over the past two decades, Malawian authorities arranged, with both the government of Zambia and the Frelimo government of Mozambique, for the forced repatriation of thousands of Jehovah's Witnesses in spite of the obvious dangers they faced upon their return to Malawi.

Similarly, in the course of Mozambique's struggle for independence, the Malawian government agreed with the Portuguese secret service to forcibly repatriate Frelimo members who sought refuge in Malawi. The differences between Malawi's current and past treatment of refugees indicate that the study of Malawian refugee policy must be integrated within the broader framework of its foreign and domestic policy and within the context of the government's dogged adherence to the one-party regime.

LOCAL AND NATIONAL DETERMINANTS OF REFUGEE POLICY

NATURAL CONDITIONS AND SETTLEMENT POLICY

African governments face two options when deciding upon settlement policies: the self-settlement solution whereby refugees are "allowed" to settle spontaneously wherever they wish, and the organized settlement option characterized by the settlement of refugees in camps or rural settlement schemes. The majority of Africa's asylum states favour the second solution because it facilitates the distribution of refugee relief, minimizes the impact of refugees on national public services and permits better control of refugees' political and economic activities. Yet, as John Rogge states, while they discourage the spontaneous settlement of refugees, not all African countries of asylum come up with effective alternative strategies; hence many refugees have little choice but to self-settle and fend for them without international assistance.

Malawian settlement policies have combined laissez-faire and interventionist approaches. On one hand, the role of the government has been limited to formalizing a fait accompli: the locations of all the camps (with one exception) derive from the spontaneous patterns of initial arrival and settlement along the borders.

On the other hand, the government has documented all sites of spontaneous settlement and pursued an active campaign of refugee registration. As a result, the majority of self-settled Mozambicans have been the recipients of international assistance.

In the first years of movement, roughly prior to the end of 1986, refugees self-settled freely within their districts of asylum while all these spontaneous settlements were located along the Mozambican borders, two patterns rapidly emerged. The first was refugee settlement within or alongside already established Malawian villages. The second was the aggregation of refugees

- in some form of *de facto* camps - in one particular area. The occurrence of one or the other form was determined by a geographical factor. The border areas along the central region spread over 490 kilometers, from the Zambian border to the district of Mwanza, and refugees entered Malawi across a multitude of entry points. In contrast, the southern border has a limited number of entry points. Refugees moved into areas where physical dispersion was difficult, leaving large concentrations of over 10,000 at Muloza (Mulanje district) and 30,000 at Mankhokwe.

In the last months of 1986, when the government decided to intervene, the patterns of settlements were therefore already well-established. Rather than attempting to relocate the refugees, the Malawian policy consolidated settlements that had been spontaneously created by the refugees themselves. The government officially opened refugee camps in the districts of Mangochi, Nsanje and Mulanje while recognizing self-settlement areas in Ntcheu and Dedza - comprising about half of the total registered refugee population - as refugee sites.

The question of the safety of both refugees and their local hosts -usually an important issue in settlement practices - was never very significant in Malawi. Indeed, both the camps and the areas where refugees self-settled are located near, or along, the Mozambican border, directly contradicting a recommendation of the OAU Convention: "For reasons of security, countries of asylum shall, as far as possible, settle refugees at a reasonable distance from the frontier of their country of origin."

Yet, security problems did occur on a regular basis in all areas of settlements, whether self-settlements or camps. The last quarter of 1992 especially, saw a serious deterioration in security along the border with Mozambique. In most border districts, attacks on Mozambican refugees and local Malawians resulted in loss of life and much damage and looting. Unidentified gunmen attacked the city of Mwanza on two occasions, prompting the government to impose a curfew on the city and to send in Malawian troops. These security threats, however, have never forced the government to relocate refugees.

Malawi's rather lenient policy regarding the location of the camps and the presence of self-settled refugees stems mainly from the natural and economic conditions in the country. The scarcity of uncultivated areas greatly limited governmental options regarding the locations of the refugees. Refugee camps and self-settlement areas are usually located on non-farmed or sparsely-farmed sections, very often on dambos (low-lying seasonal swamps). Rather than developing new sites and therefore exacerbating tensions over lands, the government opted for a formal recognition of spontaneous settlements and *de facto* camps.

In November 1991, however, the Malawian government departed from this laissez-faire settlement policy, closing all the camps in the southern region and opening a new camp, Lisongwe, in Mwanza district. With the exception of those seeking asylum in the integrated settlements of the central region, all newly arrived refugees were transported by bus from their first district of asylum to Lisongwe camp. In contrast to its former approach, the government created Lisongwe in an area previously unoccupied by refugees and located relatively far from the border.

Two factors mandated the choice of Lisongwe: the overpopulation of already existing camps and the overcrowding of the districts which had until then received the bulk of the refugees. Lisongwe's establishment responded also to logic of regional development planning. In addition to being both sparsely populated and farmed, the area was, by Malawian standards, one of the most poorly developed in terms of transport and health facilities. By creating a camp in such a location, the government hoped to ameliorate public services and ultimately generate development.

REFUGEE ECONOMIC ACTIVITIES AND MALAWIAN ECONOMIC POLICY

In addressing the economic activities of refugees, Malawian policy follows an approach similar to that of its settlement policy: consistently laissez-faire, with a few revealing instances of state intervention. Significantly, the government has neither implemented settlement schemes, whereby refugees are allocated agricultural lands or access to wage labor in order to achieve self-sufficiency, nor forbidden or monitored refugee endeavours and movements. For instance, a number of the pre-1986 refugees self-settled and engaged in farming activities. Even after 1986, the most fortunate among them (in most cases the richest ones) rented lands belonging to Malawian locals or obtained permission to use the land from the local traditional authorities.

In Chifunga and Kunyenda refugee camps, the camp administrators and district commissioners themselves successfully negotiated with the local traditional authorities to allocate small parcels of land to refugees. Officially, refugees are not to leave their camp without authorisation from the camp chairperson, and they are barred from engaging in wage-labor activities. In practice, however, the regulations are not enforced, resulting in a *de facto* freedom of movement within Malawi and to Mozambique, and a significant number of refugees working on the tea and coffee plantations or in the cities. No controls or sanctions have ever been imposed on refugees' employers, be they plantation owners, medium-scale farmers or urban traders.

In fact, in one instance, the Malawian government itself granted permission to the Sucoma Sugar Estate to recruit directly from the refugee camps. Nevertheless, the government opposed a de jure economic integration of refugees and did not implement a development-related refugee program based on the integration of refugee settlements within development planning.

Part of the reason for the absence of such programmes is the reluctance of donor countries to fund these types of activities.

While they have in theory accepted the "burden sharing" principle, the issue of "additionality," that is, whether or not development-related refugee assistance should be additional to development aid remains unresolved. Since 1989, UNHCR has been experiencing global financial difficulties resulting in part from the unwillingness of donor countries to financially match the extension of the UNHCR mandate as well as from an increasing number of operations lasting several years. The issue of additionality was of special importance in Malawi for two main reasons. First, the global budget crisis facing UNHCR has led to repeated program reduction in Malawi - and elsewhere in the world - and to a decline in many services to Mozambican refugees.

Moreover, the implementation of development projects in refugee-affected areas became even more problematic after 1992, following the decision of Malawi's major donor countries to freeze most of their bilateral development aid because of the government's refusal to accept democratic changes. But several other factors mandated the government's opposition to a formal integration of the Mozambicans: the dramatic economic situation of the country - characterized by a population explosion (growth rate of 3.7 percent per year), land scarcity coupled with land erosion, a small industrial sector and underemployment - and the nature of the political regime. Indeed, the government economic policy based in the growth of the estate sector and dominated by Press Holdings (a holding company in which the Malawian President Dr Banda owns all but one share), constitutes a major variable in determining the response of the Malawian government toward the refugees.

The establishment of wage-earning settlements similar to the Sudanese experience could have been attempted in the plantation areas of Malawi, but from the perspective of the government such a strategy was politically unwarranted, given the high number of Malawians who rely on plantation employment for survival. In effect, however, as stated above, the presence of refugee camps in the plantation areas provides a pool of refugee labor for the plantations, but does not require the implementation of a formal employment policy. Their establishment has been achieved, therefore, at a low political cost.

Implementing a refugee assistance program based on generalized access to lands for refugees - as was done in Tanzania - was simply unfeasible in Malawi, for political and practical reasons, on the local and national levels, Malawian farmers had increasing difficulty ensuring household food security due to land scarcity, drought and low producer prices. The long-term settlement of Mozambicans in Malawi would have required one of two options: First, their mass displacement to, and resettlement in, the northern region of the country where land pressure is less acute; or second, a total restructuring of the current land distribution patterns.

In other words, such a policy would have required the distribution of estate lands to landless Malawians, small farmers and refugees. The Mozambicans most likely would have opposed the first option, as it would have signified an additional movement (presumably forcibly induced) far away from their areas of origin. The nature of the Malawian state and of the economic interests at stake in the plantation economy, dominated by the presidential estates, unequivocally ruled out the overt mention of land redistribution - the second option - without speaking of its implementation.

The importance of economic interests in shaping refugee policy is further underlined by the government's approach towards refugee trading activities. Food oil is the only item whose trade was strictly controlled by the government. Small-scale trading, whereby individual refugees sell and exchange to local Malawians part of their food rations (as well as non-food items) for either cash or other commodities, is carried out in all the refugee-receiving districts. Oil, which has the highest market value of all distributed commodities, is sold by "predominantly male) refugees at a much lower price than that offered by Malawian retail sellers.

As a result, the government officially declared the trade of refugees' oil illegal, and on several occasions the police confiscated this item if it was purchased from refugees. But no such regulation was instituted for other food items distributed to refugees, principally maize and beans. Additionally, the government does not attempt to control the trade of agricultural crops grown along the Malawian border in Mozambique. The reason for the government's dual policy lies in the identity of those whose interests are at stake. Whereas maize and beans are locally produced by small farmers, the production and sale of domestic and imported oil is the monopoly of Kovo, a branch of Press Holdings (a corporation owned by the President himself) and constitutes one of the principal imported intermediate goods of which the government has a monopoly on domestic sales.

International interests also account for the government's restrictions on the sale of refugees' oil. Kovo produces about 40 percent of its consumption of oil and has successfully attracted American shareholders on the clear understanding that the local prices of oil will go up. Refugee market activities not only threatened the economic interests of retail sellers and of Press Holdings, but also the interests of American corporations. According to a (confidential) source in Malawi, pressure from American businesses caused the U.S. Agency for International Development (USAID) to decrease an intended donation of oil to refugees from 5,000 metric tons to 2,000 metric tons.

These examples indicate that whenever the activities of refugees served the economic interests of the state (that is, of the president and a few of his advisors/allies), the laissez-faire approach prevailed. When refugee activities challenged these interests, however, the government implemented a more aggressive and interventionist policy. These examples further demonstrate that natural and economic conditions are not the only variables determining and constraining the national response to Mozambican refugees. In fact, as the third part of this chapter will demonstrate, the nature and content of Malawian refugee policy originates within the raison d'etat, which in Malawi may be defined broadly as the building and continuing existence of a (seemingly) stable, one-party, autocratic regime.

THE SURVIVAL OF THE ONE-PARTY SYSTEM

THE MOZAMBICAN JEHOVAH'S WITNESSES

As underlined previously, Malawi's economic and natural resources constrained the scope of governmental initiatives in the domain of rural settlement schemes, refugee self-sufficiency and economic integration. Under these conditions, it would have been logical for the government to encourage repatriation. In reality, the attitude and policy of the Malawian government regarding this durable solution have been ambivalent at best. On one hand, it signed a tri-partite agreement with UNHCR and the Mozambican government on repatriation as early as December 1988. On the other hand, until 1992, the government minimized, if not openly denied, the existence of a spontaneous process of repatriation.

According to an article from the official Mozambican News Agency published in October 1990, Malawian officials were waging a psychological campaign to persuade Mozambicans to stay in Malawi, spreading false information about the security situation in Mozambique. However, in September 1990, the Malawian government departed from its stand against the return of refugees and officially repatriated approximately 566 Mozambicans. These conflicting responses were mandated both by the function of the country within the southern African regional system and by the nature of the state itself. With regard to the 1990 repatriation, the director of Mozambique's Refugee Support Nucleus stated: "We were surprised when the Malawian government pressed Mozambique to repatriate its citizens because they have never taken such an attitude in the past."

Given the identity of the returnees, Malawi's change of policy comes as no surprise: They all belonged to the Jehovah's Witnesses religious sect, a sect that has been banned in Malawi. The conflict between the Malawian government and the Jehovah's Witnesses began in the late 1960s, sparked by the Witnesses' refusal to buy membership cards of the ruling Malawi Congress Party. From 1967 onwards, members of the sect have been persecuted, murdered and forced into exile. As the Minority Rights Group reports, many African politicians, including President Banda of Malawi, view the Witnesses as obstacles to the building of one-party regimes.

By refusing to succumb to the card-checking campaigns, mounted by the MCP [Malawi Congress Party] to force party membership on an increasingly reluctant population, the Witnesses were an ~example' that could not be tolerated. They had to be crushed. The autocratic nature of the Malawian state accounts for the decision of the government to repatriate Jehovah's Witness refugees and also explains why two years after the 1990 repatriation; the government still required that a list of all refugees refusing health care for religious reasons be submitted to the camp authorities by the NGOs in charge of the health program.

Evidently, the Malawian government was more concerned with the refugees' religious beliefs and practices than with their economic activities within the territory or their possible involvement in either Renamo or Frelimo operations in Mozambique and Malawi. Mozambican Jehovah's Witnesses were perceived as a threat to the autocratic rule of President

Banda, a perception which emphasizes further refugee-related issues from the perspective of the one-party system.

REGIONAL AND INTERNATIONAL POLITICS

Until the end of the Cold War, President Banda's regime owed its international support and status to its stand against communism and national liberation movements in the region. Malawi was the only African country to establish diplomatic relationships with South Africa. Its president-for-life Banda was also the only African leader to make an official visit to the colony of Mozambique, which led to the collaboration of the Malawian security forces with the Portuguese army against Frelimo. In more recent years, along with South Africa, Malawi has been an important Renamo backer. In effect, Malawi's strategy of support translated into foreign aid and foreign assistance, and allowed President Banda to implement an autocratic regime characterized by the ruthless suppression of an democratic ideals.

The end of the Cold War and the political changes in South Africa signified Malawi's loss of its primary function within the global and regional systems and, as a result, its value in the eyes of its Western backers. Since 1991, external pressure against President Banda's one-party regime has increased, culminating in a decision by Western donors in May 1992 first to freeze $74 million in aid and then to leverage any additional assistance as an instrument for achieving political change. After almost 50 years of silence, they agreed that Banda's regime failed to fit their criteria of "good governance" given its persistent violation of human rights and obstinate refusal to accept democratic changes.

Malawi's response to Mozambican refugees is shaped by its domestic and foreign policies through a concoction of fantasy and Realpoltik, to borrow from William Finnegan's assessment of Malawi's pro-apartheid policy. The fantasy is territorial expansion. Researchers have shown that President Banda's aspiration toward creating a "Greater Malawi" and Malawi's landlocked situation prompted Malawi's active support of the Portuguese and later Renamo. In 1963, the Portugese colonial rulers in Mozambique persuaded Banda that if he helped them against Frelimo, he could stand to gain the entire northern half of Mozambique. According to Finnegan, when the Portuguese started a small anti-Frelimo separatist movement in 1968 called the African National Union of Rombezia, Rombezia was intended to be the name given to Banda's new territory.

Given this historical precedent, it is plausible that various agreements over territorial boundaries and expansion formed the basis of the collaboration between the Malawian government, South Africa and Renamo. Such a deal could easily have taken place, pushed by South Africa's hegemonic rule within the southern African regional system. On several occasions since 1986, the Malawian government has proposed that the Malawian army, with the help of an international peacekeeping force, seal off and protect a section of Mozambique administered by Malawi where refugees would repatriate and resettle. Until October 1992, when Renamo and Frelimo finally reached a peace agreement, the possibility of the Malawian government taking advantage of an internationally sponsored plan of action could not have been ruled out, especially in light of the increasing numbers of international military interventions conducted on the basis of "peacemaking" and "peacekeeping."

As far as Realpolitik is concerned, one aspect of the answer is self-evident: The refugee policy of any state is governed more often than not by politics and ideology, rather than ethics. For instance, until 1980, the admission of refugees to the United States was limited to those individuals fleeing communist regimes. States tend to adopt what Astri Suhrke refers to as "politicized-refugee policies," that is, refugee policies based on domestic and foreign considerations and used "to discredit or destabilize an unfriendly government or to support friendly governments." Malawi is no exception. Its policies towards Mozambican refugees in the 1980s and 1990s and its treatment of South African refugees until recently were indeed modeled along its ideological orientations. South African political exiles clearly have been forbidden from entering the Malawian territory, as a result of the signature of an extradition agreement in May 1966 between Malawi and South Africa.

Mozambican refugees, on the other hand, have been welcomed in Malawi, as a means of discrediting the Frelimo government and its Marxist social reforms, and of destabilizing the regime. In contrast, Zimbabwe (a Frelimo ally) has demonstrated some reluctance in providing asylum to Mozambicans; in 1991 it closed sections of its borders and forcibly repatriated approximately 2,000 Mozambicans. In late 1986, the Malawian government - at least officially - shifted its policy away from its pro-Renamo stand, committing 600 troops to help guard the rail route to the Mozambican port of Nacala.

This shift did not lead, however, to a reformulation of the country's refugee policy for three main reasons. First, the government had already adopted the international instruments of refugee law and therefore had endorsed both refugee status determinations as defined by the OAU Convention as well as the principle of non-refoulement. Second, the presence of refugees allowed Malawi to continue supporting Renamo troops, since the latter were able to find safety in the country and hide among "genuine" refugees whenever necessary. Finally, economic factors primarily induced the 1987 shift: The Frelimo-Renamo conflict led to a paralysis of the communication networks within Mozambique, resulting in a dramatic increase in Malawian transport costs. In the absence of a peace settlement, the defense of the Nacala-Malawi railway constituted the only way to reduce these costs and ensure Malawi's access to the sea.

Similar economic reasons account for Malawi's response to the fresh arrival of Mozambicans following the end of the Cold War, political changes in South Africa and the decision by Western countries to freeze foreign aid. In the absence of domestic democratic change, the implementation of a generous open door policy toward Mozambican refugees constituted the only way for the Malawian government to counterbalance international criticisms and concerns regarding treatment of its own people, to improve Malawi's international image in the West and to ensure that the flow of international aid into Malawi did not cease. The mere fact that the Office of President and Cabinet (OPC), one of the most powerful ministries in the Malawian government, is in charge of the management of the refugee program indicates the preeminence of the relief budget in domestic politics.

The economic function of refugee assistance, however, is a complex one. From a long-term perspective, the presence of refugees constitutes an important economic burden for both the people and the Malawian government. Several World Bank missions in Malawi have pointed out that the UNHCR relief program has been unable to cover all the governmental expenditures induced by the refugee population. Furthermore, refugee assistance takes into account neither the long-term negative environmental impact of refugee settlements, nor the ensuing depletion of natural resources - both of which Malawi will have to address on its own in the future. From a short-term perspective however, refugee assistance does instill some economic impulse, although difficult to quantify, predominantly in the forms of business contracts for national enterprises (grain milling and transport, for instance) and employment offered by local and international NGOs.

Furthermore, the program of assistance to Mozambicans includes Malawians among its beneficiaries. The assistance program has expanded from camps or self-settlement areas to integrate local villages as well. In effect, this approach signifies that infrastructure, such as roads and water points, have been constructed within the villages surrounding refugee settlement areas. Malawians also have had access to the health facilities provided to the refugees, as well as to the various projects, both as trainees and employees. At least half, if not most health workers trained by international NGOs have been Malawians. The same principle has applied to income-generating activities, construction and training projects. In an environment dominated by the absence of social infrastructure as well as work and business opportunities, the refugee assistance program certainly mitigated economic tensions and contributed to the maintenance of relative political order and stability.

The above analysis underlines the existence of a regional and international system of refugee politics upon which the regime of President Banda founded its strategic importance in the last decade. Malawian refugee policy is a crude reflection of the country's relationships with, and dependence upon, South Africa and the West - its main financial backers - all requiring an open door policy from Malawi as part of a regional destabilisation strategy and as a prerequisite for international assistance. With reluctance, the Malawian government finally decided to implement a multi-party system in January 1993, three months after Frelimo and Renamo signed a cease-fire agreement ending the 16-year Mozambican civil war.

The October 1992 peace accord and the resulting repatriation movements radically transformed the Southern African regional system and, hence, regional and international refugee politics. It is a transformation which, in conjunction with rising internal strife and an enduring economic crisis, imposed political changes in Malawi. As Mozambican refugees began to return home, so did Malawian political exiles. The simultaneity of these two movements is indicative of their interdependence. For Mozambicans to remain at home peace in the country must be sustained, a condition which necessitates, among other things, Malawi's rethinking its role within the

Southern African regional system - especially its idea of a Greater Malawi.

On the positive side, the recent political changes in Malawi and the establishment of a multi-party system should foster new relationships between the Malawian and Mozambican governments, since Malawi's expansionist "fantasy" has been linked intrinsically to the Malawian leadership and the existence of a one-party, autocratic regime. Yet, whether peace in Mozambique and the establishment of a multi-party system in Malawi will be sustainable are questions which are heavily dependent upon broader regional and international variables. These include the future configuration of South Africa and the capacity of its government to control violence within the country.

A conflict between the South African government and contending political organisations, such as the Inkhata movement headed by Buthelezi or the white ultra-right wing, will spread to the rest of the region, resulting in South African refugee movements and serving as political and military leverage for Renamo and its supporters in Malawi.

In addition to this regional determinant, the sustainability of peace in Mozambique and the existence of a democratic regime in Malawi will be heavily dependent upon the economic recovery of the two countries and, therefore, upon assistance from international actors. A rapid economic recovery not only will permit the reconstruction of the social and economic infrastructures in Mozambique, but also will provide means of survival to the thousands of former Frelimo and Renamo soldiers (a number of them still armed) thus preventing widespread violence and banditry.

Similarly, given the high level of expectations inspired by political changes in Malawi, the survival of a multi-party system in Malawi will rely heavily on international economic assistance that would enhance the capacity of the Malawian leadership to bring about tangible economic improvement in the daily life of the Malawian population. Malawian refugee policy reflects the natural constraints and economic conditions of the country, results from the interaction of domestic and international considerations and combines government activities and interventions with a historically grounded phenomena.

The first two variables account for the intervention of the international community in 1987 and the absence of formal policies of economic integration for the refugees. The management of the refugee movement was far beyond the capacity of a small country facing devastating economic crisis and poverty as well as unequal land distribution and increasing land pressure. These political, demographic and natural conditions also limited the scope and range of policies aimed at integrating and promoting the self-sufficiency of the refugees. In terms of admission and status determination, international and regional factors worked in favour of formulating an open door and relatively generous policy towards Mozambican refugees.

Tragically enough, these factors are also directly or indirectly responsible for the very circumstances leading to these flights. The domestic and foreign policy considerations contributing to the outbreak of violence and the civil war in Mozambique also influenced the response of the Malawian government to the influx of refugee movements. The survival of the Malawian one-party regime mandated an open door policy, first to destabilize the Mozambican Marxist regime and gain the favour of external backers (in particular South Africa and the United States), and, later, to reestablish Malawi's rather blemished international status.

Yet, the study of Malawian refugee policy also indicates that the arrival of Mozambicans in Malawi followed historically grounded communication routes between the Malawian and Mozambican peoples. As early as the eighteenth century, Mozambicans migrated to Malawi in search of a safe haven, land and work. The slave trade, the Portuguese colonial practices and, finally, the civil war compelled them to leave. At the same time, the existence of farming lands and employment possibilities on Nyasaland, later Malawian, plantations acted as pull factors. The mass influx of Mozambicans in Malawi complied with an historical process and actually followed historical routes of migration, which not only preceded the British and Portuguese presence, but also intensified under colonial rule.

Hence, Malawi's admission policy and group-based approach to refugee status was also an official recognition of a historically grounded fait accompli. Yet, it is also evident that Malawi's role within the Southern African regional complex contributed to the explosion of violence in Mozambique and to the arrival of refugees, further mandating its open door approach. Therefore, Malawian refugee policy is founded upon both this fait accompli and the government's foreign and domestic policies. This combination highlights a central function of the past and current movements of Mozambicans within Malawi: The refugee movements have acted as both the necessary condition and end-product of the integration of Malawi within a capitalist and nation-state system; an integration further characterized by the creation, consolidation and quest for survival of the Malawian state as a one-party, autocratic regime.

5

Competing Visions of International Political Order

Both political leaders and academics often claim exceptional times. But what does it mean to speak of exceptional politics in international relations? In one sense exceptionality is a descriptive category referring to a radical change in the systemic conditions of international politics. In this chapter a different notion of exception is examined. It refers to a particular method of conceptualizing the nature of international political order. The exception defines political order by means of constitutional-legal reasoning in which different understandings of the nature and status of international law and its political transgressions describe competing visions of international political order.

The focal point of this international politics of exception is not the traditional distinction between liberal and realist views of international politics but the constitutionalist triad of normativism, decisionism, and institutionalism. For many, the acts of violence on September 11, 2001, in the United States created exceptional times in international politics. The prime minister of the United Kingdom, Tony Blair, marked a moment of millennial change: "In retrospect, the Millennium marked only a moment in time.

It was the events of September 11 that marked a turning point in history, where we confront the dangers of the future and assess the choices facing humankind." Two years later, during the legitimacy crisis over the war on Iraq, Kofi Annan, the Secretary General of the United Nations, similarly spoke of the end of the global security order that was institutionalized after World War II: "We have come at a fork in the road.... This may be a moment no less decisive than 1945 itself, when the United Nations was founded." But what does it mean to speak of exceptional international politics?

In one sense the concept of exception is a descriptive category referring to a radical change in the systemic conditions of international politics. References to a fork in the road and a turning point in history are used to describe a factual situation that may have made it impossible to continue as before. In this chapter I examine a different concept of exception. Here exception refers to a method of conceptualizing the character of international political order by means of constitutional-legal reasoning. This method combines a particular philosophical understanding of the relation between order and exception with constitutional accounts of the question of political order at the interstice between the rule of law and the transgression of law.

Philosophically, exception refers to the idea that order is constituted in the definition of what is exceptional to it, what is seemingly its outside. The exception is not a secondary phenomenon that identifies challenges to an established order that exists independently of its exceptions; rather, order is rendered through the articulation of exceptions. Order is thus not constituted by declaring basic normative, cosmological, and/or religious principles against which one can measure exceptional events, but the other way around. Order-defining principles are constituted by means of declaring and identifying exceptions. In other words, the norm does not define the exception but the exception defines the norm.

This philosophical concept operates at a high level of generality. It reaches across or can be applied to different areas of human practice, including art, politics, love, and religion. As a concept in the theory of political order, this philosophical perspective mostly translates into a method that defines international politics by means of identifying the nature and status of an international rule of law and the legitimate conditions of its political transgression. The concept of "international politics of exception" refers to competing definitions of this relation between law and politics. In this understanding, debates about the ordinary or extraordinary nature of events such as those of September 11, 2001, are traversed by competing visions of international political order that rest on different interpretations of the international rule of law and the nature and legitimacy of its political transgression.

This particular conception of the exception is at work in some of the central interpretations of the political significance of the events currently signified as "9/11." Moreover, as I argue, debate about these events is not primarily structured along the traditional distinction between liberal and realist views of international politics but by the difference between the constitutional theories of normativism, decisionism, and institutionalism. In this chapter, I propose to develop this argument by reading some of the prominent European legal and political constitutional theories of the 1920s and 1930s into debates about international order, security, and law after September 11, 2001.

Why is this concept of exception and the theoretical triad of normativism, decisionism, and institutionalism of interest for international studies? Since 1989 "fantasizing about how to order international politics" has been very much in vogue. Sociological and legal debates about the extraordinary nature of situations, the status of international law, and the legitimacy of the suicide pact rule ("the exception for that very small group of events that warrant or even require unilateral action when the legally designated institution or procedure proves unable to operate") have played an important role in framing international politics since the end of the Cold War. Debates about the legitimacy of humanitarian intervention, the constitution of an International Criminal Court, the crisis of the United Nations, and the legitimacy of pre-emptive warfare are just a few examples of cases in which constitutional-legal reasoning has played a prominent role.

The concept of exception that is examined in this chapter also opens an important question for security studies. Constructivist and post-structural analyses of insecurity have emphasized that the rendition of enmity has constitutive effects; that it is an order-constituting device. The concept of international politics of exception shows that the ordering effects of security policy do not simply follow from identifying threats and from role-taking as enemies. They also depend on the specific method of framing the interaction with and between enemies. Constitutional-legal reasoning is such a method, one that is currently playing a prominent role in the debates about international politics and insecurity.

The argument is developed in four sections. The first introduces two ways in which the constitutional-legal concept of exception has been used in international studies and how they differ from the notion of "international politics of exception" that is developed here. The following sections introduce the three main constitutional-legal approaches to the question of exception-normativism, decisionism, and institutionalism-and how they go beyond the distinction between liberal and realist theories that has come to inform many accounts of international relations. These approaches are discussed with reference to some of the central competing interpretations of the political significance of international developments post 9/11.

A CONCEPT IN THE THEORY OF INTERNATIONAL POLITICAL ORDER

The exception is a complex concept in the theory of state, but for the purpose of this chapter I focus on a constitutional-legal concept of exception. The latter identifies the tension between rule of law and the political practice that seeks to transgress it as the central problem of political order. This notion of exception embraces two issues: (1) the principle of legality and its limits, and (2) a constitutional concept of sovereignty.

The principle of legality is one of the defining principles of liberal democracy. It refers to the subordination of political decisions to the rule of law. The latter restrains the arbitrary exercise of political power by means of a generalized system of rules and a system of checks and balances between the authoritative functions of the state (i.e., executive, legislature, and judiciary). Only exceptional conditions can legitimize a disproportionate increase of executive power and other transgressions of the rule of law beyond what would be normally acceptable within the constitutional framework. Among the classic examples of such transgressions are rule by emergency decree, state of siege, and suspending parliamentary decision-making in case of war.

The constitutional notion of sovereignty identifies a constitutional boundary issue. It refers to a highest form of political authority that is reined in by a legal system but that is also constitutive of this system. The concept of sovereignty thus names the boundary between legally circumscribed political practice and political practice that transgresses these circumscriptions. In the name of sovereignty, concepts of political order are constituted by means of working these two conflicting notions of politics into one another. The "politics of exception" refers here to contexts in which the question of sovereignty, that is, how to conceptualize the boundary between constitutionally defined political authority and transcendent political authority, is a political stake.

Although the constitutional-legal concept of exception is formulated most explicitly within theories of the state and has been worked out mostly within the context of domestic politics, it also operates in theories of international relations. First, international crises and, especially, wars provide archetypical grounds for the politicisation of the limits of legality in domestic politics. This aspect of the exception is, for example, central to the theorisation of security developed by Ole Waever, Barry Buzan, and their colleagues at the former Copenhagen Peace Research Institute in the 1990s.

They theorize security as a speech act that makes the survival of the constitutional order the stake of the political game. Securitizing moves are a rhetorical device that seeks to legitimize exceptional policy measures. Securitisation implies a move from "normal" politics contained within constitutionally defined rules of political engagement to exceptional politics, for which the constitutional rules do not hold (or at least do not provide the restraint one would normally expect). Conceptualizing security practice in these terms thus makes the exception a key concept in the theory of security politics.

This way of introducing the concept of exception in international studies does not really relocate it from domestic politics to the international system. The international system hosts the crisis situation that triggers domestic debates about the limits of legality and the legitimacy of radical increases in executive power. The political debate about the legitimacy of exceptional politics thus remains focused on the impact of securitizing moves on the nature of liberal democracy within states.

The concept of exception is also present in international studies in another modality. It functions sometimes as a foundational category that separates domestic from international politics. One of the historical functions of the concept of sovereignty has been to territorialize the legal boundary problem I have referred to above. Sovereignty identified a split between the inside of a territorial state in which politics is firmly embedded in the rule of law and an outside or interstate world in which politics largely operate arbitrarily, that is without being tightly circumscribed by rule of law. In this reading, sovereignty constitutes the international as a realm in which the exception (the exercise of political power unrestrained by rule of law) is the rule.

The exceptional nature of international politics is one of the bases upon which international studies claims a separate disciplinary status, one that makes it different from political science and law. In this reading the exception is a concept that bears more directly upon understandings of the character of international political order as such. However, it has only a limited use in the theory of international politics. It identifies two forms of politics (politics within the rule of law and politics as the arbitrary exercise of power) and locates them in separate realms (domestic and international).

It thus introduces a boundary question for international and political studies. But as a result it suggests that the question of exceptional politics (that is, the limits of legality and different methods of constituting the relation between sovereign political power and the rule of law) is not relevant for political practice within the international system. All international politics is exceptional. Consequently the exception cannot be an issue around which different visions of international political order are defined. It is itself the defining kernel of international politics and therefore not a political problem that invites multiple responses but a single constitutive given.

This chapter addresses this limitation by focusing on how the concept of "exception" refers to a particular "technique" of formulating competing visions of international political order. It develops the notion of an "international politics of exception" that makes different understandings of the legal-constitutional problem of exception relevant for distinguishing different interpretations of international politics. The fact that one can transpose legal theories focusing on the state and domestic politics to international relations is not surprising given that theories of the state are also theories of the political more generally.

Three methods of formulating the limits of international rule of law and the legitimacy of transgressive international political authority define this international problematique of exception: normativism, decisionism, and institutionalism. They are derived from an intensive debate about the nature of legal and political order in interwar Europe. This particular categorisation has been attributed to Carl Schmitt. His work, however, is not simply an outsider's categorisation of a highly politically charged debate. He was extremely active in defending one specific position in this debate; one that became explicitly connected to a juridical defense of German fascism. Therefore I want to emphasize that I am not defining the concepts through Schmitt's work, which would move the problem formulation into a defense of a peculiar combination of decisionism and institutionalism. The conceptual triptych was and has been used more widely and can be easily detached from Schmitt's particular rendition of it.

NORMATIVE AND SKEPTICAL VIEWS OF THE INTERNATIONAL SECURITY ORDER

One of the debates that immediately followed the acts of violence in the United States on September 11, 2001, was whether it was an act of war or a crime. This contest of definitions was not simply about finding the adequate analytical label. It was first of all a debate about the normative framework in which policy responses could be formulated and justified. Some questioned whether the new situation could be accommodated within existing frameworks because 9/11 indicated a fundamental change in the nature of war or because existing institutional frameworks and policy instruments failed to prevent or effectively counter this form of transnational violence.

As with many other security crises, a more radical questioning of legal and quasi-legal frameworks also surfaced. Is the violence of 9/11 and the political reactions to it not simply a reconfirmation that normative frameworks have only a limited relevance, if any at all, in international politics? Is 9/11 an exceptional event that calls for a temporary use of exceptional powers such as unilateral intervention and pre-emptive defense? Or, is it rather a sharp indication of the illusory nature of normativist position in international politics?

Here enters the first, and most familiar, engagement with the international politics of exception. On the one hand, normativist positions try to reconfirm the relevance of international law and to frame exceptional use of political power. On the other hand normative skeptics assert the arbitrary nature of international political power and thus the exceptional nature of international politics as such. What is at stake here is no longer simply the practical realisation of law in specific situations but the nature of the relation between legally transgressive international political power and legal frameworks. The exceptionality of 9/11 is no longer limited to a problem of legal categorisation. It becomes a challenge to normativist positions that defend the continuing relevance of normative frameworks for holding international political power in check.

Let me start with the skeptical point of view. For skeptics, 9/11 and its aftermath simply reconfirm that international law and institutions are largely fig leaves that hide the way that international politics is determined by the material and moral capacity of states to pursue their interests. Multilateralism and unilateralism are just methods for the United States: They use them a la carte, as it suits them. The United Nations is just an instrument at the service of the American policy. They will use it when they need to, through a multilateral approach and if they don't need it, they will act outside the framework of the United Nations.

Such skepticism questions the relevance of international legality through a critique of the relevance of the UN. The exceptionality of 9/11 consists in reconfirming this reality after an illusionary period following the end of the Cold War in which the normativist belief that international political power could be subsumed within an international legal system gained new momentum. I come back in the section on systemic sociological approaches and institutionalism to ways in which this skeptical position, often associated with claims about political realism in international relations, can turn into a peculiar form of normative thinking, institutionalism, when it needs to position itself in relation to questions about what needs to be done.

But for now this skeptical position functions as the background against which to introduce normativist views of international politics and how they define exceptional circumstances. Normativism refers to a way of thinking that emphasizes the central importance of an autonomous legal order for constraining the arbitrary and personal exercise of political power. It prioritizes the principle of legality, and its institutionalisation in positive law and legal institutions, as the condition of legitimate exercise of political power. While, for skeptics, events like the one indexed by "9/11" are a confirmation of the "reality" of international politics.

For normativists these events are a serious problem because they are politically translated into a call for legal exceptions that challenge the restraining and constitutive capacity of the existing normative order. Assertive political responses are called for, but they cannot be framed adequately within the rules defined by the existing international normative security order. Consequently the problem becomes how to allow arbitrary, that is exceptional, political power but without cutting it too far loose from the requirement of international legality. From a normativist point of view, events like 9/11 are exceptional insofar as they significantly intensify the tension between law and power politics. But, unlike the skeptical point of view, normativism resists concluding from this that law is irrelevant.

Normative responses to such events can differ considerably but they share an ambition to limit, if not eliminate (as in Hans Kelsen's attempt to abolish the dualism between state and law), the legitimate space for extra juridical power politics. One way of defending the continuing relevance of normative frameworks for international politics is to limit the exceptionality of 9/11. The act of violence of 9/11 may indeed have indicated some limitations of the existing normative order that regulates the use of force in international politics but it is not so exceptional that it completely undermines its relevance. Christopher Greenwood's defense of the international legal framework is a good example of this move: "The fact that the events of 11 September may demonstrate a need to re-examine some of the assumptions on which the international legal order rests does not mean that those events occurred in a legal vacuum."

This defense moderates exceptionality by detaching 9/11 from both criminal law and the law of war and linking it to the notion of armed conflict, which is much less regulated but not entirely unregulated in the international normative order. Therefore, rather than discrediting the normative system as such, what is needed is a refocusing of law-making and law-application on the question of armed conflict. Another defense of the importance of normative frameworks involves arguing that the political debates continue to refer to international normative orders. However exceptional 9/11 was, and however much the political reaction has transgressed the existing normative order, most political decisions do refer to existing legal frameworks when legitimating their policies.

The important point is not whether policies remain within the legal framework-they can transgress it-but rather that such transgressions cannot be taken for granted and need to be argued on grounds of exceptional circumstances. According to this argument, as long as political debates about the legitimacy of the use of force continue to refer to questions of legality, they reconfirm that international law matters. If the normative order would be irrelevant, as the skeptics claim, the most powerful states would not try to justify the exercise of political power by reference to its legality; they would just exercise it. A good example is the following statement from Adam Roberts:

> The UN therefore remains, damaged but not destroyed, as one vehicle for reaching decisions on the use of force. Paradoxically, even when attempts to obtain UN authorisation for force fail, the appeal to UN principles may have considerable value.... These claims [i.e., legal justifications for the use of force] serve more than the tribute that vice pays to virtue: they were recognition that even in the new circumstances and hard cases of the twenty-first century, force has an unavoidably close relationship to law.

These views integrate the exceptional exercise of political power (the use of force that declines legality for the sake of higher interests or urgencies) back into the normative order by showing that the decision to use force, despite its possible illegality, is a special situation that did not cut the ties between politics and law. The opposition between legal skeptics and normativist assertions of the continuing relevance of the existing normative framework is rendered more complex by the idea that the global normative security order has reached an interregnum, a constitutional moment in which the existing normative order is dying and a new normative order can be created.

This point of view seeks to retrieve a normativist position from a condition in which the normative security system of the United Nations as it took shape in the second half of the twentieth century has been critically discredited. With the skeptics it shares the judgment that 9/11 and its aftermath have given the existing normative security order a fatal blow. Unlike them it does not generalize the crisis of the normative order into a confirmation that normative restraints do not work in international politics. It holds on to the idea that international political power can be restrained by a formalized and rationalized normative system. But for the moment the problem is that the existing normative framework is put under such extreme pressure that it may need re-inventing.

A closer examination of Kofi Annan' speech for the General Assembly of the UN on September 23, 2003, provides an illustration of this idea. This speech responds to the legitimacy crisis of the United Nations after the debacle over the second resolution legitimating the war on Iraq in the first quarter of 2003. The central statement of the speech is the following: "Excellencies, we have come to a fork in the road. This may be a moment no less decisive than 1945 itself, when the United Nations was founded."

Annan recognizes the legitimacy crisis of the existing normative system that is institutionalized in the United Nations. At the heart of his speech is a fear that the nature of the security threat and the unilateral practice of some of the members of the Security Council in their response to it would lead to "a proliferation of the unilateral and lawless use of force." Annan clearly wants to avoid going down this path. His is a road of normativism. But that road has reached a fork. September 11 and its aftermath have led to a radical choice for normativists, "Now we must decide whether it is possible to continue on the basis agreed then [the founding of the UN), or whether radical changes are needed."

The choice that he introduces here is one between integrating the responses to 9/11 within the existing framework that is rooted in the aftermath of World War II or accepting that it radically challenges that framework and calls for drawing up new rules governing international politics and for founding a new network of international institutions. The latter would result in creating an interregnum in which political power is freed from the restraints of the existing normative order. Yet its arbitrary exercise remains tied to a normativist imperative: the requirement to constitute a new normative order.

The radical conclusion of the skeptics is thus kept at bay by constituting the arbitrary exercise of power as a temporary condition aimed at the institutionalisation of a new normative order. This position thus remains highly normativist. It recognizes the viability and importance of normativity for restraining international political power by asserting simultaneously the effective existence of a normative order before the current crisis and the possibility to create a new one.

The way in which politics and normative orders are intertwined in normativist readings of this distinction between constitutive and constituted power raises far more complex issues than can be mentioned here. One example of what is at stake is H. L. A. Hart's distinction between primary and secondary rules and the use he makes of it in dealing with the limits of understanding legal systems as the habitual obedience of the majority of rules backed by threats of a sovereign. Primary rules require of human beings "to do or abstain from certain action, whether they wish or not."

Secondary rules confer powers introducing new primary rules, thus legally framing constituting power. Another example is Bruce Ackerman's intertwining of democratic politics into his understanding of constitutional moments. However, for purposes of the present analysis, the important point is not to unpack the different readings of these issues but to contrast normativist framings of exceptional events with two alternative renditions: decisionism and institutionalism. Therefore let me summarize the argument so far as a way of introducing these two alternative points of view.

So far, the central issue of international politics of exception is the viability of normativism in international politics. Skeptics turn the exceptionality of 9/11 into a challenge to the relevance of international legality and a confirmation that international politics are by definition exceptional. Normativist points of view reduce the radical edge of the exceptionality of 9/11 by reaffirming the status and applicability of international normative frameworks in the current situation while recognizing that the events of and following 9/11 have shown limitations of the existing order. The basic fault line, between skepticism and normativism, is familiar to theorists of international relations.

It is one of the central elements of one of the discipline-defining codes: realism versus idealism (or liberalism), the former leaning heavily toward the skeptical view, the latter toward normativism. Is this all there is to the concept of international politics of exception? Is it simply another word for the clash between realist and liberal idealist visions of international political order? The next section breaks open this familiar dichotomy by introducing another position, decisionism. It challenges the normativist point of view from within a legal constitutional perspective rather than from a sceptical angle that seeks to deny the relevance of this perspective for understanding international politics. It is, consequently, neither realist nor normativist.

NORMALIZING EXCEPTIONALITY AND UNIVERSAL SOVEREIGNTY

Let's start from the observation that, unlike the skeptic and normativist positions presented above, not everyone accepts the exceptionality of 9/11. Kenneth Waltz and Robert Kagan, for example, "normalize" 9/11. They frame it as an important event in a systemic continuity. I want to dwell extensively on both Waltz's (in combination with a piece by John Mearsheimer and Stephen Walt on the war on Iraq) and Kagan's points of view. They represent two alternative ways of handling the question of normativity in international relations: institutionalism (Waltz) and decisionism (Kagan).

This section focuses on Kagan's Of Paradise and Power, which illustrates a decisionist point of view in the current international politics of exception. Like normativist positions, decisionism seeks to incorporate normative exceptions into a legal order, but unlike normativism it makes arbitrary exercise of power, and thus exceptions, a normal phenomenon that is inherent in legally defined political orders. For Kagan, 9/11 does not have the same symbolic importance as for normativists. The consequences of 9/11 largely confirmed long-term developments. "America did not change on September 11. It only became more itself."

"The present transatlantic tensions did not begin with the inauguration of George W. Bush in January 2001, nor did they begin after September 11." The desire for national greatness of the United States, the international orientation of US nationalism, the decline of European powers and the rise of the United States in the twentieth century, the turn of Europe to an international rule of law as a historically typical move of the weaker powers, are among the many continuities between the twentieth and the beginning of twenty-first century that the reactions to 9/11 affirmed and possibly brought out more sharply.

But Kagan's discourse does more than reaffirm US identity and its dominant position in the world. He justifies US dominance by means of a decisionist political theory that posits the continuing need for a universal sovereign in global normative orders. A universal sovereign is the "highest, legally independent, underived power" that imposes itself globally. It upholds the international rule of law in crisis situations when the normal processes of lawmaking and application are challenged.

A universal sovereign state is exceptional, not simply in the sense that it has preponderant power resources but more importantly because it includes itself in the global normative order by excluding itself from its norms. The universal sovereign is an integral part of the normative order but differs from other states because it can legitimately exempt itself from the application of the international norms. The universal sovereign judges without being judged, disarms without disarming itself, controls the authority of the global institution at the heart of the normative order (the UN) without being controlled by it, and imposes financial policies without imposing them upon itself.

In the current condition, the United States is usually seen as the main power that is able to exercise this universal sovereignty. As Kagan states in relation to transatlantic relations, "What this means is that although the United States has played the critical role in bringing Europe into this Kantian paradise, and still plays a key role in making that paradise possible, it cannot enter the paradise itself. It mans the walls but cannot walk through the gate." Why can it not enter the paradise? The answer lies with a global application of decisionism.

A universal sovereign is a necessary condition for the continuous existence of a paradise of rule of law. In contrast to legal skeptics, a decisionist position does not question the validity and value of international rule of law. Like normativism it recognizes the importance of legally defining political order. Both decisionism and normativism are theories that support the legal form. What makes Kagan's work (like Carl Schmitt's decisionism) fundamentally different from normativism is that the exceptional modality of sovereign international power-that is, it manning the walls, it being simultaneously included and excluded from the normative order-is a necessary and permanent condition of international rule of law.

While normativist visions of international political order seek to limit the assertion of arbitrary exercise of power as much as possible, and ideally fully submerge it in legal constraints, decisionist visions make the arbitrary exercise of power a permanent and immanent condition of normative order. Therefore one can argue that normativist readings of the exception as an interregnum do not simply oppose legal skeptic point of views but also, and in the current context probably primarily, decisionist groundings of universal sovereignty as a permanent and immanent condition for international rule of law.

To explain why this politico-legal vision of world order holds that fully containing sovereign power in a legal order would imply the collapse of that order, I turn to Carl Schmitt's discussion of the legal form in Political Theology. One of the central questions around which Schmitt constructs his decisionist theory of sovereignty is "to what extent, with legal-logical necessity, every ascertainment and decision contains a constitutive element, an intrinsic value of form." This is what he calls the problem of the legal form in its substantive sense.

The central characteristic of the legal form is the certainty of a decision. Legal practice consists of applying a normative idea to a factual situation, but since the idea cannot realize itself, it requires a decision that crosses the distance between norms (such as the law of war) and facts (such as the presence of Osama Bin Laden in Afghanistan) to justify an intervention (like the intervention in Afghanistan). The essence of the legal form for Schmitt is not the assertion of dominant interests (US or global security) but the guarantee that a decision is made, irrespective of its substantive content.

Normativist positions organize this legal form by enclosing the sovereign, legally underived decision within predefined procedures. They aim at substituting as much as possible objective formal and rational processes for subjective decisions. This "objectification" of political authority through formal and rational rule of law is what is at the heart of the principle of legality. It is informed by the legal positivist dream of creating a gapless legal system that includes definite norms that define the process of lawmaking and law-application in a way that excludes subjective judgments-that is decisions informed by personal, ethical, or emotional impulses.

For decisionists, normativist approaches cannot deal with situations in which the legally highest authority does not have the actual capacity to make a decision and impose it according to the established procedures. In such a case the gap between fact and law cannot be closed. For decisionists this means that the normative system comes under critical strain. In these situations the relation between actual power and legally highest power, which Schmitt calls "the problem of sovereignty," becomes an intense legal problem.

Should the one who holds the actual power to impose a decision prevail over the objectified normative processes and the legally highest authority so as to rescue the essence of the legal form, that is, the certainty that a decision is being made? For Schmitt the existence and effective functioning of the normative order depends on the presence of an actual, legally underived power that can decide on the exception, that is, on whether one is in a situation in which the formal and rational processes fail and on what needs to be done in response?

Decisionism thus makes a double move through which the exception becomes a permanent condition of normative order. First, normative orders require a sovereign who is included in the normative order as the guardian of its legal form but who cannot be completely restrained by that order, and who has the actual capacity to decide on the exception-that is, when the gap between fact and law cannot be closed through the normal procedures. That is why Kagan can endorse the view that the United States "must live by a double standard," that the United States sometimes acts unilaterally "not out of passion for unilateralism but only because ... [it] has no choice but to act unilaterally."

Second, this notion of sovereignty is personalized. The main focus is firmly on who decides and not on the objectified process through which decisions are reached. It thus reintroduces a subjective competence (the who question) in a normative order that tends to focus on objectified processes (the how question). "What matters for the reality of legal life is who decides." In the domestic context this is the question of who is capable of holding emergency powers that can decide to suspend the law and impose a decision irrespective of the judicial procedures. In international relations this raises the question of which state or group of states can claim universal sovereignty and make sure that the international rule of law (Kagan's paradise) retains its validity in the international system, even in the face of mortal challenges.

It is important to emphasize that decisionism is not a theory of legal crises; it is not a theory that accounts only for those extreme situations in which the existing normative order faces a challenge threatening its survival. Rather it seeks to formulate the normal reality of legal life that is inherent in the legal form. It makes what for normativists is a crisis situation into the general condition of legal life. In decisionism, the sovereign exception is a permanent and inherent element of an effectively functioning normative "paradise."

International decisionism, as can be found in Kagan's work, is therefore not a political and theoretical argument against the international rule of law. Its target is not the relevance of normativity in international politics but the idea that international normative orders can operate as a closed legal system that is fully organized by formal and rational legally defined procedures and offices. Instead it asserts that the international rule of law can only operate under the watchful eye of the universal sovereign who guarantees the conditions of existence of the normative order, against enemies and against factual situations in which existing legal procedures do not result in a decision.

The universal sovereign guarantees that a decision will be made and that the essence of the legal form, the imperative to come to a decision, irrespective of its content, is continued. For decisionists, the exceptional exercise of political power by a universal sovereign is thus a normal, permanent, and necessary phenomenon in international relations. This interpretation of Kagan helps to clarify that the central contention of his text is not simply a critique of European support for the international rule of law.

As a decisionist, Kagan endorses the value of an international rule of law and respects, to a certain extent, that Europe wishes to remain within its "paradise." The central bone of contention is that Europe endorses a normativist reading of international rule of law that assumes that the international rule of law and multilateral forms can indiscriminately rule all international politics at the cost of universal sovereignty. For Kagan, as a proper decisionist, the international rule of law can only exist and operate effectively because a sovereign power guarantees that decisions are made. That is the meaning of Kagan's insistence that the United States makes it possible for the "Kantian paradises" to exist.

The political purpose of his discourse is therefore not to deny the relevance and validity of international rule of law-what Kagan sees as the European position-but to ground the United States as the only power capable and willing to embrace and exercise this particular modality of power that, following Etienne Balibar, I have referred to as "universal sovereignty." This interpretation also explains why the exceptional character of 9/11 is played down in decisionist interpretations. For decisionists, exceptional events are normal phenomena, things that happen regularly, and which confirm that the legal order cannot effectively eliminate personalized arbitrary political power.

The necessity of the latter is implied by the legal form itself. For Kagan, given that the United States is the only power capable of and willing to be the universal sovereign, 9/11 indeed confirmed what was going on before. The United States is the universal sovereign because of both the formal necessity of a universal sovereign in a system of international rule of law and the specific historical situation in which it finds itself to be the only power capable and willing of exercising this sovereignty.

Kagan combines his decisionist point of view with an endorsement of American identity. He mixes an endorsement of what he call a distinctly and common American assumption into his decisionist critique of normativist readings of international politics. As a result he grounds his decisionism as being an authentically American position: "The policies of the Clinton and Bush administrations, well or ill designed, nevertheless rested on a common and distinctly American assumption-that is, the United States as the 'indispensable nation.'"

Kagan's text thus also reveals that the formal scheme of decisionism is politically tied in with domestic and global nationalist politics. The universal sovereign globally expresses and constitutes not simply the legal form but also the authentic character of a nation. In a way not dissimilar to Schmitt, Kagan ties legal and political theory directly into identity politics and the ideological mobilisation in the name of national unity. The notion of "universal sovereign" thus makes a formal constitutional critique of normativism into a nationalist statement.

The decisionist position moves the interpretation of international politics of exception beyond the realist/liberal or skepticism/normativism distinction. One cannot easily map the debate between normativism and decisionism onto the realist/ liberal distinction. Decisionism is not a legally skeptical theory. Normativism and decisionism share a need to define a place for normative order at interstice between politics and law. The central legal and political problem for both is the nature of normative order and the relation between an international normative order and the role of extra-normative political power.

Unlike skepticism, which seeks to delete constitutional legal dimensions from international relations, both decisionism and normativism define the nature of politics and political order through a constitutional legal gaze. While the latter interpret international politics on the basis of their understanding of the nature of constitutional legal orders, skepticism understands the nature of international politics on non legal grounds, such as a utilitarian framing of rational self-interested actors.

The next section further widens the concept of international politics of exception and further complicates the simple distinction between realist skeptics and liberal normativists by showing how systemic sociological approaches of legal skeptics, like Waltz and Mearsheimer, can shape-shift into normative visions that resemble a third tradition in constitutional legal thinking: institutionalism.

SOCIOLOGY AND INSTITUTIONALISM

In both normativism and decisionism the central political problem is the relation between extra juridical political power-constituting power and universal sovereignty, respectively-and the legal order. They conceptualize the relation differently but share the idea that the concept of international politics is shaped at the interstice between the two. That is why for both, the question of the exception, which refers to the instable nature of this relation, defines a central political and legal problem.

Systemic sociological interpretations of international politics enter this normative debate by challenging the legal-constitutional concept of exception. Instead of defining the interstice between politics and law, the exception refers to a question of the systemic continuity or discontinuity of the objective sociopolitical order of international relations. I use two short pieces, one by Waltz and one by Mearsheimer and Walt, to illustrate this a -exceptionalist theoretical move.

The important point that I wish to illustrate through a reading of neorealist theory is that such a sociological move posits law-like general rules that can be translated into normative political positioning that resembles a particular legal theory, institutionalism. The latter was a central part of the legal-constitutional debates that framed the distinction between normativism and decisionism in interwar Europe. The argument here is thus that the normative core of a systemic theory like neo-realism is reminiscent of institutionalism.

The core idea of institutionalism is that law is an expression of an objective sociopolitical order and not of a legal system, as in normativism, or a decision, as in decisionism. Law expresses existing hierarchies of institutions that each are defined by a founding principle and that taken together are expressions of a natural order. In "The Continuity of International Politics," Waltz asks: "Have the terrorist attacks produced a strategic revolution, or do they leave the underlying conditions of international politics largely intact?" He concludes that 9/11 is not an exceptional event. It is one of many recurrent crises that are typical of international politics. The terrorist attack did not "change the two main bases of international politics [the gross imbalance of power and the existence of nuclear weapons]."

This "normalisation" of 9/11 is effected through a double move. First he identifies terrorism as an instrument of the weak who because of their weakness do not seriously challenge the security of powerful states. Second Waltz questions the revolutionary potential of the events of 9/11 that some ascribe to them. They are not structurally changing the conditions and modalities of international politics; or, as Waltz conclude: "although a mile wide, the anti-terrorist coalition is only an inch deep."

The important point for the discussion here is that this interpretation introduces a sociological understanding of exception. In sociological interpretations, the key political debates about exception do not focus on alternative conceptualisations of the relation between arbitrary power and the restraining effects and political status of law. Instead, the debates are about conflicting accounts of the objective reality of international politics and whether or not events have broken its normal, institutionalized development. Normality rather than normativity of sociopolitical relations is the focal point.

How does Waltzian neorealism foreground the objective sociopolitical order as the defining criterion in the question of exception? Two positions are of central importance: legal skepticism and epistemological positivism. Legal skepticism does the groundwork for the shift from normativity to normality. The rule of law and the legal form are seen to be largely irrelevant in international politics. International relations is the nonhierarchical realm in which like-unites (states) interact without a global sovereign power imposing a rule of law. Extra juridical exercise of power dominates and is cut loose from any significant legal restraints. International politics is thus exceptional by definition.

As a result exceptional power, the legal form and the nature of the rule of law, are not the central categories through which the modalities of international power can be defined, except to differentiate it in a very general way from domestic political power. Equally important is a methodological choice for epistemological positivism and the defense of a social science of international relations against an international political theory or philosophy. The sharp separation of facts from values implies that different interpretations of the modalities and conditions of political power cannot be judged on the basis of normative criteria.

They have to justify themselves as the best account of the factual reality of the sociopolitical order of international relations. The requirement of a single method of research provides the common symbolic framework on the basis of which one can retain the competition between alternative accounts of international politics as a debate about "facts." It guarantees some common understanding about what a "fact" is and how the factual impact of an event can be established. It keeps moral, normative, and metaphysical judgments at bay.

This epistemological positivism plays a crucial role in letting the criterion of "normality" of practice-that is, a relation to the normal, objectified reality-prevail over normativity-that is, the relation to norms. It makes judgments of the political significance of events like 9/11 dependent on a "social scientific" debate of whether existing theories accounting for the objective sociopolitical order are still good enough. In this "social scientific" debate, the question of exception transfigures from a normative issue about the legitimate transgression of rule of law into an empirical question of radical change. An event is no longer exceptional because it justifies the suspension of the rule of law or because it raises the specter of the universal sovereign but because it radically changes the sociopolitical order.

So far this section has simply introduced a sociological reading of the exception and how such an interpretation changes the terms of the debate, as captured in the phrase "from normativity to normality." But what is the relevance of such sociological readings for an article that seeks to introduce a concept of international politics of exception that refers to competition between constitutional legal framings of international political order, to a contest of visions of international political order that derive from competing interpretations of the nature of legal order? When sociological approaches, like Waltzian neo-realism, seek to enter a political contest of the legitimacy of extraordinary use of power they transfigure the factual normality that they endorse into normative political criteria.

The sociological rules that identify the objective political order shape-shift into norms that evaluate the legitimacy of political practice from within a pre-given institutional order. Let me focus on the key concept of neo-realism's account of the objective sociopolitical order of international relations: anarchy. International anarchy is not simply the absence of a global sovereign and a global rule of law. It also frames the objective sociopolitical international order as a market place in which states compete for power and security. The neorealist market is an objective sociopolitical order that predisposes its units, in this case states, to act instrumentally and calculate power in relative rather than absolute terms.

Although the market is presented as an objective structure that characterizes international politics, it is also a normative institution. Market competition is inscribed with normative principles restraining competition. Two stand out among these: the prohibition against monopolizing power (monopoly would transform the system into a hierarchical one in which a state or a world government can claim universal sovereignty) and the obligation to calculate policy options rationally in terms of their contribution to national security. In intense moments of political contestation, the sociological concept of the market relying on rules of action based on economic rationalism can shift to a normative institution expressing general norms constraining the arbitrary exercise of power in the market.

This normative concept of the market translates politically into an opposition to both ideological politics (driven by value rationality rather than instrumental rationality and expansionist policies that strive to monopolize power and that calculate politics in terms of absolute rather than relative gains. The political and power-restraining effect of such neorealist inscriptions of power politics can be seen at work in Mearsheimer's and Walt's argument against the intervention in Iraq in 2003. They argued that the intervention is unnecessary because Saddam Hussein is a rational actor that can be contained. Mearsheimer and Walt introduce various examples that show Saddam Hussein as a rational leader calculating power relations in terms of Iraq's vulnerability.

These examples suggest that when the United States and its allies use credible threats and clearly set out the lines that cannot be crossed, Iraq could be deterred from acquiring and using WMDs. As long as Saddam Hussein remains a rational actor who will calculate power relations in terms of reducing Iraq's vulnerability, there is no need for a preventive war; hence, the title of the piece "An Unnecessary War."

This argument shows how the economic form and rationalism of neo-realism introduces normative restraints of power politics. Whether he is evil toward his own people, or whether he breaches UN resolutions, or whether Iraq is in urgent need of democratisation, or whether the US administration wishes to pursue ideological objectives are not the central criteria for "regulating" the use of force in international relations. Instead the criteria are derived from the economic form and instrumental rationalism. This shape-shifting of sociological rules and conditions into general norms allows neorealist visions to intervene politically as a normative vision of restraints on the arbitrary exercise of power.

Does that mean that neo-realists and other systemic sociologists are closet normativists? They are definitely not. They posit the rules differently from normativists. Rules are not formulated through and from within legal institutions and an objectified legal system. They are means and expressions of an existing historical political order. Neo-realism's normative shape-shifting is in that sense somewhat reminiscent of an important alternative theory of normative order in interwar Europe that competed with decisionism and normativism: legal institutionalism. Since this chapter seeks to introduce how international politics of exception bring traditions of constitutional legal thinking and legalistic conceptions of political order into political play, I want to briefly indicate what it implies to read normative positioning, like the one within neo-realism, in terms of this tradition.

Georges Renard's "institutionalism" is a legal theory that treats institutions rather than individuals as the central legal subjects. It also emphasizes the importance of administrative law and rulings. But more important for my purposes here, Renard's institutionalism formulates a Thomistic vision of normative order that emphasizes the idea of a common good that is expressed and actualized in the founding ideas of existing institutions. For Renard, institutions are founded in an idea that is worked out and sanctioned in their development. "The institution is a communion of people in an idea."

The founding is not procedural, in the sense of being an outcome of following formalized legal or quasilegal procedures like in normativism. Neither is it to be thought of in terms of the human faculty of creating out of one's own will like in decisionism. Rather the founding is an orientation of forces in terms of a principle that is immanent in the natural order: "Sovereignty resides neither in the prince nor in the people, it resides in a Principle."

Hence the idea that this theory lets rules emerge from the existing sociopolitical order that is conceptualized as the natural order. The international system (and in neorealist terms, anarchy) can then be interpreted as an institution that articulates a founding principle of equality between states and the common good of security that institutes power balancing and economic rationality rather than empire or a system of total wars driven by value rationality. For Renard, the rules of international relations derive from the existence of a *res publica*, a common good "whose conservation and development requires, not simply mutual concessions, but a rational and harmonious orientation of national politics."

The model of judicial judgment in Renard's theory is administrative law and courts like military tribunals or civil services setting out their own internal court procedures. Procedures and judgments need to develop from within an institution since they need to be in line with the institutional working out of the original founding principle and the objective reality of the institution. Institutional normativity becomes self-enclosed. A universal legal system that develops general rules for individuals that can be applied independent from the specific institutions in which the individuals function does not have priority over administrative courts and their procedures of decreeing and judging.

One of the consequences is that the tension between formal legal frameworks and arbitrary politics, which is here exemplified by administrative law and commissions, is not really a defining element of normative order for institutionalism. The defining elements remain the principles expressed in existing institutions and their practical functioning. For Renard founding ideas are not arbitrary. His vision is Thomistic in the sense that these institutions each articulate a common good that reflects a natural order.

The different institutions and the hierarchies between them are part of an organic whole that is united in a divine common good that it articulates and a natural law that it realizes. I will not dwell on this Thomistic element but it is important because, unlike Schmitt's appropriation of institutionalism as simply being a constitutional condoning of the factually existing institutions, Renard's institutionalism is based on a tradition of natural law that unites diverse institutions and the hierarchies between them in a divine order organized around a concept of common good. It also emphasizes that institutionalism subordinates human decision, which is so central to decisionism, to naturally given institutions and rules.

When religious beliefs give way to scientific reason the divine element moves to the background. Natural law is then accessed via scientific inquiry into the nature of things; natural law is given by observation (une donnee de l'observation). While decisionism supports the dictum that authority rather than truth prevails as the condition of order, the institutionalist approaches challenge this by making truth rather than authority the criterion for defining the modalities of political power. Also normativist approaches, like legal positivism, emphasize the importance of truth against authority. But while the latter's truth derives from legal reasoning, the institutionalist truth derives from applying scientific methods that "observe" natural law.

In turning normative along institutionalist lines, neorealist sociology does not forfeit its scientific reasoning but turns it into a method of unpacking the objective reality of an institution as the expression of a founding idea. The scientific truth therefore becomes a method of expressing and sanctioning this original founding idea, which in the more explicit Thomistic version of George Renard ultimately cannot be but an expression of the divine order. As Franz Neumann remarks, such a vision tends to reduce statements about normative order to reassertions of what it considers to be existing institutions. But it does not have to condone existing policies.

That depends on what it "sees" as being the idea that founds an institution as part of the natural order. As Mearsheimer and Walt's intervention showed, systemic sociological frameworks that posit a universal natural order grounded in an idea can sanction particular policies as going against the rules defining the natural state of affairs. Interpreting systemic sociologies, which formulate political choices on the basis of universal and timeless rules that characterize the objective reality of the international system, in terms of legal institutionalism brings out how their "social scientific" interpretations resemble a particular normative tradition that lets rules emerge from and fully embeds them into an existing objectified, or even better, naturalized institutional order.

At first sight, neorealist interpretations shift the question of exception from the international normative order to the transformation and continuation of the existing order. The concept of exception refers not to a constitutional question but to a question of radically disruptive change of the objectified institutional conditions of international politics. Normativity seems to have been displaced by normality. But when looking closer at how neo-realism translates into political positioning in an international politics of exception it starts looking very much like Renard's institutionalism but without recognizing its Thomistic flavor. It introduces a normative vision of international political order in which the concept of exception disappears in an understanding of international society as an organic unity organized as the expression and continuous development of a founding idea that actualizes natural law and a universal common good. In that sense, when drawn into an international politics of exception neorealism's legal skepticism may still end up with a normative vision of international politics that is strongly reminiscent of a particular tradition in constitutional legal theory: institutionalism.

THE INTERNATIONAL POLITICS OF EXCEPTION

The question posed in this chapter was "What does it mean to speak of exceptional international politics?" In response, I have set out a concept of "exception" that refers to a method of formulating competing views of international political order at the interstice between law and politics. In this political constitutional reading of the exception concepts of international political order are formulated in the shadow of constitutional legal theory. The concept of "international politics of exception" then refers to situations in which factual statements about the extraordinary nature of events like the clandestine violence of 9/11 become integrated into a legal and political debate in which competing interpretations of the nature of international political order are primarily derived from competing understandings of the nature and limits of normative, legal order.

Not realism and liberalism but normativist and decisionist visions are the main contenders in such a politics of exception. They structure debates about the nature of international order in terms of competing interpretations of the location and status of extrajuridical political practice in international rule of law. Normativist approaches prioritize legal restraints of international political power. They seek to limit law transgressing political practice to highly exceptional circumstances, such as violence that cannot be contained within the existing legal frameworks. But even in these situations normativism asks for limiting the scope and time of extra juridical exercise of international power as much as possible by tying it as closely as possible to normative requirements.

Decisionist positions on the other hand make extra-juridical exercise of power a permanent requirement for the constitution and proper functioning of international rule of law. International rule of law depends on a state claiming and willing to enact universal sovereignty. This state is part of the international normative order but cannot be fully restrained by it. The reason for this is that it needs to guard that the legal form-the necessity to close the gap between international law and international political events-is maintained under all conditions. While the normativist positions represent a tradition in liberal thinking, the decisionist position cannot be equated with realism. It is a legal-constitutional theory of political power that formulates international order as a normative order. Unlike realism, decisionism is thus not a legal skeptic theory.

The realist position is an element in a third position in the international politics of exception that combines legal skepticism with legal institutionalism. This is a vision that deploys the legal constitutional concept of "exception" to draw a gap between domestic politics and international politics. While the former is ruled by law the latter is beyond rule of law. There is no international rule of law and therefore it does not make sense to derive visions of international political order from interpretations of the nature and limits of international normative order. Conceptualizing international political order then becomes a sociological exercise in which one observes the rules that define the natural practice of international politics.

However, as argued in relation to two neorealist texts, when these sociological visions formulate sociological rules in universal and timeless terms and when they politically position themselves within an international discussion of the legitimacy of practices that transgress a given normative order, they become reminiscent of a third legal constitutional theory, institutionalism, that competed with normativist and decisionist conceptions of normative order in the early twentieth century. The institutionalist position remains anti-exceptionalist; the constitutional concept of exception is not central for the definition of normative political order.

However, it does share with the other two a framing of international political order in line with traditions in legal thinking. It relocates the rule of law from a universally institutionalized system to administrative expressions of and judgments based on natural principles that are expressed in existing institutions. The latter are ordered hierarchically as the expression of a natural, if not divine, order. Insofar as realist skepticism translates into legal institutionalist points of view, it frames international normative order in a way that resembles a secularized version of Neo-Thomistic thinking at the beginning of the 20th century.

Why is it relevant to return to this legal constitutional conception of "the exception" today? Why draw attention to legal constitutional interpretations of international political order for order is formulated at the interstice between rule of law and its political transgressions? Since 1989 claims about extraordinary times and the need for the use of extraordinary power have been rife in the international politics of security.

The shift from ideological-military containment of rival political systems during the Cold War to debates about the legitimacy of humanitarian intervention (Somalia, Haiti, Rwanda, Bosnia, and Kosovo being exemplary cases), the use of force to uphold international law (Iraq in the early 1990s), the reinstitutionalisation of international humanitarian law (the formation of the International Criminal Court), the legitimacy of pre-emptive defense, and the detention of people in "administrative" centers (Guantanamo Bay and detention centers for refugees) have made the judicialisation of international politics, the question of the limit of rule of law, and the assertion of transgressive international political authority key issues in the reconfiguration of the international political order.

The concept of "exception" introduced in this chapter does precisely refer to these issues. It draws attention to how political contestations of international security policy may be reconfiguring international political order in the shadow of legal constitutional visions of politics. If this is indeed happening then the ordering effects of the politics of security do not simply follow from fixing new global enemies and friends and the inscription of one's relation to these enemies in historical narratives.

At least equally important is then the method of inscribing extraordinary global political authority in and out of an international legal order. When the latter issue becomes a central stake in the international politics of security, it makes sense to revisit debates in legal and political thought that developed conceptions of the nature of political practice precisely through framing the nature of extra-juridical exercise of power and the conditions of its legitimacy. Such revisiting will contribute to understanding the specific modalities of legal-constitutional conceptualisations of international order that are at play in such a politics of security.

6

Shifting the Politics of International Development

When he introduced the idea of the Global Compact at the 1999 World Economic Forum in Davos, UN Secretary-General Kofi Annan opened a new chapter in the history of the United Nations. Never before had the organisation expressed such a willingness to join with business in promoting international development. Centered on the ambitious objective of "[giving] global markets a more human face," the Global Compact has since become, thanks to the direct leadership of the secretary-general, a key instrument in the UN's overall strategy to foster a more inclusive and sustainable world economy. The mission of the Global Compact is framed on the basis of two primary objectives.

First, the Compact is a corporate citizenship initiative that invites the private sector "to embrace, support and enact ... a set of core values in the areas of human rights, labour standards, the environment, and anti-corruption." The 2,400 companies that had joined the Global Compact as of the end of 2005 were committed to voluntarily applying, within their sphere of influence, ten principles drawn from four major international agreements: the Universal Declaration of Human Rights, the Fundamental Principles and Rights at Work of the International Labour Organization (ILO), the Rio Declaration on Environment and Development, and the UN Convention

Against Corruption. Participating companies, whether transnationals like Shell, Nike, and Novartis, or small and medium enterprises from the South, are expected to report annually on the progress they have made in the implementation of the Compact's principles.

Second, the Global Compact constitutes a forum whose aim is to facilitate cooperation among the various economic and social actors in the global arena in order to promote UN values. Thus, besides the private sector and the UN Secretariat, the Compact involves six UN specialized agencies-ILO, UN Development Program (UNDP), UN Environment Program (UNEP), Office of the High Commissioner for Human Rights (OHCHR), UN Industrial Development Organization (UNIDO), and UN Office on Drugs and Crime (UNODC)-as well as a number of non-governmental organisations (NGOs), labor associations, business associations, think tanks, and government representatives. Because most of the participants belong to over fifty national and regional networks, the Global Compact is often referred to as a "network of networks." Through the action program that it spearheads, the Compact seeks to promote dialogue on corporate social responsibility and development and to foster new forms of partnership among member stakeholders. To reach these goals, the Global Compact relies above all on its ability to bring people together, which it effectively demonstrated in 2004 by organizing the largest meeting of business, labor, and civil society leaders in the history of the United Nations. Rooted in a tradition that stresses the role of multilateral institutions as "intellectual actors," this chapter argues that the Global Compact epitomizes the current state of the politics of international development in three distinct ways.

First, the Compact illustrates a major turn in development thinking and in North-South relations. It should be recalled that the UN actively nurtured the "negative chemistry" that long prevailed between the Third World and the business community. In opposition to this deep-seated trend, the Global Compact is premised on the assumption that the UN and the private sector have a common interest in the promotion of sustainable development on a global scale. The Compact thus reflects a historic change of attitude within the UN regarding the role of business and markets in the fight against world poverty.

Second, the Compact bespeaks the need to adapt the mechanisms of international governance to the contemporary challenges of development. Old forms of multilateralism have clearly failed to bridge the gap between rich and poor countries. This failure has been one of the catalysts in the emergence of a new set of international practices that has been referred to as "complex multilateralism." Often considered the most vivid example of the public-private partnerships initiated by the UN over the past few years, the Compact is a striking manifestation of this evolution toward a bottom-up, nonhierarchical model of multilateral cooperation.

Third, the Global Compact offers an excellent vantage point for an assessment of the competing worldviews that currently structure the development debate. It is generally recognized that the end of the 1990s led to an unprecedented convergence between the "UN paradigm"-the interventionist policies traditionally promoted by the UN and its specialized agencies-and the "Bretton Woods paradigm"-the promarket policies defended by the International Monetary Fund (IMF), the World Bank, and the World Trade Organisation (WTO). This changing multilateral environment, however, has yet to generate a truly global development consensus. The debate over the Compact reveals how profoundly divided the development community remains as to the best response to the specific needs of third world countries.

Building on these insights about the significance of the Global Compact for the politics of international development, the article comprises three parts. The first, proceeding from a historical perspective, analyzes how the Global Compact partakes of the recently initiated reorientation of the UN paradigm. The second part explains the innovative nature of the model of governance proposed by the Compact, a model that draws upon the practices of several international bodies. Finally, the third section summarizes the ongoing debate between supporters and critics of the Global Compact. Overall, the Compact experiment clearly shows that beyond its ever changing dynamics, international development ultimately remains a political, rather than a technical, process.

FROM HOSTILITY TO PARTNERSHIP: THE UN AND BUSINESS

Beginning in the 1950s, the UN was prompted to keep its distance from the corporate sector by the Cold War environment and the need to display a relative impartiality toward market economy and planned economy advocates alike. That attitude turned into institutionalized animosity in the 1960s when developing countries entered the organisation en masse. Indeed, the rise of the North-South conflict led the UN to make the regulation of the private sector and of transnational corporations in particular, one of its top development priorities for over a generation.

After the inauguration of the United Nations Conference on Trade and Development (UNCTAD) in 1964, the UN systematically defended the notion that the transnationals, left to themselves, would further enlarge the gap between developed and developing countries. As a corrective measure, the UN put forward a series of interventionist policies aimed at regulating such issues as the price of commodities exported by the third world, restrictive business practices, and technology transfers. During the 1970s, in the wake of discussions on the New International Economic Order, the founding of two institutions-the Center on Transnational Corporations (CTC), entrusted with helping developing countries to build up their capacity to negotiate with the transnationals, and the United Nations

Commission on Transnational Corporations (UNCTC), mandated to establish a code of conduct for transnational corporations-only exacerbated the climate of confrontation between the UN and business.

In line with the belief that underdevelopment resulted from external factors related to the international environment, the "anti-business prejudice" remained a conspicuous feature of the UN paradigm until the end of the Cold War. The UN's mistrust toward the private sector, it should be stressed, stood in sharp opposition with the policies defended on the basis of the Bretton Woods paradigm. In fact, one of the chief objectives behind the creation of the IMF, the World Bank, and the General Agreement on Tariffs and Trade (GATT) was precisely to facilitate the opening of markets on which the corporate sector's prosperity was said to depend. Thus, the question of the appropriate attitude for the UN to adopt toward business long persisted as a major source of friction between its agencies and the Bretton Woods institutions.

In recent years, the international dynamic of social forces caused all the multilateral organisations to revise their approach toward development. As suggested above, the dialogue between the UN paradigm and the Bretton Woods paradigm is more intensive today than ever before. The UN acknowledges more and more the "great opportunities" that globalisation affords, while the Bretton Woods institutions are more ready than before to admit its risks and perils. In keeping with this logic of convergence, the international financial institutions increasingly regard the fight against poverty as "the paramount challenge of the 21st century"; for its part, the UN now recognizes that development is primarily the responsibility of each state.

One significant outcome of the climate of cooperation currently prevailing in the multilateral system has been the emergence of a novel consensus among the UN, the IMF, and the World Bank on making poverty reduction a priority of the international agenda. A pivotal component of the transformations at work within the UN has to do with the organisation's opening up to the corporate sector, a process sometimes described as "a change of 180 degrees." Following a meeting with leaders of the International Chamber of Commerce (ICC) in 1998, Kofi Annan clearly affirmed the change in the UN's position: "There is great potential for the goals of the United Nations-promoting peace and development-and the goals of business-creating wealth and prosperity-to be mutually supportive".

In the name of this new intersection of interests, which attracted a good deal of media attention due to generous donations by Ted Turner and Bill Gates, the UN drew closer to business by promoting two approaches: setting up operational public-private partnerships and developing joint forms of diplomacy. According to one observer, "every UN organization is currently involved in multiform private sector partnerships." The aim of this new approach is to allow UN agencies to attract capital to development projects and to benefit from private sector expertise.

By way of illustration, the Global Alliance for Vaccines and Immunisation, a program whose goal is to provide vaccines to the children of the poorest countries, has brought together the Bill and Melinda Gates Foundation, the Rockefeller Foundation, and the International Federation of Pharmaceutical Manufacturers and Associations, along with the World Health Organization (WHO), the UN Children's Fund (UNICEF), and the World Bank. Similarly, the UNDP has launched, in partnership with a number of high-tech companies, the Global Digital Opportunity Initiative, aimed at initiating e-strategies in third world countries. Beyond these examples, it is worth noting that public-private partnerships have expanded to the point where the UN has recently felt the need to set down detailed guidelines for their operation.

In addition, the UN has drawn closer to business through the development of new forms of cooperation in the area of diplomacy. The UN Conference on Environment and Development, held in Rio de Janeiro in 1992, constituted a precedent in this connection inasmuch as the private sector was deeply involved in the official proceedings of the event. The UN persuaded the participating companies to join together in the World Business Council on Sustainable Development (WBCSD), an association it now consults on a regular basis. The WBCSD's active role was effectively highlighted at the Johannesburg Summit 2002 (Rio +10), which attracted more than 100 CEOs and 700 business delegates.

A number of other recent UN conferences also opened the doors wide to the private sector. For example, at the Conference on Financing for Development, which took place in Monterrey in 2002, representatives of business presented a set of joint proposals and organized an International Business Forum, held in parallel with the intergovernmental meeting. By and large, it is clear that the new involvement of business in conference diplomacy represents a shift in the practice of multilateralism.

The Global Compact can thus be viewed as an expression of an emerging trend in the evolution of international cooperation. Whereas for decades business was seen by UN agencies as part of the problem of development, it is now considered part of the solution. Within this shifting environment, the Global Compact stands out due to its original combination of the two modes of collaboration just described between the UN and the private sector: operational partnerships and more open channels of diplomacy. For example, as a Compact member, Hewlett-Packard (HP) has partnered with the UN to issue a "global citizenship strategy," a corporate code that seeks to make the protection of human rights "part of the 'HP way.'"

Concurrently, HP is also involved in multipartite discussions with a variety of Compact stakeholders, including the UN Secretariat, the OHCHR, and the World Bank, to reduce "businesses' complicity in human rights abuses." The Global

Compact thus clearly seeks to serve developmental as well as political functions, a twin characteristic that helps explain why the initiative has moved to the forefront within the UN's overall strategy toward business.

THE GLOBAL COMPACT

Over the recent period, criticism of the functioning of multilateralism has spread among governmental, NGO, and academic circles. Multilateral institutions have often been decried for their lack of efficiency and representative ness. Given the large resources at their disposal, it is no surprise that development agencies have been particularly blamed for the ongoing crisis of multilateralism. Among the different initiatives that have been taken so far to improve the workings of international governance, the Global Compact certainly appears as one of the most important. Ian Hurd has perceptively described the Global Compact as an "intriguing piece of constitutional design," which draws on the experience of a variety of international institutions. In keeping with this insight, we suggest that the Compact's distinctiveness results from a unique combination of various decision-making mechanisms used in the UN, the ILO, the Organization for Economic Cooperation and Development (OECD), and the WTO.

The Global Compact is based, first, on UN methods, in the sense that it shares with the UN the objective of promoting internationally shared values. Since 1945, one of the UN's main contributions to international politics has been to establish new basic standards, particularly in the field of individual and collective rights. This "norm-setting" function involves two particularities that make the UN qualitatively different from all other international institutions. First, by virtue of its holistic mission, the UN develops standards dealing with every aspect of social relationships. Second, despite their well-known drawbacks, the norms articulated by the UN enjoy a high degree of legitimacy, as they are founded upon a broad international consensus.

These two features of the UN's governance model are at the very heart of the Global Compact. To begin with, the Compact promotes an integrated vision of international life, since its underlying principles have to do with the basic makeup of the social fabric: human rights, labor rights, the environment, and the rule of law. Furthermore, the Global Compact derives a part of its originality from the fact that all its principles are covered by international agreements within the UN. To quote Kofi Annan, the goal of the Global Compact is "to unite the powers of markets with the authority of universal ideals."

Another model of governance for the Global Compact is the one provided by the ILO. What most distinguishes this specialized agency within the UN system is its tripartite management system: in accordance with its 1919 constitution, governments, employers, and workers all have a place in the ILO's governing bodies. The ILO can thus draw on a long tradition of collaboration with non state actors, such that it has been referred to as "the UN's first private-public partnership."

For decades, this partnership has been credited with significantly helping the ILO to promote new forms of collective bargaining. The Global Compact strives to reproduce the kind of dialogue promoted by the ILO by gathering around the same table "all the relevant actors" in the area of development. The diversity of those actors-private companies, unions, NGOs, and other members of the civil society-aims to enhance the representative quality of the Compact's decision-making process. Following the path carved out by the ILO for almost a century, the Global Compact's multi-stakeholders approach bespeaks a wish to go beyond the classic model of intergovernmental multilateralism.

The OECD offers a third model of governance for the Global Compact. Long concerned with the need to improve corporate governance, the OECD seeks to promote "corporate responsibility," a concept that refers to "the actions taken by business ... in order to enhance the mutually dependent relationship between business and societies." The OECD defined the principles of corporate responsibility in a set of guidelines adopted in 1976 and revised in 2000. The most important of those principles is no doubt the idea that to be effective, corporate responsibility must be based on voluntary implementation.

The OECD's non coercive approach toward corporate responsibility has provided the general basis for the Global Compact's philosophy and activities. The Compact's ambition is to globalize the practices of corporate responsibility in order to achieve a new "social contract" that would stipulate the terms under which the right to maximize profits could be exercised. The Compact's approach has been well summarized by John Ruggie, who argues that "as markets are going global, so, too, must corporate social responsibility." Highlighted at the 2003 G8 Economic Summit, the parallel drawn here between the OECD's work and the Global Compact appears to be more and more widely recognized.

Finally, inasmuch as it emphasizes consensus, the Global Compact's model of governance takes its cue from the WTO. It has been said that the consensus principle is part of the WTO ethos, because that principle is viewed by WTO members as "a fundamental democratic guarantee that is not negotiable." The desire to avoid confrontation is best exemplified by the WTO's method for managing trade disputes. According to the formal procedure, the organisation settles disputes by creating a panel whose goal is to decide whether or not a member's rights have been violated. But, as John Jackson explains, this "rule-oriented" approach often gives way to a "diplomacy-oriented" approach based on negotiation and compromise.

Founded on the same spirit of flexibility, the Global Compact proposes to resolve conflicts through dialogue among stakeholders. This method is patently demonstrated in the mandate assigned to the Learning Forum, the "core" of the Global Compact. Through periodic meetings, the Learning Forum's essential purpose is to allow participants to openly discuss the application of the Compact's ten principles. As in the WTO, the Global Compact thereby strives to favour an organisational culture where the opposition between points of view is resolved through discussion.

By combining the values and experience of various international institutions, the Global Compact distinguishes itself as one of the recent period's most innovative initiatives in the practice of "complex multilateralism." The future evolution of this program will no doubt be closely scrutinized by all experts of international cooperation. Thus far, the most salient aspect of the Compact's short history may be the exceptionally lively political debate it has sparked.

THE DEBATE ON THE GLOBAL COMPACT

The Global Compact has from the start generated highly polarized positions on issues both of substance and of process. In terms of substance, the question is to determine whether the Global Compact is an instrument that furthers development or not. In terms of process, the debate bears upon the legitimacy of the eclectic model of governance described above.

THE ENTHUSIASM OF THE ADVOCATES

The keenest support for the Global Compact has, quite naturally, come from within the UN Secretariat-which houses the Global Compact Office-and from the UN agencies that are directly involved. In their capacities as official spokespersons, Kofi Annan, his special adviser John Ruggie, and the head of the Global Compact Office, Georg Kell, have enunciated the most sophisticated arguments in favour of the Compact.

Advocates of the initiative articulate their defense around two main ideas. First, the Global Compact is, in their view, an initiative that can effectively contribute to sustainable development and to a better distribution of global wealth. Second, the Compact has the advantage of being grounded in more inclusive, and thus more legitimate, mechanisms of governance than those usually at work in multilateral institutions.

Substance

To begin with, the promoters of the Global Compact argue that it fosters global prosperity because it responds to the mutual interests of the developing countries and the private sector. They view the Compact as a win-win solution to the problem of world poverty. This analysis is based on the notion that state-centered policies have failed to promote development and on the conviction that "governments and intergovernmental bodies can no longer do it alone."

An oft-cited illustration of the failure of the government-led approach to development, the relative reduction of foreign aid budgets since the end of the Cold War, has prompted the UN secretary-general to suggest that "trade is better than aid." Believing that only private corporations have the technology and the expertise required to deal with today's economic challenges, some observers have concluded that markets provide "the only hope of pulling billions of poor people in the developing countries out of abject poverty."

Supporters of the Global Compact are persuaded that the UN has every interest in encouraging public-private partnerships and in favouring a greater openness of markets. They see in the Compact a program that is consistent with those two priorities while, at the same time, offering a series of additional advantages. They contend, for instance, that the Global Compact adds "social legitimacy" to global markets. Kell and Ruggie point out in this regard that popular support for globalisation is fragile because globalisation has disconnected the networks of production and finance from other social relationships. According to them, the imbalance resulting from globalisation will persist so long as the economy is not ruled by universal values.

To prevent an intensification of the "backlash against globalisation," a better integration of social needs within markets appears necessary. And that is precisely the *raison d'etre* of the Global Compact, which proposes to close the "governance gap" by embedding global markets in principles to which the whole international community can adhere. Indeed, advocates of the Compact like to describe its project as that of "taking embedded liberalism global." For them, the Global Compact should be all the more attractive since its main areas of activity-human rights, labor, and the environment-coincide with the very issues that engender the greatest fears regarding globalisation.

Commentators have also pointed out that the Global Compact makes the most of the natural convergence of interests between developing countries and the business community with respect to trade liberalisation. Underlying this rationale is the observation that the international trade regime currently faces enormous protectionist pressures due to social concerns in countries of the North. Although they may be legitimate, the argument goes, those concerns threaten to spawn trade restrictions that would be particularly harmful for the poorer nations. Ruggie, for instance, holds that "the rejectionists of globalisation in the North are on a collision course with the needs of the poor in the South."

Viewed from this angle, the Global Compact provides a much more flexible framework than the WTO for dealing with the social and environmental issues linked to international trade. Not surprisingly, the private sector generally agrees that a UN-based system of regulation without rigid structures is preferable to overloading the WTO regime with new legal obligations.

For its advocates, the Global Compact offers the great advantage of facilitating dialogue between business and civil society while remaining "free from 'command and control.'" In short, supporters of the Compact argue that the initiative works.

They stress that not only has membership in the Compact increased constantly, but it is more and more diverse in terms of geography and economic sectors. Moreover, they suggest that the Compact has proven its ability to foster positive changes in behaviour and attitude. In this connection, a recent survey conducted by McKinsey and Company on behalf of the Global Compact Office indicates that, for nearly half of the participating companies (40.2 percent), the Compact has accelerated policy reforms related to its objectives. The survey also shows that in developing and transitional countries, where the Global Compact recruits, respectively, 43.6 percent and 5.3 percent of its members, Compact membership has significantly helped to familiarize companies with the very notion of corporate responsibility. All this has led advocates of the Global Compact to conclude that in a matter of a few short years, the program has succeeded in advancing its core principles.

Process

The Global Compact, as noted above, strives to distinguish itself through its inclusive methods and the diversity of its membership. Even though its supporters admit this approach has drawn the UN into "uncharted territory," they see in it the basis of the Compact's political legitimacy. In fact, some analysts have suggested that, by its very nature, the participation of non state actors in UN forums, which is encouraged by public-private partnerships such as the Global Compact, adds a "democratic surplus" to the practice of multilateralism. Because it provides a system of checks and balances, the interaction between NGOs and the private sector could help to correct one of the chief deficiencies of global governance.

The results obtained through such interaction would be all the greater to the extent that it promotes a learning process based on dialogue and emulation rather than confrontation and sanctions. Defenders of the Global Compact believe that instead of punishing or excluding delinquent companies, it is more productive to put them in touch with corporations known for their progressive behaviour in the area of corporate responsibility. The Compact hence prides itself on being an "interorganisational network" that relies on persuasion and the example of good practices rather than on hierarchy and coercion.

Another argument is that the Global Compact gains even greater legitimacy by allowing the UN to move back again to the center of debates on global governance. Its promoters are delighted, for example, that the Bretton Woods institutions, the G8, and the OECD, ordinarily unenthusiastic about the UN's economic initiatives, have expressed a keen interest in the Compact. But more fundamentally, supporters emphasize that the Global Compact enlists participating companies in "an advocacy role on behalf of the United Nations." From the beginning, the hope has been that the unprecedented support of business for the UN would help restore the organisation's credibility in the international arena. The McKinsey report cited above is encouraging for those who share that hope, as it highlights the fact that the Compact has indeed given UN officials a "heightened profile" in the private sector.

Finally, some observers argue that the Global Compact draws legitimacy as well from its usefulness as a laboratory supplying abundant information on how to improve the workings of international cooperation. The fact, for instance, that the UN Staff College now relies on the Global Compact to introduce students to the logic of partnerships gives practical expression to the institutional goal of making the Compact "an overall value framework for cooperation with the business community." Furthermore, it has at times been suggested that the Global Compact may foster reform within the UN and thereby enhance the organisation's "relevance."

In stating that he sees the Compact "as a chance for the UN to renew itself from within," Kofi Annan explicitly articulated his wish to instrumentalize collaboration with private corporations in order to transform the UN's organisational culture. For its advocates, one of the Compact's major benefits is that it can act as a catalyst for the emergence of a "UN culture favourable to business values and methods." The Compact could thus help the UN to better adapt to the challenges of globalisation.

THE MISTRUST OF THE CRITICS

Intellectually close to the alterglobalisation movement, critics of the Global Compact include NGOs, intergovernmental agencies, and some third world governments. Their views converge on two key ideas that are related to the same issues of substance and process as those identified in the discourse of the Compact's supporters. On the one hand, they maintain that the Global Compact aggravates the inequalities of development and widens the gulf between North and South. On the other hand, they contend that by giving greater power to the private sector, the Compact tramples on the democratic principles that should underpin the management of the international economic order.

Substance

Those who oppose the Global Compact base their analysis on a deep mistrust of the business community and on a negative assessment of the results of the neo-liberal policies adopted in recent years. In their view, the opening of markets can bring about no more than a superficial contribution to development, since fundamental problems such as the concentration of wealth and the lack of social justice simply fall outside the concerns of the private sector.

Former UNICEF executive director Carol Bellamy stressed that private capital concentrates where the returns are highest: "Private capital seldom gravitates to the very neediest countries [and] in those countries that it does reach, private capital often does little for the poor." For such critics, the basic premises of the Global Compact-namely that the third world shares mutual interests with the corporate sector, and that markets can play a major role in poverty reduction-are greatly in doubt.

The denunciation of the Global Compact is all the more pronounced because of the widespread perception that it epitomizes a regrettable ideological shift on the part of the UN. According to its detractors, the Compact clearly "embrace[s] the corporate trade and investment agenda" and therefore represents a break with the UN's traditional position on issues of economic policy. This turn is deemed objectionable as it threatens to limit discussions on development within the organisation by "stigmatizing" all options that would involve "redistributive policies and binding regulations."

Various commentators also worry that the "pro-market spin" adopted by the UN in conjunction with the rise of public-private partnerships will in the long run lead to an increased "privatisation" of the development process. This fear stems from the notion that the rapprochement between the UN and business will lessen the onus on governments to deal with the problem of poverty. Another criticism often directed against the Global Compact has to do with its nonbinding mode of operation, which calls for neither serious monitoring nor any kind of sanction. Although it has agreed to take part in the initiative, Amnesty International, for example, is among those who have denounced the absence of specific criteria for identifying possible violations of the Compact's principles.

Critics of the Compact are upset as well that instead of being made stricter, the rules of compliance have gradually been loosened. Until 2003, the primary method of monitoring consisted of asking participating companies to post annually on the program's website at least one example of the application of one of the Compact's principles. Yet in 2002-2003, with almost 1,000 firms participating in the Compact, a mere 138 examples were made public. The UN subsequently lowered its requirements and is now content to ask firms to explain in their annual reports how they have applied the Compact's principles. The change of procedure has obviously not done away with all the irritants: in 2004 fewer than 60 percent of participating companies reported taking at least one action to implement Compact principles.

This turn of events validates for many observers their opinion that "so-called 'voluntary initiatives' ... are often very weak and do little to significantly improve corporate social and environmental performance." Sensitive to this outlook, Kofi Annan himself has recently recognized that an initiative like the Global Compact can in no way replace state regulatory action. Some analysts also point out that one of the harmful side effects of the Global Compact's voluntary approach is to short-circuit all debate on the negotiation of a binding code of conduct for transnational corporations, something the South has been demanding for decades.

Finally, according to its critics, the Global Compact impedes development because it disguises the true goal of private enterprise-profit making-under a thin veneer of social conscience. In this respect, the criticisms aimed at the Global Compact overlap with other theses that portray corporate social responsibility and philanthropy in general, as marketing tools that allow the business community "to project an image of fairness and solidarity." To justify their mistrust, some detractors have been quick to note that among Compact corporate members that declare having undertaken policy change, 40 percent openly admit that participation in the Compact had no significant impact on their decisions.

As far as its adversaries are concerned, the Global Compact offers private companies a "free PR ride," in that it lets them inexpensively "bluewash" their reputation by associating their name with that of the UN. And, as we shall see below, bluewashing is considered dangerous not only because it allows private enterprise to dissimulate its motives but also because it tarnishes the UN's image.

Process

Those who contest the Global Compact's legitimacy argue that it is not very democratic. The UN has been rebuked for its lack of transparency and the "culture of secrecy" that surrounded the launching of the initiative. Some analysts have deplored, more particularly, that UN member states themselves were pushed to the sidelines of the project and were consulted only several months after Kofi Annan's speech at Davos. Furthermore, the Global Compact is sometimes depicted as an expression of "global corporatism" in light of the fact that none of its stakeholders-be they corporations, NGOs, or international agencies-is directly accountable to the public. Yet, notwithstanding the variety of the arguments condemning the Global Compact's lack of democracy, all are definitely focused on the new power relationship the Compact establishes between the private sector and the UN.

There are many critics who doubt that this issue can be seriously broached within the current review process of the governance structure of the Compact. In the eyes of its opponents, the Global Compact proposes a partnership weighted on the side of business and transnational corporations. One of the basic objections raised by the critics is, for example, that the requirements for participating in the Compact are more restrictive for NGOs than for corporations. They contend, more broadly, that transnational corporations-which are the mainstays of the Compact-have access to human and financial resources unavailable to other members, including UN agencies, to defend their points of view.

Another frequently heard criticism is that the norm of consensus wrongfully favours the private sector, because it leads inescapably to "a fairly minimalist agenda of corporate social and environmental responsibility." In the wake of the fears set off by the influence of corporations, some observers have noted that the Global Compact maintains the South on the margins of the international system. They point out in this connection that the Compact recruits its most important members and supporters from the firms, NGOs, and governments of the developed world. The Global Compact is accused of low-grade democracy on the additional grounds that it weakens the UN, an institution regarded as "the guardian of global public good."

A number of critics contend that the UN's behaviour is contradictory inasmuch as it promotes cooperation with corporations that, behind the scenes, lobby for ever greater degrees of liberalisation, or take action against multilateral agreements such as the Kyoto Protocol or the Convention on Biological Biodiversity. Peter Utting also explains that the Global Compact pushes the UN toward a form of self-censorship. "As UN agencies have got closer to business," he argues, "some officials feel more inhibited about writing anything that runs counter to the current." Opponents of the Compact look negatively upon this trend for at least two reasons. First, they believe controversy is an essential component of a true international democracy. Second, they are concerned that self-censorship may be the prelude to a veritable "commercialisation" of the UN-that is, a blind institutional commitment in favour of the private sector.

Finally, the Global Compact is denounced by its critics for weakening the UN by putting a stain on the organisation's reputation. In the words of CorpWatch, "The UN's positive image is vulnerable to being sullied by corporate criminals." One frequently flagged danger is that the UN may eventually be confused with international organisations dominated by business, like the IMF and the WTO, and consequently lose the public support it now enjoys. Many analysts agree that this latter outcome would represent a major backward step for democracy and global governance.

This analysis of the Global Compact facilitates a better understanding of the politics of international development by emphasizing three distinct issues. First, far from being an isolated initiative, the Global Compact stands as the illustration par excellence of a deep trend in the current evolution of the multilateral system. Initiated in the early 1990s, this trend is shaped by the unprecedented increase in UN support for business and the market economy. Second, the Global Compact represents a major innovation in the field of global governance.

In allowing for experimentation with new forms of international cooperation, it shows that multilateralism is an institution whose norms and rules may evolve, albeit slowly. Third, although the Global Compact aims for openness and dialogue, the stakeholders inside and outside the Compact remain on very different wavelengths. While proponents applaud its pragmatism, critics believe it negates the values traditionally promoted by the UN.

The Global Compact provides ground for further reflection on the politics of development and on the theory of international relations in various ways. With respect to development, the Compact raises the issue of whether nonbinding measures such as the promotion of corporate social responsibility can effectively lead to a redistribution of global wealth. It also puts into question the existence of a so-called post-Washington consensus. In fact, it may be hypothesized that all of the major developmental initiatives of the recent past-such as the Millennium Development Goals, the Poverty Reduction Strategy Papers, or the Doha Agenda-give rise to divergences similar to those generated by the Global Compact regarding the (in)compatibility of capitalism and justice.

In more political terms, the Compact highlights the difficulties of making global governance democratic. Although the Compact does give more voice to non state actors on the international stage, clearly the language of "partnership," "networking," and "policy dialogue" cannot by itself erase the inequalities that cause some groups to be "in" while others are left "out." From the perspective of international relations theory, the Global Compact allows a better understanding of the nature and the role of international institutions.

Although limited, the impact of the Compact suggests that international institutions are purposive agents that have an autonomous capacity to effect normative change in global affairs. The study of the Compact also illustrates the fruitfulness of applying a constructivist approach to the complex mechanisms of power in world politics. In rallying business around its bid for a world social contract, the UN may have gained some material power. For the Global Compact to become a universal value framework, however, the UN still lacks another, more ideational, form of power: the capacity to legitimate "the order of global things" among groups that defend conflicting interests.

7

Mass Politics in India

The famous Soviet dissident Andrej Amalrik predicted that 1984 would be the year of the collapse of the Soviet Union. He was right about its eventual collapse, but wrong about the year. Instead, 1984 turned out to be a crucial year for another huge imperial state: India. This chapter tries to explain some elements of what happened that year in India by looking at two religio-political movements, one Hindu, one Sikh that tried to change the shape of the Indian nation-state. In order to understand these events one has to analyze both the secularity of the Indian state and the religiosity of the two movements involved. My interpretation will be based on a historical analysis of post-colonial modernity and on a political science account of the development of the Indian political arena over the last twenty years.

In June 1984 the Indian Army attacked the Golden Temple Complex, the central shrine of the Sikhs, in an operation with the codename Blue Star. This huge complex contained, along with numerous other buildings, the Harimandir (Golden Temple) and the Akal Takhat (the Eternal Throne). The latter was occupied and heavily fortified by militant Sikhs who demanded the separation of a Sikh state, Khalistan, from what they described as Hindu India. The army encountered so much resistance in the complex that it had to bring tanks into the operation, which caused much greater damage to the religious buildings than the generals had expected. The operation lasted from 4 June until 7 June.

It destroyed the Sikh Library, which contained a great number of sacred manuscripts and objects from the lives of the Gurus in the Sikh tradition. The numbers game of counting the casualties on both sides has not been conclusive and leaves us with estimates ranging from a few hundred to a few thousand. On the Sikh side the number of dead militants was greatly outnumbered by the number of dead pilgrims who were caught in the crossfire during their visit.

The leader of the Khalistani Sikhs, Sant Jarnail Singh Bhindranwale, was killed in the encounter. This, however, did not mean the end, but rather the beginning of his importance, as martyrs are central to Sikh tradition. His ghost turned out to be much more effective than he had ever been alive. Operation Blue Star took its place among the founding massacres in Sikh historical memory: the pre-colonial massacre of Sikhs in the battle of Malerkotka by the Afghan war leader Ahmad Shah Abdali in 1762, the colonial massacre of peaceful demonstrators in Jallianwala Bagh in Amritsar by the British general Dyer in 1919, and now, in 1984 the post-colonial massacre of Sikhs in the Golden Temple.

These memories repress a lot, but end up constructing a narrative of Sikh suffering, inflicted upon them by outside states. It conveyed the message that Sikhs no longer belonged to the state of India, which was exactly what the militant Khalistanis wanted. The clearest and perhaps most threatening sign of the Sikh understanding of the events was the mutiny of Sikh soldiers in various regiments across the country, significant because of the crucial role Sikhs played in the Indian army from the late nineteenth century onward.

Operation Blue Star turned out to be Indira Gandhi's last battle. On 31 October 1984, India's prime minister was assassinated by two of her Sikh bodyguards. The assassination was followed by a widespread pogrom against Sikhs and their property, especially in major northern Indian cities with sizeable Sikh minorities, such as Delhi and Kanpur. These pogroms were organized and led by political leaders of Mrs. Gandhi's Congress Party and were meant to "teach the arrogant Sikhs a lesson they would not forget," as people said at the time.

The repression was allowed, and sometimes assisted, by the agencies of the state, including both the police and military. Trains and buses were stopped, and Sikhs were taken out and killed. In the Punjab the reverse happened, with the militant Sikhs killing Hindu passengers. In the elections of 1985, Mrs. Gandhi's son, Rajiv, a former airline pilot without any political experience, gained a landslide victory in what was called a "sympathy vote." The anti-Sikh pogrom, and the following electoral success of the political party that had orchestrated the violence, left a great number of Sikhs who had never sympathized with the idea of a separate Sikh state fundamentally disillusioned with the Indian state. Whatever happened afterwards, Khalistani militancy had gained a permanent place in the Indian polity.

The Hindu nationalist movement also had a crucial year in 1984. The Vishva Hindu Parishad (World Hindu Council, VHP), a religious movement led by Hindu monks, and its political ally, the Bharatiya Janata Party (Indian People's Party, BJP) began a campaign to remove the sixteenth-century Babar mosque from the alleged birthplace of the Hindu god Rama, one of the major gods of the Hindu pantheon. The mosque was located in the northern Indian pilgrimage center Ayodhya, and, according to an inscription on the mosque, it had been built by the Mughal general Mir Baqi in 1528. Local belief which dated back to the pre-colonial period had it that the mosque had been built on a destroyed temple for Rama and, actually, was situated on the birthplace of this god.

The mosque had been closed by the government since 1949, when unknown Hindu activists placed an image of Rama inside it. Despite some agitation after independence, there had not been much of an effort to change the status quo. This changed completely when the VHP and BJP entered the stage. Both the VHP and the BJP are part of a parivar (family) of organisations, supported by the Rashtriya Swayamsevak Sangh (National Volunteer Corps, RSS), a militant group which has been in the forefront of Hindu nationalism since its founding in 1925.

Despite this "family-connection" between the VHP, the BJP and the RSS, they have considerable independence and important differences in aims, strategy and leadership. In September 1984, the VHP organized a demonstrative procession of trucks called: "Sacrifice to Liberate Rama's Birthplace." This procession went to the state capital, Lucknow, where it attracted large crowds. It was supposed to end in a huge rally in Delhi, but the rally fell flat due to the assassination of Mrs. Gandhi. The anti-Sikh pogrom going on at the same time drew attention away from Hindu-Muslim tensions surrounding Babar's mosque in Ayodhya, but only for a short time. A surprise decision of a district judge in Faizabad led to the opening of the mosque for the Hindu public in 1986. This decision could not have taken place without the assent of the central government.

In 1988 the BJP and the VHP organized a number of demonstrative processions throughout the country, and even among migrant communities abroad, in which bricks were consecrated for use in the temple that would be built in the mosque's place. In the elections of 1989, the Congress Party of Mr. Gandhi lost its majority in Parliament, and the opposition Janata Party of V.P. Singh replaced it, with the parliamentary support of the BJP. Despite its official support of the new government, the VHP-BJP alliance continued its agitation for the replacement of the mosque with a temple. In 1990 they organized a large procession, led by L.K. Advani, the leader of the BJP, which started in Somnath in western India and was meant to end in Ayodhya, with the ultimate goal of destroying the temple.

The procession was stopped in Bihar, and Advani and a number of his lieutenants were arrested, leading to the BJP's withdrawal of parliamentary support for Singh's government. The 1991 elections brought the Congress Party to power again in the wake of the assassination of its leader, Rajiv Gandhi, who had been killed by Sri Lankan Tamil separatists in southern India. The BJP, which had grown enormously in the years of Ayodhya agitation, continued its campaign for the destruction of the Ayodhya mosque.

On 6 December 1992 the VHP and the BJP organized another rally in Ayodhya. The aim of the rally, which was publicly announced by the VHP leadership in all major Indian newspapers, was to destroy the Babar mosque. Despite this public announcement, the rally was allowed by the authorities, under the eyes of the gathered press and without much hindrance by the huge paramilitary police force present in Ayodhya. Activists proceeded to demolish the old structure until, after a day of hard work, all that remained was rubble and a question: Why didn't the police intervene?

A high ranking police officer told the press that the police could easily have intervened and prevented the demolition, but they had not received orders to do so. Naturally, they did not get any orders from the state officials of Uttar Pradesh, as the state was governed by the BJP, the political party behind the demolition. The paramilitary forces, however, were under the direct command of what in India is called "the Center," the Union government in Delhi. Why did the Center not act?

The story is that India's prime minister, Narasimha Rao (Rajiv Gandhi's successor), was taking a nap and, as he is a very old man, nobody wanted to disturb him. When he woke up, the demolition had already proceeded too far. I do not relate this story to illustrate indecisiveness on the part of the Indian Government, as on the next day the Union government did act very decisively: It dismissed the state governments of four states in which the opposition party BJP ruled. It put the leadership of the BJP and the VHP in jail for a short time and banned a few radical movements, on both the Hindu and the Muslim side. Rao's nap had been a strategic one which allowed the Union government to re-establish the supremacy of the Congress Party after a serious challenge from the BJP.

Nevertheless, all these political actions did not prevent the civil war that broke out in many parts of the country, in which thousands (mostly Muslims) were killed, nor did they prevent the relations between Hindus and Muslims from reaching their lowest point since partition. Many Muslims had by then totally lost their confidence in the state and its institutions, because politicians seemed unwilling to protect the rights and lives of the Muslim minority.

The stage was thus set in 1984 for the introduction of two series of events which can be connected in a narrative involving the destruction of sacred centers of religious minorities, either by the state or with the assent of the state. Such a story shows the extent to which the so-called secularist Congress Party and the institutions of the Indian secular state are instrumental in the marginalisation of religious minorities. A story told in this way demystifies the narrative of religious nationalism. It shows, from the standpoint of the cynical, well-informed observer, that what seems to be a religious conflict is in fact a political game. Such stories show the political dynamics of conflict situations, but they do not answer the question of why these religious centers would become an issue in the first place.

One answer to this question, perhaps more gratifying to a western audience than the political game described above, is that the forces of secular modernity are up against the forces of religious obscurantism (otherwise called fundamentalism). The leadership of the Congress Party, from Nehru up through Rao, which wants to bring India into the world of modern progress, are opposed by Muslim, Hindu or Sikh extremists, who dream of religious nation-states. This explanation, dignified by forms of Weberian modernisation theory, is so much a part of western mythology (otherwise known as common sense) that it is constantly broadcast by the mass media when they report events in Egypt, Iran, Algeria, India, Sri Lanka and other places. It is a story that is hard to question, since any alternative is often viewed as a relativist attack on equality, liberty and fraternity, the founding myths of the liberal nation-state.

In this chapter I present a somewhat different reading of these events by looking at the secularity of the modern nation-state in India and the religiosity of nationalist movements. This reading depends on an analysis of the relationship between state and society as well as on an analysis of social movements which try to alter that relationship. The movements I have introduced above present radical and violent answers to some of the basic questions posed in postcolonial modernity. Some of these answers are readily classified in the category of fascism, but by labelling them as such we have not made the questions go away. The sacred ruins we see today in India are, to an important extent, the result of both the successes and failures of the postcolonial state.

THE SECULARITY OF THE INDIAN NATION-STATE

The nation-state is a hyphenated phenomenon, both aspects of which, nation and state, have to be taken into consideration. Crucial to the nation-state is the notion, as expressed by Ernest Renan that "the nation is a daily plebiscite." This sense of community and collective will is produced in nationalism. Like every community, the nation can be imagined in many ways, but liberal theory emphasizes that the nation can only be modern if it is secular. Therefore, the role that religion plays in nationalisms in many parts of the world today is often felt to be an embarrassing anomaly by those who adhere to a Weberian modernisation theory.

Nationalism has to be connected to secularism to be truly modern. In the West, religion has been defined as an autonomous sphere, separate from politics and economy; this should also happen in the rest of the world, if it is to become truly modern. This idea is expressed in many ways, but most succinctly in what is known as the secularisation thesis. The boredom that takes hold of almost any audience when one speaks about contemporary religion is perhaps the most striking effect of the secularisation thesis which, basically, argues that we already know everything that there is to know about religion: It declines. The success of industrialisation, science and technology has made religion in the modern world obsolete.

In sociological theories of modernity the transition from the pre-modern, rural community to the modern, industrial and urbanized society is said to be marked by the decline of religion as an expression of the moral unity of society. In the age of nationalism, the nineteenth century, nationalism in Europe was often far from secular. Contrary to many nationalism theories, nationalism does not replace religion, but has its origin in religion and develops by nationalizing religion.

The secularisation these are even less applicable to the history of Islam, Hinduism, and Buddhism and most other religions than it is to Christianity. The organisation of religion, the place of religion in society and the patterns of recruitment are so different that not only secularisation theory itself, but also the empirical and theoretical problems which are derived from it in the context of western Christianity, become meaningless. As we have already seen, all this has not kept social scientists from universalizing this ill-founded theory about the West to include the rest of the world. Because all societies modernize, and secularisation is an intrinsic part of modernisation, all societies secularize; so the rhetoric, dressed up as argument, goes.

Just as the nation is, in many instances, not secular, the secularity of the state, as expressed in the separation of church and state may not be as clear-cut as it appears. This separation takes shape in very different forms in different societies. The different histories of state-society relations in different parts of the world cannot be captured in a single master-narrative of secular modernity. What we have to consider in the case of India is a colonial history of state-society relations. The events in Amritsar and Ayodhya are not a sign of backwardness, but are the product of a specific history of what I would, provisionally, call "post-colonial modernity."

The Khalistani militants who are fighting for a separate nation-state, the Hindu activists who destroyed the mosque in order to establish Rama's kingdom on earth, Mrs. Gandhi who ordered Operation Blue Star, Rao who took a nap when the VHP activists exerted themselves, the millions who watched the events in Ayodhya on CNN, all of them are fully modern. They all live under the material conditions and participate fully in the discursive practices of the modern world-system of nation-states. There is no reason to say that any of them is caught in a time warp, medieval or backward as compared to others who are the bearers of reason and progress. However, their positions are different, because they are the product of different histories.

Since the nineteenth century, then, religion has been the site of difference on which the struggle for alternatives to Christian modernity in many parts of the colonial world took place. In that very struggle new religious discourses and practices have emerged which have been placed in the category of fundamentalism (a term derived from American Protestantism), precisely because they are different from the dominant religious forms of the late twentieth-century West. For at least some of these new movements the term religious nationalism is preferable, as they articulate discourse on the religious community and on the nation.

What kind of secularity do we find in the colonial state in British India of the nineteenth and early twentieth centuries? Religious neutrality was seen as essential, first for trading purposes, and later for British rule in India. The British East India Company resisted direct support for missionary projects. The company's neutrality, however, did nothing to prevent attempts to reform Indian society through education, an endeavour fully supported by the utilitarian anglicists. Education, however, turned out to be a field in which evangelical missionaries were extremely active. Whatever the debates between evangelicals and utilitarians - and they were considerable - none of them would have denied that civil society and the forms of knowledge on which it was based were ultimately part and parcel of Christian civilisation.

Despite their official policy of religious neutrality, the British interfered with every aspect of Indian religion and society. Considering the nature of the colonial project, there was actually no choice but to do so, and the tropes of withdrawal, secularity and neutrality were only used to mask that necessity. Let us, for instance, look at the British project of identifying and classifying communities in Indian society. This project is immediately relevant to the religious nationalist movements introduced in the beginning of this chapter.

The Khalistani movement of today cannot be understood without looking at the colonial recruitment of Sikhs in the Indian army. After the Mutiny of 1857, the British disbanded the Bengal army and shifted their recruiting to the Punjab. In their recruiting policy they acted upon a notion of material races, and the Sikhs were not only counted among these races, but were considered the superior example of it. The British were still impressed by the military resistance they had encountered from the Sikhs during their earlier advance into the Punjab.

They introduced in the recruitment process the idea that there was a clear boundary between "pure" Sikhs and "not quite" Sikhs and stipulated that only pure Sikhs should be recruited. Pure Sikhs were those who belonged to the Khalsa and wore the five signs of Sikhism, including the unshorn hair (and thus the turban), the dagger and the steel bangle. Clearly, this boundary already existed in the pre-colonial period, but it was now reinforced by the secular state in the crucial process of providing labor opportunities. Baptism in the Sikh Khalsa meant eligibility for entry into the army. There can be little doubt that the colonial reinforcement of Khalsa identity provided a basis for later mobilisation to defend the purity of Sikh faith in the Singh Sabha movement and for the postcolonial development of Sikh mass politics around the symbols of purity.

Even more important for the British than identifying who was a Sikh and who was not, was the imperial notion that India was divided into two large nations, one Hindu and the other Muslim. Again, Hindu nationalism, as we know it today, is largely a product of that notion and the colonial projects connected to it. Most importantly, the British set out in the eighteenth century to codify Hindu law and Muslim law. The secular principle of equality before the law was thus replaced by a principle of differential legal treatment of religious communities.

This codification of communal difference had significant postcolonial consequences. For example, in 1986 a major political crisis broke out in India about the Muslim Women (Protection of Rights on Divorce) Bill. The new legislation was the Congress government's answer to agitation by Muslim leaders who protested a decision of the Supreme Court in the Shah Banu case. This case arose out of an application made by a Muslim woman, Shah Banu, for maintenance under section 125 of the Code of Criminal Procedure. The woman had been separated from her husband and demanded a monthly allowance.

The new legislation is based on the assumption that Muslim personal law derives straight from immemorial religious law, as codified in the sharia, conveniently forgetting that this immemorial law, as codified in civil law, is in fact a colonial construction. The government action was immediately condemned by the BJP as an attempt to appease the Muslim minority, as indeed it was. This created the curious situation in which Hindu nationalists asked for the secular application of a uniform civil code for all Indian citizens, while the secular Congress Party wanted to protect the minorities from this uniformity.

This irony can possibly be explained by the historical fact that the Hindu personal code, derived from the dharmashastras, has never gained the foundational value for the Hindu community that the sharia has gained for the Muslim community. This, in turn, has to do with the nature of textual authority in Hinduism as well as with the construction of the Hindu identity. In the Muslim case, the law has become the public symbol of the integrity of the Muslim community and is thus directly linked to the political treatment of a minority, either in terms of protection or in terms of appeasement.

This has ossified Muslim personal law in India to an extent unknown in Muslim states like Pakistan and Bangladesh. It provided Muslim leaders with an issue for which to fight. At the same time, it gave BJP politicians an issue which they could use to show the backwardness of the Muslim community, especially in its treatment of women, and also to show the willingness of the Congress Party to pamper the Muslim minority in order to win their votes. The extent to which the political terrain for this was already laid out in the colonial period is striking.

The colonial construction of the Hindu community did not proceed along the lines of homogenisation, as in the Muslim case, but along those of differentiation. The Hindu majority was seen by the British as endlessly fragmented and diverse. In their documentation of these differences the colonial authorities created long lists of castes, ethnic groups which were hierarchically linked.

These hierarchical listings led to widespread agitation and the formation of caste associations on an all-India basis, whose main purpose was to enhance the status of their respective castes. In southern India much was made of the racial distinction between Aryans (Brahmins) and Dravidians (Non-Brahmins) which led to the formation of Dravidian parties which continue to dominate politics in Tamil Nadu even today. In the rest of India, caste consciousness was also raised by the colonial project of enumerating the different castes. This has resulted in an ongoing dialectic of caste politics against the politics of Hindu unity (sangathan) until the present day.

The greatest threat to Hindu unity was the possible formation of a separate, huge community of "Untouchables." Outside of the caste hierarchies were large groups which were Untouchable outcastes, groups with culturally despised occupations, such as sweepers and scavengers, as well as tribes, groups mainly living outside of peasant economies in hill regions and jungles. In the twentieth century the British gave these groups special, preferential treatment to redress their immense social disadvantages. This was immediately seen by Hindu nationalists as a policy to weaken Hindu unity. In particular, the British decision in 1932, made under pressure from the Untouchables, to create separate electorates for them was strongly resisted by the leader of the Congress Party, Mohandas K. Gandhi, who undertook a fast unto death to have it revoked.

The legal historian Marc Galanter argues that "it is evident that Congress opposition, if not Gandhi's personally, was inspired by fear that the great Hindu base of Congress support would be weakened." The result of Gandhi's fast was that Ambedkar, the Untouchable leader, stopped his campaign to create separate electorates for Untouchables. Instead he accepted

Gandhi's proposal for a system of reserved seats which is still in force today. The importance of Untouchable participation in Hindu nationalism has to be seen in light of Hindu-Muslim conflict and competition. Their votes were and continue to be crucial to Hindu majoritarianism.

Again, colonial (secular) interventions set the stage for postcolonial politics. The ante was raised was raised by extending the principle of preferential treatment and distributive justice from the so-called scheduled tribes and castes to a new category, the Other Backward Castes (OBCS). This came to occupy a large part of the political arena, as, for example, in the southern Indian state of Tamil Nadu, OBCS included all castes except Brahmins. The new policy led to caste warfare, especially in Gujrat, but also in other states.

The 1989 decision of the Singh government to implement the recommendations of the Mandal Commission for massive reservations for OBCS in the public sector, universities and elsewhere, led again to the pitching of caste against Hindu unity. This was well expressed in the slogan, commonly heard throughout northern India in this period: Mandal or Mandir (temple), meaning that one was either for this policy of reservation or one was a Hindu nationalist striving for the building of the Rama temple in Ayodhya.

However, this general analysis of the colonial history of secularism and the secular production of religious politics cannot explain fully the role of the secular state in the 1984 happenings. Why indeed 1984, or better, why the 1980s? There are a few general features in the development of Indian politics which can contribute to the events of 1984 and their aftermath. Many political scientists have argued that the 1970s showed the decline of the Congress system which had governed India since independence. Mrs. Gandhi had to fight off her rivals for the succession of her father, Jawaharlal Nehru, who had made India into a largely one-party system.

She definitely succeeded in doing so, as her landslide victory of 1971 shows, but only at the cost of a further centralisation of power in Delhi and the weakening of rivals by playing them off against their opponents. This strategy led increasingly to a decline of the ability of the Congress Party to govern India. The precariousness of Mrs. Gandhi's rule became evident when she decided to dispense with democracy, declaring a state of emergency, after her seat in Parliament was challenged in court by the opposition. The Emergency of 1975 to 1977 politicized the police and the powerful civil service and led to a general erosion of the credibility and legitimacy of the Congress Party and the state itself. Many politicians, including leaders of the BJP, were arrested and jailed.

There can be little doubt that the distrust Hindu nationalists feel towards the Congress Party's secularist and progressive posturing was much strengthened in this period. Mrs. Gandhi was soundly defeated after her decision to return to democracy in 1977. However, the coalition that succeeded Congress for three years under the name Janata Dal was too internally divided to be an alternative to the Congress system, which at least had a long history of containing and balancing various factional strife. In 1980, Mrs. Gandhi again won the parliamentary elections and came back to power, but now more than ever, her government had a feeling of being embattled, of presiding over a system which was falling apart.

In the case of the Punjab there can be little doubt that the political strategies employed by Mrs. Gandhi's Congress Party were a major element in creating the Khalistani separatism of the 1980s. Since independence, the Congress Party and the leading Sikh Party, Akali Dal, have been the main contenders for power in the Punjab. While Congress has been the dominant party over much of this period, the 1977 and 1980 elections were won by the Akalis. It is widely said in India that Bhindranwale was used by Congress in this context to weaken support for the Akali Dal.

Evidence for this comes from the fact that Bhindranwale's men ran as candidates against Akalis in the elections for the committee that manages all Sikh shrines in the Punjab and is the main resource in Sikh politics. To many analysts this explains also why Bhindranwale was soon released after his arrest in connection with the murder of Lala Jagat Narain in 1981. Interestingly, the Punjab provides also an excellent example of the way Mrs. Gandhi divided her own party at the regional level in order to prevent challenges to her central power. She appointed the leader of one faction of the Punjab Congress Party, Giani Zail Singh, to the position of home minister in the Union government and then later president, while she put his opponent, Darbara Singh, at the head of the Punjab government.

These maneuvers explain at least partly the inability of the state to deal decisively with the growing separatist militancy in the Punjab until the movement that the army was brought into the Golden Temple, a self-defeating action by all accounts. Uttar Pradesh, India's most populous state with more than 100 million inhabitants, shows a similar picture of divisive politics and a growing willingness of all political parties, including Congress, to see religious nationalism, in this case Hindu nationalism, as a possible unifying force.

The main contenders for ruling Uttar Pradesh were the Congress Party, Janata and the BJP. The Congress Party had lost its dominance in Uttar Pradesh in the 1970s, just as it had in the Punjab. Uttar Pradesh in this period is a good example of the mobilisation of the OBCS, led by the middle peasantry. The short-lived Janata government, which ruled Uttar Pradesh after the Emergency, implemented reservation policies favouring these OBCS. The BJP, however, saw this kind of policy as dividing the unity of the Hindu nation.

As discussed earlier, the politics of caste reservations and of Hindu nationalism played themselves out in the politics of the 1980s and Uttar Pradesh was one of the crucial arenas. Congress could not stay out of this conflict, even if it had wanted to, and, as in the Punjab, ultimately favoured religious nationalism. The crucial decision in 1986 to open the mosque in Ayodhya for the Hindu public could not have been made without direct assent of the Congress leadership. This was clearly done to gain political advantage by acting according to Hindu populist sentiments, although this backfired in the end by giving the BJP more momentum.

THE RELIGIOSITY OF NATIONALIST MOVEMENTS

There is a common fallacy that religion and politics are two different fields of social activity. This leads observers sometimes to speak of the politicisation of religion, and to say that this is against the original intent of the founder of religion, or God himself. Undoubtedly, there are movements which try to steer away from the official political arena and call themselves apolitical, but even in these cases this withdrawal can be seen as political. Much clearer, however, is the political nature of the movements with which I began this chapter - the Khalistani movement and the Hindu nationalist movement.

Both movements attempt to create new nation-states to replace the current one. In these cases the common question is not whether these movements are political, but whether, or to what extent, they are religious. It is largely spurious to come up with old or new definitions of religion, culture or politics. It is more useful to look at the imagined common history, territory and identity which characterize these movements, and to recognize the extent to which this imagination is rooted in religious institutions and sacred scriptures, and is formulated by religious leaders. The following section will address these issues in both Sikh and Hindu nationalism.

THE KHALISTANI MOVEMENT

The Sikh tradition was founded by Guru Nanak in the fifteenth century and exemplifies a particular form of religious thought in India which is devotional, but does not wish to use images in worship. The Sikh brotherhood (khalsa) emerged out of that traditional in the eighteenth century. The current Khalistani movement is a radical faction in that brotherhood. Its ideas can be traced partly to the Singh Sabha movement in the colonial period. The first Singh Sabha was established in 1873 and preached the purification of the Sikh brotherhood from Hindu practices.

One of the key issues was thus the assertion of boundaries between Hindus and Sikhs, clearly in reaction to reformist activities on the part of the Arya Samaj, a Hindu reformist movement which tried to "convert" Sikhs to Hinduism. A major victory for the Singh Sabha movement occurred in 1905, when Hindu images were removed from the Golden Temple in Amritsar. In the early decades of the twentieth century the Singh Sabha movement increasingly turned its attention to the management of Sikh temples (gurdwaras), the places of congregational worship. These temples were, under British law, the property of priestly families whose moral and ritual behaviour did not conform to the purist standards of certain reformists who originated in the Singh Sabha movement.

These families called themselves Akalis. Akal is the term in Sikhism for the ultimate, timeless reality. The most important campaign of the Akalis was a struggle for the control over the temples. In 1925 the agitation succeeded in placing the temples under the authority of the Shiromani Gurdwara Parbandhak Committee, a representative body of the Sikh brotherhood. This success led to the formation of the Sikh political party, the Akali Dal. The control of the temple-committee has become the most coveted prize in the factional politics of this party.

The slogan of the Singh Sabha was that Sikhs were not Hindus. The boundary between members of the brotherhood and those followers of Sikh traditions who were not members of the brotherhood was now transformed in a boundary between pure Sikhs (members of the brotherhoods with beards, turbans and the rest of the markers) and Hindus. Religious groups, such as the Nanakpanthis, the Nirankaris and the Namdharis who followed the Sikh teachings but did not accept the brotherhood, were asked to declare that they were not Sikhs, but Hindus which, of course, they refused to do.

The guiding fear behind all this seems to have been (and continues to be) that the Sikhs would lose their sense of a separate identity and simply become one of the many sectarian movements in Hinduism. One of the main grounds for this abiding fear is the practice of many Punjabi families to initiate only one son into the brotherhood, while the rest of the family is clean-shaven and follows Sikh and Hindu teachings as they see fit. The boundary between Hindus and Sikhs is thus constantly negotiated in the day-to-day practices of a large portion of Punjabis who are only potentially pure Sikhs.

It is striking that the Khalistani movement began, in fact, not as a separatist movement, but as a protest movement of a purist faction of the Sikh brotherhood against privileges given to the Nirankaris. According to the tradition of the Sikh brotherhood, there have been ten Sikh gurus; since the last one, Sikhs have had to rely on the sacred sayings of these gurus (gurbani), collected in the sacred book of Sikhism, the Guru Granth Sahib, and, in the event of a dispute, to trust the opinion (gurmatta) of the brotherhood. The Nirankaris, however, continue to have a living guru. This is considered blasphemy by the brotherhood.

On the day of the big festival of Vaisakhi, 13 April 1978, the Nirankaris staged a large procession in Amritsar and were confronted by a group of radical members of the brotherhood. Thirteen Sikhs and two Nirankaris were killed. The Akali Dal government of the Punjab registered a case against the Nirankaris, but they were later found to have acted in self-defense. This verdict is often quoted by Khalistanis as a sign that true justice could not be expected from a Hindu government.

In April 1980 this led to the assassination of Gurbachan Singh, the Nirankari guru. The immediate origin of the Khalistani movement lies therefore in a conflict about religious orthodoxy, framed in the narrative of true or false Sikhs, and in the failure of the state to protect pure Sikhism, or worse, in the alleged conspiracy of the state to use the Nirankaris against the brotherhood. An important role in the attack on the Nirankaris was played by the Damdami Taksal, a religious institution under Bhindranwale's leadership. Bhindranwale felt strongly that the Sikh religion was under mounting pressure.

After the assassination of the Nirankari guru, he was suspected of involvement in the 1981 murder of Lala Jagat Narain, editor of the largest Hindu-owned newspaper of the Punjab, the Punjabi Kesari. Bhindranwale was arrested, which led to the hijacking of an Indian Airlines plane by Khalistanis who demanded his release. His arrest made him a rising star in the growing separatist movement in the Punjab, and after his release he quickly became its leader. He and his followers entrenched themselves in the Golden Temple, and from there launched terrorist attacks on Hindus and on state institutions. This ultimately led to the events of 1984.

The narrative of Khalistani aspirations is framed in terms of history, territory and identity. The history of the Sikhs as popularly seen and told by themselves is one of constant struggle against foreign state power. Early on it is a struggle against the Mughals, later against the British, and finally it is a struggle against the Brahmins of the dominant Congress Party. In these struggles the Sikhs are portrayed as the courageous minority who fight against overwhelming state power. The stories dwell on massacres and martyrdom, but also on ultimate superiority and victory. The events in the Punjab in the 1980s could have been scripted along these lines. The Khalistani challenge to the central state elicited a growing involvement of the central state in the affairs of the Punjab.

It led to a police state in which the prisons were filled with young Sikhs, innocent or not, who was subjected to torture and numerous atrocities, setting the stage for a civil war. Finally, the attack on the Golden Temple and the killing of Bhindranwale made him into a textbook martyr for the Sikh cause and demonstrated to his followers that he had been right all along about the bad intentions of the Indian state. A major feature of nationalism is the political of space. Bordered territory symbolizes the fixity, stability and sovereignty of the nation-state, so that borders have become contested sites for international warfare, refugees and immigration policies. Those who see themselves as a nation often seek a spatial, territorial expression of their nationhood.

The Indian Muslim League spoke of a "homeland" for Muslims when it demanded Pakistan in the 1940s. This expression was adopted by Sikh leaders when the Punjab region was cut in two by the partition of 1947, but it did not play a significant role in the negotiations that led to Indian independence. In the 1960s Master Tara Singh, the leader of the Akali Dal, began a movement demanding a separate state within the Indian Union, with a Sikh electoral majority. Not religion, but language (Punjabi) was the basis of this demand, since language had been generally adopted as the marker for deciding state boundaries within the Union.

This movement succeeded in 1966 when the Punjab was divided into the largely Hindi-speaking (and Hindu) state of Haryana and the largely Punjabi-speaking (and Sikh) state of Punjab. As we have seen, however, a separate state within the Indian nation-state proved to be not quite enough for some in the 1980s. While these territorial strivings are typical for all nationalisms, some of them at least are grafted upon pre-nationalist senses of sacred space. According to Harjot Oberoi, Sikhs were not bound to the territory of the Punjab, but to the lineage of gurus and then to the scriptural guru, that is the words of the guru in the *Guru Granth*.

In his view, the territorial demand is entirely a modern, nationalist demand which has nothing to do with religion. This transterritorial aspect of Sikhism made it easy to travel beyond the Punjab and to build temples wherever they had a large enough community. It is, at the same time, true that this religious transcendence of local belonging makes it possible to tie religious identity either to nationalism or to transnationalism.

Both possibilities are fulfilled in the Sikh case, which has produced both a Punjabi territorial nationalism and a transnational diaspora. Both nationalism and the transnational Diaspora are tied to the Punjab, however, in the center of Sikhism: the Golden Temple in Amritsar. There is no place which expresses so strongly the existence of a global Sikh community as the Golden Temple. That is why the attack on the Golden Temple by the Indian state proved to many Sikhs that they need a territorial nation-state to protect their sacred center. Identity politics is, obviously, the main element in the Khalistani movement. As argued earlier, the guiding fear among Sikhs of the brotherhood is that they may backslide into Hinduism.

This fear is clearly expressed in the exhortation to young people to show the visible markers of being a Sikh, as in this speech by Bhindranwale: "If you do not want beards then you should ask the women to become men and you become women. Or else ask nature that it should stop this growth on your faces. Then there will be no need for me to preach, no need to break my head on it." This passage also shows the extent to which religious identity is tied up with gender identity, as Veena Das rightly observes in her comments on Bhindranwale's speech. The message is that to be a real man one has to be a visible member of the brotherhood. That allows one also to wear the dagger and protect the honor of the Sikh community against attacks from outside.

The idea that Sikhs need their own state to be able to maintain the social and symbolic boundaries which distinguish them from Hindus is not only found among extremists like Bhindranwale. In the 1960s, the period of agitation for a separate Sikh Punjab within the Indian Union, the acclaimed Sikh writer, historian and longtime member of the Congress Party, Khushwant Singh, wrote in the conclusion of his two-volume history of the Sikhs: "The only chance of survival of the Sikhs as a separate community is to create a state in which they form a compact group, where the teaching of Gurmukhi and the Sikh religion is compulsory and where there is an atmosphere of respect for the traditions of their Khalsa forefathers." Khushwant Singh, writes about a separate state within the Indian Union and he is anything but a Khalistani, however one still sees in this quotation the common ground shared by extremists and moderates.

THE VISHVA HINDU PARISHAD

The Vishva Hindu Parishad was founded in Bombay on an auspicious day, the birthday of Lord Krishna, 29 August 1964. One hundred fifty religious leaders were invited to Sandeepany Sadhanalaya, the center of a Hindu missionary movement headed by Swami Chinmayananda. The host had been instrumental in organizing the conference and became its president. Shivram Shankar Apte, a worker of the militant Hindu Rashtriya Swayamsevak Sangh, was elected as its general secretary. The aim of the new movement was to strengthen Hindu society and spread Hindu values, not only in India itself but also abroad. The VHP's primary aim is to formulate a modern Hinduism as a common religion of the Indian nation.

For its first 15 years, it had only limited success, but this changed drastically in the 1980s. The VHP received a considerable boost when an Untouchable sub caste in Meenakshipuram in southern India converted en masse to Islam in 1981. Conversion and petro-dollars are the major concerns of Hindu nationalists who believe that their nation is under threat from Islam. In historical terms Islamic aggression is seen by the VHP as the cause of many Hindus leaving their religion and converting to Islam. In its view, the unity and integrity of the ancient Hindu nation has been most fundamentally threatened by conversion by the sword. Indian Muslims are therefore constantly exhorted to realize their fundamental Hindu nature.

While these conversions happened in the past, the Meenakshipuram case was seen as proof that the Middle East used its oil wealth to continue the conversion project. Although the Meenakshipuram conversions were insignificant in terms of overall numbers, this case has become the most publicized issue in the VHP's defense of Hinduism. Its propaganda about the Islamic threat led to the organisation of the highly successful nation-wide "Sacrifice for Unity" in 1983, which in turn became the basis for the events in 1984, described above. Hindu nationalism, as found in the VHP, also expresses itself in terms of history, territory and identity. Like their Khalistani counterparts, Hindu nationalists describe Hindu history as a story of oppression by Muslim rulers, followed by British Christian rulers, and now by Indian pseudo-secularists.

Their story is less one of militant rebellion against foreign rule or martyrdom, although these are not entirely absent from it, but rather it is a story emphasizing Hindu tolerance and spiritual superiority in their relations with their oppressors. At the same time, however, the VHP argues that Hindus have been taken advantage of because of their tolerance and should now stand up to claim what is their right, namely the Hinduisation of the Indian nation-state. The VHP condemns the Congress Party, which has ruled India for most of the period since independence, as a pseudo-secularist party. The Congress Party's Nehruvian program of reducing the salience of religious beliefs and practices in politics, as well as the state's projected neutrality toward religious difference, which it inherited from the colonial state, are both seen to be contradicted by policies that pamper the minority.

More specifically, the Congress Party and the state are viewed as using the Muslim community as a vote bank and dividing the Hindu majority by pitting the Untouchables against the rest of the Hindus. Independence, as VHP ideologues keep reminding their audience, has not brought freedom for the Hindu majority. They believe that the state should express the Hindu values of purity and incorruptibility as found in the divine realm of the God-king Rama and that history books should be rewritten to convey the proud heritage of Hindu civilisation and the wrongs inflicted upon it by "foreigners."

The territory of the Indian nation-state is also in the VHP's conception of Hindu sacred space. This notion of nationwide Hindu sacred space is based on the existence of Hindu centers all over the country connected to each other by intersecting pilgrimage routes. These routes have been utilized for the VHP's processual agitations and most elaborately in the "Sacrifice for Unity" in November and December 1983 when 3 large processions and at least 47 smaller processions traversed the country. Processions of temple chariots are an important feature in Hindu temple festivals. The VHP made use of brand-new trucks, named temple chariots, which carried huge water pots filled with Ganges water and smaller pots of local sacred water. In this way, all rivers and sacred waters of India were symbolically connected to the Ganges as the unifying symbol of Hindu India.

The "Sacrifice for Unity" laid the groundwork for the ritual processions aimed at the destruction of the mosque in Ayodhya. The VHP's plan to destroy this mosque as the first of a series of similar mosques, allegedly placed on Hindu sacred spots, is an attempt to map out the national territory in such a way that India is a country for Hindus only. Advani's campaign of 1990, which ended in his arrest in Bihar and the downfall of Singh's government, started in Somnath, perhaps the best known of Hindu temples destroyed by Muslim conquerers. After independence a new Hindu temple was built there by Hindu activists, led by major Congress politicians. Advani's message was clear: What had been done in Somnath by Congress should have been followed up in other places, and the BJP-VHP alliance was going to do just that.

The identity politics of the VHP movement are complex in nature. On the face of it Hindus do not have to worry, as the Sikhs do, that they will fade away. They are a comfortable majority, but, to use Stanley Tambiah's phrase, they have a minority complex. Part of this can be explained by the fact that before partition the Hindu majority was not at all secure, considering the presence of a large number of Muslims and the unclear position of Untouchables as second-class Hindus. Part of it also involves the very basis of the formation of a Hindu majority, namely Hindu identity.

The term "Hindu" refers to a very wide-ranging and divergent set of beliefs and practices which are not easily translatable from region to region. The minority complex of this insecure majority is particularly expressed in the fear that Untouchables will convert to Islam. This is shown in the success of the VHP propaganda about the Meenakshipuram conversions which blew up this incident to unbelievable proportions. The pre-independence political rivalry and mutual antagonism between India's two major communities, Hindus and Muslims, is given new political life by the VHP.

While conflicts between the two communities had been confined to particular cities and localities since the creation of Pakistan, the VHP succeeded in making it again into a nationwide phenomenon. The other side of Hindu identity politics relates to the long-standing fear that the Untouchable communities, which make up a crucial percentage of India's population, may decide that they are not part of the Hindu nation. Policies which focus on these disadvantaged communities are portrayed by the VHP and its political ally, the BJP, as trying to divide the Hindus against themselves. They are said to be a threat to unity. This is why for Hindu nationalists the debate about affirmative action is closely related to their cause of unifying the nation under a Hindu banner.

Religious nationalism in India went through important changes in 1984. Operation Blue Star fulfilled the hopes of Khalistanis by creating a very real divide between Hindus and Sikhs in the country. That year saw the beginning of the agitation which led to the destruction of the Babar mosque in Ayodhya in 1992 and to a new phase of intercommunal enmity between Hindus and Muslims in India. Both of these conflicts have an international dimension because of the inimical relations between India and Pakistan.

India accuses Pakistan of assisting Sikh terrorists in their actions in the Punjab which borders Pakistan. Pakistan follows closely what happens with their fellow Muslims in neighboring India. This situation is obviously made worse by the tense standoff in Kashmir, where Muslim militants want a separate state. Ultimately, the international tension between Pakistan and India must, of course, be seen as the result of a partition of the subcontinent, caused by religious nationalism. It shows that separation, eagerly sought by Khalistanis, and does not necessarily solve political problems. It only changes their definition from national to international.

Since India's independence many political scientists have predicted that the country would fall apart. This mood was perhaps best captured in the title of Selig Harrison's 1960 book, India: The Most Dangerous Decades. A similar sense of impending doom is expressed by the subtitle of a recent book by Atul Kohli: *India's Growing Crisis of Governability*. Kohli rightly calls attention to the politicisation of the main institutions of the state, including the police and the civil service. He also emphasizes the gradual decline of the Congress system, which previously contained various regional and social conflicts.

A major element in this, and Kohli acknowledges this, is the success rather than the failure of mass politics in that a growing number of groups have become involved in the political system. Their mobilisation has taken shape in two types of mass movement: the backward caste movements and the religious nationalist movements. Unfortunately, this enhanced participation has also led to a growth in political militancy and violence. The change in the political arena is undoubtedly among the most important elements in explaining the growth of religious nationalism among both Sikhs and Hindus in the 1980s. The phenomenon itself, however, is not explained by it. For that we need a long-term perspective which analyzes both the secularity of the state and the religiosity of social movements.

8

Movement in the Key Concepts

The scrutiny of the historical foundations of the UN world-unity vocabulary is not very helpful in itself, but in order to understand the historical dimensions of the present, the study of the historical foundations of world-unity structures represents a very useful starting point, since those world-unity structures still constitute a fundamental part of the current framework of international relations; and it will be no less useful to make visible the conceptual structures related to the use of time layers in political narration since they are key elements of almost all future-oriented political narratives.

It would be too much for any single study to claim that only since the founding of the United Nations has it become possible to view the world as a single political unit. Since the 1940s, the United Nations has represented political hopes predicated on various appeals to a "world cosmos." Since the end of the 1980s, it has been widely argued that the concepts, narratives, and arguments used to examine international relations have shifted from a diplomatic relations among states to cosmopolitan understandings of law, world unity, and a new global "governmentality" The purpose of this chapter is not to make such grand claims about the character or analysis of international relations (International Relation) and its possible foundations; rather, claims about "paradigm change" are best approached through the methods of conceptual history.

Just a cursory glance at such materials makes it evident that the vocabularies of the two world organisations differ greatly and should give a reader at least the feeling that these two periods represent profound paradigm changes. These texts also suggest, as methodological injunctions, that these periods should not be understood as special contemporary political moments and that it is impossible to understand them without grasping the vocabulary and concepts used in contemporary debates. My main critical point is directed at the dominant methods of reading based on assumptions about historical process and development.

In such narratives, key concepts are often functional in character, enabling scholars to carry out their historical studies for the purpose of generating a suitable feeling of world politics as a cumulative process of "historical development." Additionally, in these narratives key concepts have been treated as the foundation on which theoretical contributions are based, but hardly ever as objects warranting critical examination in their own right.

In relation to these shortcomings, my analysis seeks to demonstrate that empirical readings of international relations are still appropriate. Empirical methods do not invalidate more normative studies but enable us to examine the contexts in which theories of international relations came to be used and how they have changed over time. They thus highlight the need for theorisations of international relations to be sensitive to periodisations when dealing with sources, and especially for a need for great caution about these periodisations.

KOSELLECK, PERIODISATION, AND TIME LAYERS

Koselleck calls the basic elements of modern political narratives "time layers" (Zeitschichten). Time layers are not akin to historical events and facts of a contemporary context but constitute only modes of the narration that orient and persuade the reader to adopt the perspective of a continuous historical development. In this way, IR analysts have long been persuaded to see the United Nations as the next, more-developed version of the League, and the League as a successor of the Hague Peace Conferences. When such a kind of predecessor/successor view of periodisation is removed, we can see that mainstream approaches to international organisations rest upon foundations that are strongly influenced by the narratives authored by prominent scholars.

Another major contribution to the discussions on the theorisation of periodisations is Koselleck's theory of the main characteristics of the conceptual movement of modern political concepts. I rely on this theory in my analysis of the changes in the concepts and vocabularies of IR during the dark 1930s and futurological 1940s and of the interpretations that have been produced about these reforms to the foundations of international order. In my view, Koselleck's methodological prescriptions constitute some of the best contributions for the creation of a theoretical foundation enabling the periodisation of these reforms and of how we might understand the key concepts that played a crucial role in the 1930s and 1940s when the search for vocabularies and concepts drawn from constitutional thought began.

This conceptual-historical orientation also represents a renewed attempt to acknowledge the very abstract character of twentieth-century concepts and vocabularies, allowing us to see and handle them as abstract and universal concepts independent of any specific attributes of time and place. In this sense, my analysis challenges the oversimplification of texts as well as of contexts. It also challenges approaches that have mythologized concepts of international relations without reference to historical sources, while attempting to introduce new understandings of international relations and world politics.

Surprisingly few theoretical presentations of IR as a scholarly discipline have tried to pay serious attention to the crucial textual sources of the conceptual "foundations" of twentieth-century international relations, the planning documents of the League and the United Nations. Yet these are perhaps the only texts that offer exemplary answers to the most abstract conceptual problems of twentieth-century IR, especially in their references to "world unity" and "world community" and in the organisational vocabularies that are thereby enabled. Only by challenging the account of historical process that has been superimposed onto the basic concepts of international relations can we examine historical texts in a more detailed way.

In the account of historical method pursued here, the intention is especially to examine the motivations behind the concepts and their uses and to build our description around these texts and concepts in a manner that opens up many new interpretive possibilities for the history of international relations. Such a procedure shows that particular concepts and theories lose their sense of historical necessity and appear instead as unsettled and fascinating objects. As a starting point, some preliminary theoretical observations will be further developed later. First, before the planning of the UN there was scarcely any kind of diplomacy making any significant use of the societal, unitary, and organisational vocabularies of international relations.

Second, all the preparations for a new UN vocabulary and its key concepts were made quite rapidly over a planning period of about four years, and the process was not based on any strong claim about a continuous, longer process of history. Third, utterances about a longer historical process were instead generated as a vocabulary that became useful in the 1940s and was mostly motivated by the contemporary political problems of the dark 1930s as well as the conceptual problems posed by the specific experiences of international relations since the outbreak of World War I.

Fourth, the motivations behind the periodisations of history and the use of the above-mentioned time layers in the narrative structures about dealing with international relations and world organisations in the accounts of the 1930s and 1940s advocating reform are not reasonably understood as the products of visions of a long and continuous process, but were related to the desire to create a new vocabulary addressing specific contemporary problems. Fifth, this specificity reshaped the utopian, idealistic, even transcendental characteristics of vocabularies that were earlier deemed to be highly philosophical.

Finally, the recognized need, in the context of UN planning, for a philosophical mythology providing a conceptual base for world organisational planning, which define later as a complex simplicity, was the main reason and motivation behind the innovations of vocabularies and concepts of the societal and organisational world-unity project. The new vocabularies became useful in this context for planners attempting to devise a model of international relations in the future since the temporal peace-league model was no longer deemed practical for a general peace plan for the future of international relations.

As an example of present-day use of time layers in narration and the exploitation of concepts as key tools for the legitimation of a development history, cite Antonio Cassese's reference to Immanuel Kant and specifically his suggestion that Kant is the philosophical father of the development of real world organisations. Kant is often-and with good reason-regarded as the most important philosophical father of the vocabularies of world unity.

The Kantian world-unity vocabulary tradition is discussed in my project in terms of being almost the only existing conceptual base held by the actual planners, but simultaneously we have to raise doubts about the presence of actual Kantian philosophical elements in IR texts. I argue for a reading of these reformulations of Kant's world-unity message by different scholars and planners as narrative adaptations intended to make the Kantian vocabulary useful for their own contemporary projects. It is also needless to restate that this is also a coherent move in relation to my aspiration to dismiss the style of development-historical narration; there is always a good reason to be skeptical of all kinds of claims about the wider contemporary use of Kantian or other philosophies as models for real world organisations, as so many have tried to show.

By referring to Kant in this context to establish two links that are important for the conceptual historical reading of IR's vocabulary and concepts. The first suggests that the new vocabulary of the United Nations includes characteristics that are conceivably Kantian in origin, but that we should not discuss this as a philosophical question in relation to the real world organisations. The second point is that between Kant's own production and the Kantianism of the UN vocabulary we need to consider specific constitutional debates in Germany that make use of German and Kantian styles of unity abstraction. Both of these aspects of conceptual history are very poorly studied, and the philosophical interests of scholars have in general dominated the readings.

Lastly, the Kantian vocabulary also brings to the fore all kinds of questions concerning the rich discussions on the proper theorisation of the effect of the Enlightenment and of the Great Revolutions, and especially the use of Enlightenment ideas in the visions of our contemporary discourses. A very important issue is that the distance between the paradigm changes in the political concepts of our own century is not great enough to enable us to establish a connection between them and their Great Revolutions counterparts.

VOCABULARY INNOVATIONS, KANT, AND IR

The historical analogies between contemporary ideas of the "Saddle Era" (Sattelzeit) and the twentieth century are surely the most delicate and complicated issue to deal with. By focusing on such a highly empirical thing as vocabulary, we surely create tools that minimize the risk of building a development-historical description, but we also have to be well aware of the methodological pitfalls of inaccurate analogies and misleading periodisations.

According to Koselleck, the modernisation of political concepts and vocabularies occurred especially during the Sattelzeit. Kant's philosophy and vocabulary themselves belong to that era. Kant is famous partly for his tendency to politicize the basic tenets of the old law of nations and of the traditional style of natural-law arguments in the context of the French Revolution. Kant urged the introduction of new visions of moral principles into the international system of monarchical diplomacy. Kant's *Zum ewigen Frieden* was a pamphlet that utilized the basic ideology, central to diplomacy, of a system of balance of power in order to revise this very same diplomacy.

In *Die Metaphysik der Sitten* Kant challenged the tradition of a law of nations through new discursive methods of rationalism based on Enlightenment thought. Both works formulated their criticisms in terms of an academic discourse, the usual format of German constitutional debate. It was pivotal in this discourse to construct competing unity models by using the natural-law styled argument and the so-called societal principle. In a revolutionary but understandable move, Kant embodied his criticism in a societal picture of world unity and in the key concept of Weltburgerrecht and others like Menschenstaat, Weltrepublik, and Volkerstaat.

According to Kant, the real system of international relations should rely on the rational and in this sense also on the societal unity of all the people of the world. Such a move changed the possibilities for diplomacy of sovereign powers to monopolize the concept of international relations. More than anything else, it offered future generations of thinkers the foundations of a new conceptual system not based on the ancient regime. Thus Kant contributed (perhaps more than any other classical philosopher) to the concept of "world unity."

WORLD ORGANISATIONS IN CONTEMPORARY IR NARRATIVES AND TEXTS

It is possible to put forward a basic point of criticism leveled at the various studies of world organisations that present an institutional character implying a historical-developmental narrative structure so that their connection to each other is best understood within a predecessor-successor relationship. It can be argued that the basic problem with this kind of narrative is that its accuracy depends on the reliability of the assumptions it makes about continuity. These narratives have subsequently been discarded whenever even a minor paradigm change in interpretive theory has undermined the accuracy of their definitions. However, the biggest problem with this approach is not its brief temporal validity but the loose connections it establishes between the theory, historical contexts, and periodisations of international relations, on the one hand, and the vocabularies and concepts used in actual IR documents, on the other.

Because of the strongly speculative slant of those development-historical studies, the key abstract concepts of twentieth-century international relations-such as "world community," "world organisation," "universal human rights," and "international law"-have been analyzed from the perspectives of various predetermined theoretical models. In addition, many studies of world organisations have focused too enthusiastically on the issue of future horizons, which has also been the basic characteristic of the abstract vocabulary of international relations since the foundation of the United Nations.

In addition, it seems to me, many researchers setting the standard for the formulation of the field's problems have articulated their objectives in such abstract terms that delving deeper into any of the details of the historical source materials of international relations is deemed unnecessary. This phenomenon is the root cause of the consensus behind development-historical interpretations of historical moments, such as the foundations of the League and the United Nations.

The contextual and historical analysis of the UN system has been particularly topical since the outbreak of the cold war. In that context, the existence of two rival military alliances had much influence on the scholars who produced interpretations of the structures of international relations. Vocabularies of "world community," as well as theories of optimal UN operation, were all transformed to better reflect a bipolar world.

CONCEPTUAL HISTORY AS AN APPROACH TO KEY IR CONCEPTS

Central to Reinhart Koselleck's understanding of the use of concepts in modern narratives is that the concepts present three defining characteristics. First, they are future-oriented programmatic principles. Second, they function as speech-acts that have a specific strategic role in a contemporary speech-act situation. Third, they are key elements in the specific instructions on the future organisation of politics. Koselleck's programme makes it possible to achieve a grasp of the theoretical views and narratives that articulate contemporary models of politics. For that reason, it is one of the best-suited methods available for the careful study of conceptual change.

Following this approach, some of the IR source materials considered as conceptual projects based on principles of pursued continuity and the maintenance of traditional values and meanings; in other words, and as J. G. A. Pocock argued, the concepts of political thought contain historical projects that can be understood by using the term paradigm. For Pocock, a paradigm is a concept that operates like a "container" for basic historical values that stay the same in different periods and over a lengthy period of time.

For the purposes of the present work, the more important paradigmatic point is connected with vocabularies. Vocabularies are like containers of ideas that are transformed from one period to the next, but later users are either not absolutely sure about the motivations of their earlier counterparts or are altogether unaware of them, or even though they do not share such motivations they still make use of the same vocabulary. Thus, the idea of the paradigm will enable us to better understand the various changes taking place in the vocabulary of IR. Pocock's idea of a paradigm is well suited to the field of international relations and diplomacy, where traditionalism is always praised and normative codes of conduct obtain.

Additionally, the historical-conceptual reading of texts is also a method that enables us to add to our interpretation a sort of rhetorical dimension, which can be defined, according to the works of Quentin Skinner, as a counter-act characteristic of all speech acts in one context and discourse. The historical-conceptual method makes it possible to determine the counter-act characteristic of speech acts in different temporal contexts. Genealogically speaking, the historical-conceptual approach recognizes that only shorter periods can be meaningfully analyzed, and while contemporary discourses can be compared with each other, the broader temporal scope favoured by historical-developmental narratives is, in the last analysis, illusional.

With respect to the present study, the genealogical approach can be used, for example, to investigate the modes of ordinary governance produced by planning structures of international relations. Because IR is dominated by the practices of diplomacy, it is very different from party politics and parliamentarism in terms of planning, politics, and mechanisms of authority. Governmental representatives and ambassadors from the contracting sovereign states (in a way that can be considered characteristic of the old system of diplomacy) authored the founding materials of the League.

In the case of the United Nations, to the contrary, the key planners were mainly officials of the US State Department, professors, and other experts. This group's purpose was to create a suitable model for the postwar reconstruction of international relations. Both these preparations happened in particular circumstances, in the aftermath of the most destructive world wars in history. The United Nation's foundation occurred, moreover, in the context of the Holocaust and of the most industrialized destruction techniques ever seen. It is almost needless to say that both planning projects were motivated by commonly shared hopes for peaceful life in the near future.

The two world wars were regarded as the most tragic moments in human history by all the invited delegates and planners, as well as by all the people of the world. The key concepts used in UN planning were thus meant to provide an answer to the problem of destructive war, as well as a new base for peaceful relations between all states. The phrase key concepts also refer to the other motivations of UN and League planners.

By means of key concepts, UN planners envisioned world unity, which produced a very abstract and almost mythological view of international relations and world politics. These concepts were not meant to help construct a model of politics that would be closely based on existing political relations; rather, the planners' main strategy was to articulate premises, which they then utilized to build models of the interrelations between states and other entities of world politics and organisation.

A remarkable thing concerning the concepts underpinning theoretical IR studies is that they have had great difficulty in accommodating the real political actors of contemporary international relations like those who were active in the founding projects of the League and the United Nations. These actors have not been treated as the founding authors of the texts and structures of international relations, nor indeed as actors; rather, that role has been given either to the presumed philosophical roots of the source materials or to autonomous institutional developments. The political actors and their texts are dismissed, as it were, or, at any rate, scholars do not seek to relate the texts to their relevant, real-world contexts when they study them.

The notion of key concepts also makes it possible for us to grasp the conceptual move from the League to the United Nations by means of a comparison between the two sets of vocabularies. One of the most important starting points for such a comparison is the operational use of time layers by UN planners. The League's founders also sought to analyze history in order to understand what kind of institution the League had to be if it was to solve the old system's problems. Hence, for them also the operational use of time layers was instrumental in constructing their political models.

It is my contention that the conceptual shift from the League to the United Nations is related to the introduction of such vocabulary and conceptual innovations as the dynamical and organisational description of international relations, human action concepts, and "societal" as well as "communal" presentation models of world unity, which all had to be accommodated in the new vocabulary. The narrative of a complex world unity was then constructed without a clear "placing" and "timing" of concrete actions, and without naming the actors.

Contrary to the essence of this vocabulary, I put forward the view that it is possible to assign clear motivations, directly related to the contemporary context, to all those operations. It is thus possible to present the precise reasons for the uses of abstract concepts and vocabulary innovations. In this way we can specify their temporal and spatial attributes, which in turn will enable us to begin to understand the basic characteristics of contemporary international relations on a more practical level.

For example, and phrased as a question to be answered: Why was it deemed important to provide the UN world-organisational project with new concepts at a particular moment in history, whereby it was possible to attain a universal appeal or a high level of world unity abstraction? We will also be able to start understanding how the inner logic of these vocabulary innovations was directly linked to the task of constructing political and administrative structures of the actual United Nations, which for the first time also had to have an appeal to the worldwide audience.

ORGANISATIONAL RHETORIC IN INTERNATIONAL RELATIONS

Before proceeding to the more empirical part of my analysis, it is necessary to consider the possible benefits of assimilating organisational rhetoric for analyzing the vocabulary of international relations. My specific intention is to determine how this organisational rhetoric and use of vocabulary are different from older variations of organisational vocabularies in political and constitutional rhetoric.

The shortcomings of older organisations was made famous by Robert Michels in his well-known book *Zur Soziologie des Parteiwesens in der modernen Demokratie*, published in 1911. According to him, organisations tend toward oligarchy, which of course is not a very uncommon argument in discussions concerning diplomacy, international relations, or world organisations. The concept of organisation has an old, very static conceptual history, although, as has already been indicated, its recent conceptual history is more dynamic. For the majority of history, however, political bodies indeed functioned, along the lines of Michels's statement, as sociopolitical command structures promoting authoritarian ideas and norms of behaviour.

In the early years of the conceptual history of "organisations," Plato made use of the metaphor of the body in his political pathology and in his description of the foundations of the cosmological order. In the middle Ages, the scholastic concept of corpus played a key part in the vocabulary of the

Roman Catholic Church. It made it possible to support arguments for the existence of spiritual unities with ideas originating in natural law. In the context of the Great Revolutions, organic and organisational rhetoric was used in constitutional theory as a dynamical and pompous style of presentation, specifically in arguments for the integral political unity of society considered as a state or nation.

It made it possible to view the political system as an abstract and invisible form of continual structural change, but one that contained political bodies and institutions and had very concrete material outcomes. A more dynamic vocabulary of organic and organisational rhetoric began to emerge rather late. It is best understood as the product of "modern" narratives of politics. The history of the concept of "the organisation" belongs very much together with those of the concepts of "revolution" and "progress."

These are Koselleck's two prime examples of concepts linked to political movement. Both were raised to a key position in the vocabulary of the French Revolution, despite having different conceptual historical heritages. The political philosophical concepts of "revolution," "revolutional movement," and "progress" were borrowed from the astrological branch of natural-law reasoning. Their old movemental character was kept, but it was shifted to handle the political and societal system in such a manner that the old planetarian context was substituted for the movemental character of societal progress and transformative political unity. All political and historical events were thereafter grasped within the framework of progressive revolution.

In constitutional thought, the movemental character of concepts has been an important element of political discourse since the Sattelzeit. By using these concepts, the contemporary political system has adopted a dynamic character and a rhetorical style characterized by a very strong future orientation. The movemental character of the presentation of authority and of other similar kinds of modern political vocabulary structures has, more than any other conceptual innovation, made it possible to devise the public, democratic, and societal styles of political discourse.

In the various articles collected in the handbook *Geschichtliche Grundbegriffe*, organic and organisational rhetoric has also been treated in a similar fashion to that of Koselleck's, being characterized as a dynamical style of rhetoric. This was an important aspect of the descriptions of the constitutional and political systems of the French Revolution, since it provided a way to combine various political entities and introduce the dynamical perspective of a progressive political system. Organic and organisational rhetoric and vocabulary also provided a language that made it possible to incorporate the French Revolutionary concept of the political and national "general will" into the constitutional narratives of political unity. In Germany, the monistic Hegelian theory of the state was the most comprehensive example of the new organic political philosophy in the aftermath of the French Revolution.

The dynamic nature of organic and organisational rhetoric is of course implicitly rejected by the traditional, negative appraisals of the essence of the concept of organisation. The most famous example is Michels's book mentioned above. Koselleck has argued that the function of some key concepts is to act as filters (Duse) for all the others. It is these concepts that give meaning to the broader vocabulary. Furthermore, Gorg Haverkate has described the concept of organisation as one that offers a flexible mode of discourse for constitutional arguments and a suitable way to combine different ideological constructions and viewpoints and put them into one and the same model.

Also, Ernst Wolfgang Bockenforde has put forward a view of organisational rhetoric as a dynamical rhetorical style used in juridical and constitutional texts. The style seeks to convince readers in order to create a suitable support by consent, rather than by force and necessity. Moreover, according to Gerhard

Dohrn-van Rossum natural-metaphoric rhetoric suggests the need to combine the "natural" and "political" contexts in discourse. Such a combination certainly played an important role in Kant's use of organic elements in his vocabulary as a coherent part of his "emancipatorial and political Naturrecht."

In Kantian dualism, moral reasoning is kept apart from practical politics. This tension is resolved by the historical-developmental narrative of the famous "own cleverness of historical development," which is capable of creating solutions to practical political problems. These historical and theoretical points are mentioned in order to introduce a more interpretative framework for understanding contemporary problems related to the move to an organisational vocabulary in the international relations of the 1940s.

Organisational rhetoric seems a practical and suitable solution for a new vocabulary for international relations, providing a tool that makes it possible to answer two questions that were central to post-World War II international relations: how to build a new world system with the authority to control the activities of its members and how to reform the old system of a static league of states. This move to organisational rhetoric took place in the context of the emergence of an immense need for a more dynamic, universal, societal and unitarian style of international relations and world political discourse. The movemental quality of the new vocabulary and concepts made it possible to achieve a more manageable and political, and less transcendental, character of international relations, but it was organisational rhetoric that opened entirely new possibilities for the "dynamics" of governmentality and planning in international relations.

One unique aspect of the adoption of organisational vocabulary in this context is the fact that this vocabulary was introduced in order to offer the most suitable tools for the new style of discourse. It is thus possible to state that both the organisational vocabulary and the new, organic character of international relations were deliberately selected by planners and also accepted by the broader public on account of the latter's appealing, persuasive discourse. It was a great challenge to achieve a new type of discourse that would include all existing world entities into one plan for world unity. Hence, and it is worth repeating, it has to be stressed that the vocabulary innovations we have been discussing were implemented with specific objectives and rhetorical tactics in mind.

PRELIMINARY REMARKS ABOUT THE FOUNDING MATERIALS

The conceptual historical reading of the employment of Kantian vocabularies in UN planning documents is a demanding endeavour. One of the more established facts in IR history is that in the first half of the 1940s many scholars were looking for a foundation for a new world unity and for new organisational vocabularies. Scholars working with the planning of the United Nations undertook to construct a project that made it possible to replace the conceptual system of balance of power, and especially the contractual nature of the peace league.

The period during and after World War II was more propitious than any other since the Great Revolutions for radical, political reforms and for important vocabulary innovations. Arguably, it appears as a revolution in world politics comparable to the moment of constitutional thinking embodied in the Enlightenment's declarations of modern freedom rights.

THE LEAGUE

Reading the founding materials and planning texts of the Covenant of the League of Nations (the Covenant), its paradigmatic viewpoints appears to be quite simple: The diplomatic framework was a peace treaty between contracting nations. The parties to the treaty were still, as was the case in the monarchical European era, "the High Contracting Parties," who contracted into the treaty on general peace in very much the same way the leading powers did in the era of the "Concert of Europe," even though the number of parties to the treaty (45 states) was unprecedented.

Beside this traditional diplomatic core, there were other elements in the League that gave rise to the feeling that a totally new international order was being established. Since the Hague Peace Conferences, one of the key ideas for fostering general peace had been the settlement of international disputes by legal means, and thus the League's system was supported by the authority given to the International Court of Justice. At the time of its foundation, the farthest-reaching academic discourse about the nature of the League and its future prospect was primarily of a juridical nature.

It made the concept of "League" suitable for broad international purposes by presenting the whole system as a developed "reign of law," linking all nations by means of the cultural unity of law. The legal aspects of the League's unity were also the most abstract ones, allowing for many pompous pronouncements about the future of international relations. There were most remarkable shifts in the constitutional aspects and the conceptual paradigm of the League once the concept of "League" had been attached to theories of integration, opening up for integration by legal means when political integration was seen as impossible.

The other important conceptual question was the international treatment of issues concerning the situation of the world's labor force. In order to solve that problem in the spirit of the time, the International Labour Organization (the ILO), the League's sister body, was founded, and through its basic texts introduced human action concepts into the IR vocabulary. Legal aspects aside, the League and the ILO are best understood in terms of paradigmatic texts that make use of a clear-cut vocabulary, which was devolved for the application of international solutions to the basic problems of an earlier period, namely, a world war and the revolutionary movements.

THE UNITED NATIONS

The planning of the United Nations consisted of a rather chaotic series of meetings and drafted texts that took place amid an atmosphere of excitement generated by the feeling of witnessing the final struggle for a free world. The meetings were thus generally characterized by uncertainty regarding the objectives of the planning work and of competing visions of the future world organisation. No element was definitive or presupposed before it was selected as a good target for the plans, and even the universal nature of the UN project was not certain before 1943.

It was only after the decision to confer a universal nature on the new organisation that it became possible to construct an organisational unity vocabulary, which as a paradigmatic characteristic of the texts was also very influential on other contemporary conceptual inventions. The political motivations for the foundation of the United Nations were still based on the catastrophes and problems of the preceding periods, but the vocabularies that were developed now seemed to be increasingly removed from them. In other words, the collapse of the political and cultural systems, especially in Europe, and to a lesser degree worldwide, was considered to be so complete that there was no reason to think of a continuation of the old system.

In that sense, the feeling about the visions of history might be comparable to the political climate during the era of the Great Revolutions; it was surely easier to lay the basis for a new vocabulary by using as a point of departure a feeling of radical break from the past than it would have been by using a feeling of continuation. A central political motivation behind the innovations in vocabulary was to capture a vision of history that was global in its scope, dominated by nationalistic war machines and their fatal purposes, which could never offer any hopes for a lasting peace system. It logically followed from that vision of history that the nationalistic war machines had to be controlled by a new system of international relations.

INTERPRETING INNOVATIONS IN VOCABULARY

While interpreting those innovations in vocabulary, we have to always keep in mind that the task of reforming the structures of international relations was monumental. The planners' first and most important enterprise, to substitute the vocabulary of a diplomatic league and a temporary peace treaty for that of a world-unity system and a perpetual peace, was in itself revolutionary. To additionally make such a project suitable for the practical construction of a world organisation based on democratic and liberal values promoting individual human rights-all of this represented a tremendous challenge, a fact on which scholars have seldom reflected.

The crucial starting point for the study of vocabulary innovations in the new world-organisational language is the planning group led by Leo Pasvolsky. Pasvolsky's contribution to the planning of the United Nations illustrates the increased dependency of world-unity vocabulary the further the planning work went on. Pasvolsky was not at all a specialist of philosophical world-unity vocabulary before he started to lead one of the UN planning groups. However, in the course of the project he became the leading specialist on the most abstract aspects of the new UN vocabulary and concepts, as well as on the rhetorical tactics derived from them. He eventually became perhaps the only person to be able to answer questions concerning the characteristics of the UN world-unity vocabulary.

What made Pasvolsky a user of one version of the Kantian world-unity vocabulary was the nature of his opposition to old power politics, its principles of diplomacy, and his rejection of the hegemonic view of state sovereignty. Turning this view on its head, he argued that the key factor in world politics is the world community and that the concept of world unity properly implies real organisational unity, and, accordingly, that all subparts of world unity were to be subordinated to it. In a statement delivered in January 1945, Pasvolsky spoke to US senators and others about the almost-completed UN project and explained that, according to the project's inherent logic, every member nation was an entity that was to be understood in terms of its status as a member of a universal community and the world organisation.

He additionally stated that all member-states were coherent parts of world unity, independently of their own willingness to accept this fact. In the context of the same definition, Pasvolsky further said that the "universal membership was based on the principle that the organisation was an association of nations with common ideals and common standards of behaviour." Furthermore, he went on to mention that "all member nations should act in cooperation in accordance with the norms and rules in the international community."

The statement then formulated a definition of the criterion for membership in the United Nations that was suitable from the perspective of world unity: "States by accepting certain common principles would be thereby eligible to membership in the organisation and that therefore membership had not been made to rest on the fact that a nation exist, but rather that a nation lived by certain principles."

The most obvious effect of this language was that all nations were, within its framework, totally dependent on the definitions attached to them from the perspective of world-organisational unity and community irrespective of what the other aspects of those definitions were. Pasvolsky's definitions regarding the new world unity continued by rejecting views of international relations, diplomacy, and world organisation that were anchored in the concept of international relations as a free political union. The refutation of the notion of a "free union" of "sovereign states," on which all other international and world organisational structures had been based, was one of the main and most tactical reasons for the use of organisational discourse.

In contrast to those old ideas, organisational rhetoric highlighted the interconnection between the members and entities of world unity, which led to the notion that member nations were going to tie themselves not only to each other but also to this rhetorically and tactically mythological world unity. Through their own forced willingness, or according to the new, autonomous inner logic of international structures, they were becoming members of a world unity. The organisational world-unity vocabulary also gave very few possibilities of conceiving the new union as an international league of equal powers, although the legal nature of the new organisation was fully based on the notion of the signature of a treaty between sovereign powers, and the name of the organisation itself was "the United Nations Organisation," recalling the existing military alliance.

Pasvolsky's planning group was not the only one to have adopted the new vocabulary. The group that offered one of the earliest lists of reasons for the adoption of the new organisational vocabulary was the International Commission for the Organisation of Peace. Its report of April 1941 stated five simple, novel points regarding the future international and world organisations. They were:

a. Nations must renounce the claim to be the final judge in their controversies with other nations and must submit to the jurisdiction of international tribunals. The basis of peace is justice; and justice is not the asserted claim of any one party, but must be determined by the judgement of the community.
b. Nations must renounce the use of force for their own purposes in relations with other nations, except in self-defence. The justification for self-defence must always be subject to review by an international court or the competent body.

c. The right of nations to maintain aggressive armaments must be sacrificed in consideration for an assurance of the security of all, through regional and worldwide forces subject to international law and adequate to prevent illegal resorts to international violence.
d. Nations must accept certain human and cultural rights in their constitutions and in international covenants. The destruction of civil liberties anywhere creates danger of war. The peace is not secure if any large and efficient population is permanently subject to a control which can create a fanatical national sentiment impervious to external opinion.
e. Nations must recognize that their right to regulate economic activities is not unlimited. The world has become an economic unit; all nations must have access to its raw materials and its manufactured articles. The effort to divide the resources of the world into sixty economic compartments is one of the causes of war. The economic problem arising from this effort has increased in gravity with the scientific and industrial progress of the modern world.

The next report of the same group was published in April 1942. It delved further into the theoretical issues of international relations, showing that the group was already seeking to introduce the use of organisational vocabulary in order to promote world unity, even though their discourse was not yet very far developed in that respect. According to the text of the report:

> Organisation to make international law effective was, however, hampered by exaggerated developments of the idea of sovereignty. A sovereign state at the present time claims the power to judge its own controversies, to enforce its own conception of its rights, to increase its armaments without limit, to treat its own nationals as it sees fit, and to regulate its economic life without regard to the effect of such regulations upon its neighbours.

Another group which contributed to the same task, and whose work was analogous to that of Pasvolsky's group, was the Group of Jurists, which made plans for "the future of international law." This group specialized in the legal aspects of new world-organisational structures. It published its report in the spring of 1944. According to this document, contemporary problems could not be solved any more by the old means of a system of sovereign states. In the future, the problems would have to be solved by international means, which stressed the need of an organized world community with a strong world organisation. In the words of the report:

> A process of international legislation was begun with reference to problems which could not be solved by measures taken by individual states.... For the second time in a single generation, most of the peoples of the world have become engaged in a world war. The fact offers insistent challenge to the intelligence of mankind. The Community of States should be organized on a universal basis. All States which exist or which may come into existence in the future should be included. No provision should be made for the expulsion or withdrawal of any state. The States of the world form a community, and the protection and advancement of the common interests of their peoples require effective organisation of the Community of States.

The group concluded that in the future, because it offered the only way to stave off nationalistic and aggressive strivings and in order that a system able to guarantee lasting world peace might emerge, the concept of an existing world community should be incorporated into international relations. Additionally, the group argued the need for a world community, saying such a community could not last without an efficient world organisation-which, to put it another way, meant that there could be no precondition for an efficient world organisation without the foundational assumption of a world community. Thus, we may say that organisational rhetoric was introduced little by little, and partly unconsciously, in a series of planning documents.

The main driving force behind that process was simply the search for the most practical way to produce a narrative of world unity and community characterized by the interconnectedness of all world entities. The outcome of that process, the foundation of an organisational vocabulary, was one of the most important events in twentieth-century international relations. It moved conceptions of international relations and world organisations toward somewhat mythological models. It promoted the use of very broad and movemental characteristics in order to make it possible to view the political system as an abstract and invisible thing in a state of continual structural change.

Within this theoretical framework, the oligarchical tendency of political bodies described by Michels and others becomes a rhetorical ploy directed against all forms of organisation that pertain to oligarchical command cultures. Lastly, the introduction of organisational rhetoric into world-unity vocabulary also made it possible to hinder the use of organic and organisational rhetoric in theoretical models of the nation-state. Enabling theoretical models to argue for the existence of autonomous dynamics of living organisation in the nation-state had once been very popular in continental European constitutional discourse.

THE RESOLUTION OF SOME APPARENT PARADOXES

Another narrative concerning the essence of the organisational vocabulary of international relations should be linked to and start with the UN planners themselves. It is reasonable in this context to ask questions about who the planners were, where they came from, and what they had done previously in their lives. We can analyze the different personal histories of the founding years, looking at how and why the founders came to lay the foundations of a new world organisational project and why they constructed a new vocabulary. These are all very basic questions. They have not, however, often been explored by scholars, perhaps in part due to the difficulties the new vocabulary has caused.

The identity of the planners of the United Nations, including their temporal and spatial contexts, constitutes a good starting point for our quest to fully understand the complex nature of their numerous innovations. The first apparent paradox related to the planning of the United Nations-one that raises questions about the ideology of the whole project-is linked to the fact that the plans for the construction of a new organisational vocabulary were produced by a group of planners who were working for the US State Department, and US foreign political and federal constitutional thinking has been characterized by a lack of societal, organisational, and world-unity vocabularies.

The paradox also concerns the history of US constitutional thought, inasmuch as its concept of Union has been articulated as a strongly and openly political project. In that sense, it has also been a very "antiorganic" project-one that does not suppose or aim to create a nation or society. Geoffrey Gorer addresses this issue in his book The Americans. He argues that a crucial difference between the conceptual systems of Europe and the United States is to be found in the fact that the European metaphoric model is organic and that of the United States is mechanist. According to Gorer, the European model and discourse refers mainly to the rhetorical and vocabulary innovations of the French Revolution. The difference between the two explains why the League's rhetoric of a political union for a general peace fitted very well with US constitutional concepts. On the other hand, the later move, to anew organisational world-unity description of IR and world organisations, was a strange and uncharacteristic one.

A second aspect of the paradox relates to the traditional vocabulary of US foreign policy from the early nineteenth century onward. The rhetoric of US revolutionism in the nineteenth century, as for example visible in the reference to the concept of world citizenship was characterized by the principle of anti-colonialism and the notion of "free republics." It is also through those conceptual means that the US government legitimized the Monroe Doctrine and justified its own foreign interventions.

From the perspective of the study of interwar IR sources and planning rhetoric, the counter dualism of Gorer's argument, which is somewhat impressionistic, orientates the reader toward development-historical approaches. In the 1920s and 1930s, various scholars already conceived of the old diplomacy and the static concepts that underpinned it as constituting a deeply flawed system. These views gave rise to calls for a more dynamic system of international relations and a new world-organisational approach. The most pressing issues, which made systematic conceptual change possible, were working conditions for employees-"the Economic Consequences of Peace," "The Problem of Revision in International Law" -and the problem of change in politics in relation to IR.

All these issues were interconnected. They also related to the systemic flaws of the League, which themselves were due to the contradictions inherent in the League's wartime origins and its conception as a static solution to essentially regional problems. To the UN planners in the 1940s, those issues were still considered to be the most pressing ones. Critics who publicized them became famous in part because their view made it possible to see clearly that the League's conceptual foundations had been couched in a static vocabulary.

The impetus for the development of a new, dynamic, organisational IR vocabulary thus stemmed from criticisms of the League's system. This critical activity encouraged UN planners to view and handle the League as a failed opportunity and as a product of old European diplomacy, and, as a result, to turn it into a counter model for the new, dynamic world organisation. In order to carry out their project, UN planners also had to devise replacements for the other kinds of concepts conceived of as static: the old humanitarian, moral conceptual unities, which broadened and softened the natural-law analogies of the old law of nations as an all-embracing, universal moral responsibility.

For all those reasons, they had to be replaced with more progressive ideas. The powerful criticism of the lack of dynamical aspects in the conceptual foundations of the League represented a very promising development for proponents of organisational world-unity vocabularies, in particular for those of the Kantian tradition. As previously mentioned, in my view the interpretation of twentieth-century source materials for international relations requires a careful study of the criticisms that were made of the old diplomatic order and law of nations.

Those criticisms originated from two different sources: the conceptual tradition of Kantian Weltburgerrecht, which was also strongly influenced by the German notion of socialitas and the world-citizenship vocabulary tradition of US revolutionism. The older historical dimensions have to be discussed together with the contemporary context of the world-organisational planning in order to help elucidate the intellectual roots of the planners' conceptual innovations, which made the project possible, as well as the reasons why the State Department's UN planning group had such a crucial role in the construction of the new, organisational world-unity vocabulary.

US President Franklin Delano Roosevelt was one of the key actors in the context of the foundation of the United Nations. However, while he certainly entertained strong views on the future of world organisations, he never explained his views in full. They remain, to this day, known only schematically. In relation to the UN project, FDR was in effect a spokesman for the heritage of US revolutionism. He articulated his political program around the simple notion of human freedoms. These, according to him, constituted the old "American constitutional roots," which the whole world should rediscover and abide by if it were to live in peace and harmony.

Roosevelt offered the United States as an example to the rest of a belligerent world of a free, open, and antinationalistic society. The most famous description of his vision of the future of international relations is based on freedoms and rights of the individual, which he called the Four Freedoms. A variation on the same basic ideas was also used in the Atlantic Charter, which paved the way for US participation in the war and presented the block of enemy nations as the belligerent side of a world that was to be free and open.

That the basic and unadulterated rhetoric of freedom should have seemed to be the most suitable language for a US president in a time of war is no cause for surprise. Roosevelt's message had to be kept simple enough for all audiences and had to make clear that the war was being fought against criminal governments. The simplicity also helped to keep open all strategic and tactical questions concerning the war, as well as the question of the future of international relations. After the death of Roosevelt, Harry S Truman continued with this rhetorical style until the end of the UN preparations. At the conference in San Francisco in 1945, he expressed only slightly more complex and future-oriented views about the freedom of all the people of the world.

Many researchers have attempted to study the UN planning in conjunction with the New Deal program of the Roosevelt government, in particular because the US war policy was known as the New Deal of War in some circles. From the perspective of the actual planning materials, this approach leaves much to be desired. An exclusive focus on President Roosevelt, Vice President Wallace, Secretary of State Cordell Hull, or Undersecretary of State Stettinius should be avoided: It is certainly too restrictive to allow us to see the complexity of the planning of the United Nations (although neither would it be wise to widen the scope to too many actors).

Roosevelt himself was mainly focusing on the warfare aims, keeping his position concerning the nature of the future world organisation open as long as possible. He also limited references in his speeches to the ideas of the future IR and the world organisation to that which had already been published in the planning reports. A general lack of time, due in particular to the requirements of the war effort, meant that scholars and officials such as Pasvolsky, especially in the case of vocabulary construction, did the actual planning work to a great extent.

It was not until recent years that Pasvolsky received acknowledgment as one of the key UN planners, yet if we had to pick the single most influential individual in that planning, it would have to be Pasvolsky. He was appointed head of the Office of Post-World War Planning in September 1943. His task was to formulate plans for the postwar peace settlement and the new world organisation. In that capacity, Pasvolsky was the key person in the US planning group whose task was to formulate the postwar structures of international and world organisation.

Because of the differences in their respective roles, the planning rhetoric of Pasvolsky's group was very different from that of President Roosevelt. The role of Pasvolsky in the preparations was that of a pragmatic, technical planner, and he transformed Roosevelt's pompous, humanistic globalism and the broad development-historical perspectives of other politicians into conceptual material UN planners could use in their work. The key idea of Pasvolsky's project was to introduce the notion of a "world community" on which to base all other reformative structures, which were to constitute the tools, and characteristics of, the new world organisation. It followed logically from that starting point that much of the old diplomatic system would have to be either discarded or replaced.

Another important consequence of the introduction of the notion of a world community into the vocabulary of international relations was that it made it possible for planners to move world-organisational discourse closer to the concepts of constitutional and national unity building, which originated in the "general will" tradition of political philosophy. This represented again a very abstract conceptual ploy, whose purpose was to create a feeling of (progressive) movement around the key concepts of the new constructions of international relations.

The constitutional, progressive-developmental, and unity aspects of the new world-organisational rhetoric were already discussed in more detail above; it suffices to say here that within the framework of the new vocabulary of international relations, those aspects were intended to operate in very different ways than they had in their original, constitutionalist-nationalist, and "general will"-based context. The new organisational-unity rhetoric followed its own tactical and strategic rules from the moment it was introduced into the field of international relations.

It is also important to realize that, from the perspective of conceptual planning, the purpose of all those conceptual innovations was to challenge the old IR paradigms. The new organisational vocabulary was deliberately conceived to achieve that purpose. It then became possible to add a more concrete layer around that theoretical inner core-namely, the new diplomatic and legal regulations and codes of conduct-and, finally, to implement an adaptive and progressive system of international relations, fully able to handle perpetual change, as had been promised.

Additionally, a broad rhetoric was needed to bring together the many different strands of contemporary IR thinking. It was needed in order to have all those strands included in one and the same vocabulary and in order to build a new, functional system of international relations, contrasted to the old, anarchic one. For that reason, universal human rights, for example, which were by definition considered to be the birthright of all human beings, were also reestablished by the charter of the new world organisation, representing the founding document of a newborn humanity. The same world-organisational framework was applied to the other subparts and concepts of international relations, such as the field of international law or concepts such as "peace" and "member nation."

Through the very abstract vocabulary of organisational-unity rhetoric, it became possible to refer to the existing conditions of politics at a high level of abstraction. This constituted an important advantage as well as a significant problem since it resulted in a lack of precise references to specific time, place, and action(s) and actor(s). The use of all-embracing concepts and vocabulary was the key tactic of UN planners; its purpose was to enable them to obtain complete control over all interactions of world politics, whether the specific actors were states or not. In other words, by invoking such a general and universal approach, UN planners were proclaiming that no political actor could be left outside the new world organisation, and because of this their rhetoric achieved truly global dimensions, something the League's could never do.

It is also possible to claim, from the perspective of vocabulary structures, that it is no surprise that the abbreviation UN has been treated in a moral, metaphysical, and legal way, rather than in a practical, political, and historical one. Many debates concerning the interpretation of world-organisational entities, actors, political structures, and "deeper structures," such as moral evaluations of international relations, are obviously related to the constructions created during the founding process of the United Nations.

The problems of the above-mentioned interpretations, which have been more impressionistic than analytical in their approach, are also due to a large extent to the complexity of the conceptual changes that took place after the signature of the Covenant and before that of the UN Charter. Even at the time, interpretative problems hung over the planning process concerning the relationship between what had been planned and drafted during the preparations and what was eventually to be signed. This atmosphere of uncertainty was also present in the meetings between US senators and key UN planners.

The time available for planning was expected to be limited. The signature of the Charter was to take place at the San Francisco conference "before the war is over and the world public opinion gets tired of the topic," as Jan Smuts put it. Some of the delegates in San Francisco were unsure about what the new charter and the acceptance of this new organisational framework would mean for the future. The members of the key planning group, for their part, were not worried about the abstractness of the new vocabulary and concepts. On the contrary, they used the high level of abstraction to create the core of the postwar project.

Based on the documents pertaining to the last phase in the planning process, it is possible to argue that nobody besides Pasvolsky was ready to answer the main questions about the nature and key characteristics of the new world-organisational entity. Not even the so-called "father of the United Nations," the 1946 Nobel Peace Prize laureate Senator Cordell Hull, a long-term secretary of state, was ready to answer those complicated questions. Pasvolsky's project was very abstract and theoretical, but also quite simple. Its foundations were the conceptual metastructures discussed above, whose purpose was to create the conceptual preconditions for a new paradigmatic vocabulary as well as for the whole new system of global governmental structures. Constitutionalism and world-citizenship were not words he used much, and his references to "new international law" were limited. For the new project's success, it was imperative that it be understood as a radical departure from the past and a big step toward a more united world.

Most importantly, the foundation of the United Nations represented a unique opportunity to overhaul international law-the traditional code of conduct in international relations. As the Carnegie planning report stated, this was the beginning of the "International Law of the Future." The first postulate of the Carnegie plan for the future international law articulated a new definition of the field of international relations, pointing out that, from then on, "the States of the world [would] form a community, and the protection and advancement of the common interests of their peoples [would] require effective organisation of the Community of States."

In conclusion we can say that the conceptual-history approach and the study of the vocabularies used in world-organisational planning enable us to direct serious criticisms at the various moral, legal, institutional, and functional constructions of post-WWII theories. From the foundational perspective of unity rhetoric, it is explicitly self-evident that the United Nations and its Charter must play a central role in interpretations of world politics. But only through a genealogical reading of the foundation of the United Nations does it become easier to grasp the substance of different authors' arguments and to determine how right or wrong they are when they interpret the nature of UN unity and its main texts.

From the perspective of UN planning, the meanings given to the UN system and the UN Charter are many times odd, and they often merely fit a particular author's starting assumptions. One of the most important reasons for that inaccuracy in studies of international relations has been the very poorly understood move to a world-organisational rhetoric and its political implications. All historical constructions are of course constantly in motion. They are reused for tactical reasons in contemporary political battles, which make it harder to speak about them in relation to present-day and future politics. In that sense the meaning of concepts can never be pure, clear, or stable. Out of the various time layers, the past is certainly the most suitable for the empirical methods of IR studies.

The methods of conceptual history make it possible to determine the actual conceptual models that were selected in various historical periods and the actual conceptual changes that took place in different contemporary contexts. This kind of reading enables us to recognize and stay away from the main interpretative pitfall of handling different texts and contexts as parts of one and the same developmental story. It also makes us more ready to notice the reuses and reformulations of the main tools of universal-unity arguments and argue that those tools themselves are hardly ever novel in the true sense of the word, but rather recycled from older narratives.

In relation to the way conceptual change works, it is easy to see that after the grim political climate of the cold war and in the aftermath of perestroika, there dawned a new era in international politics that made world-citizenship rhetoric pertinent again. The new discourse naturally reused some basic ideas of the UN world-unity rhetoric and popularized again Kant's Weltburgerrecht, thus adding a new chapter to the history of world-unity vocabularies. For this chapter, the most interesting aspects of the 1990s world-unity and Weltburgerrecht boom are that it demonstrates how few conceptual and vocabulary bases we actually have for the development of world-unity vocabularies, how poorly the latter are understood from the points of view of political and strategical planning, and, finally, how strong the nationalistic imaginary still is. Indeed, the nationalistic imaginary still dominates the nationalistic narrative structures of IR theories, and world politics exists in its own closed moral sphere.

9

Politicizing Secularism

National and international politics have recently undergone a religious revival of sorts and while the effects of this transformation have been far reaching, the implications have yet to be fully explored. One is left wondering how the rebirth of religion within the political realm challenges our understanding of the relationship between religion and politics in a democratic regime. In The Politics of Secularism in International Relations, Elizabeth Shakman Hurd investigates how religion and politics are dealt with in foreign policies in the United States and Europe as well as in the disciplines of political science and international relations. In doing so, she isolates and questions the assumptions surrounding secularism that are traditionally taken for granted in political contexts and analyses.

According to Hurd, conceiving religion and politics as fixed and separate categories is problematic. Secularism's role within politics, as well as the assumptions and vocabulary involved therein, should form the focal point in inquiry into the relationship between religion and politics. Hurd's method of inquiry constitutes a departure from her predecessors in that the three dominant international relations theories namely realism, liberalism and constructivism all are based upon unquestioned assumptions. In doing so, Hurd sets herself the ambitious task of uncovering the roots of the ongoing political interaction between secularism and religion.

Hurd claims that the relationship between religion and politics is unstable and essentially contestable where the conceptions and settlements of this relationship are themselves part of continuous political negotiations. Doctrines of secularism determine the nature of the perceived relationship between religion and politics in so far as such theories serve to differentiate between religion and politics. Such differentiation is in itself a political act. Hurd writes, "Secularism produces authoritative settlements of religion and politics, while simultaneously claiming to be exempt from this process of production. This is a formidable exercise of power."

Following Hurd's argument, secularism can constitute an epistemic space that defines the boundaries between religion and politics, as taken for granted by the dominant theoretical perspectives in international relations. As a result of such assumptions, secularism is considered normative and is used to garner legitimacy for the political regimes and actions of the Western world. However, without acknowledging and investigating the political role of secularism, the current religious revival in national and international politics remains a mystery Instead; secularism is to be conceived of as a form of political authority.

It operates with exceptional power within policy decisions and the formation of identities, wherein the foundational relationship between the secular and the religious is reiterated and renegotiated, rather than taken for granted. As a result, secularism forms perspectives on the proper relationship between religion and politics by engaging various ontological, epistemological, political and ethical assumptions. Furthermore, according to Hurd these perspectives manifest themselves as traditions that influence the use and analysis of political authority in international relations. Therefore, one must approach perspectives on secularism as political strategies which are continually evolving, thereby reconstructing the political order with reference to constitutive norms and principles.

Hurd puts particular emphasis on two secular traditions that work as interpretive horizons and play authoritative political roles: laicism and Judeo-Christian secularism. Laicism pertains to the tradition of the Enlightenment-era critique of religion in which religion is conceived of as despotic and is associated with the misuse of power in the name of religion. Therefore, the task of laicism is to get rid of religion by referring religion to the private sphere, where it is irrational, affective and value-laden. In contrast, the public sphere is a neutral and value-free ground, reserved for decisions based on rational arguments and deliberation, impartiality, universality and tolerance regarding common matters.

Furthermore, laicism establishes the relationship between religion and politics as one of blunt separation as guided by the ideals of liberty, equality and neutrality. This conclusion is reached by the proper use of reason and guaranteed by the sovereign state. From the Judeo-Christian perspective, secularism is made possible by the implied hierarchical distinction between an eternal and temporal order and the associated division between divine and human powers. In Judeo-Christian secularism, religion and politics are differentiated, but not separated as in laicism.

The coupling of religion and politics within the Judeo-Christian tradition is conceived of as essential to Western history, identity and unity, and as a result, the Judeo-Christian tradition is taken as a prerequisite for secular democracy. In both traditions, secularism is the organizing principle of modern politics that defines religion as a fixed category, excluding religion from the spheres of power and politics. In that sense, secularism is both a political and a theological move establishing the proper spheres for politics and religion. Thus, Hurd points to how secularism as a political strategy operates on a broader theological-political spectrum.

The implications of laicism and the Judeo-Christian tradition transcend Western civilisation and are furthermore relevant to Islamic tradition, which has of late served as the primary case for examinations of religion's role in national and international politics. Hurd makes a genealogical sketch of the interaction between secularism, Islam and the constitution of national identities in Europe and the United States. In doing so, she reveals how secularism is considered incommensurate with Islam in so far as Islam is opposed to a Western secular world.

In particular, in reference to laicism, she revisits the history of the French Republic and the tradition of Judeo-Christian secularism as it relates to the history of the American Republic's modes of encountering Islam. In general, laicism operates with the aim of making Muslim agents able to differentiate religion and politics, while Judeo-Christian secularism conceives Islam as an insuperable threat to Western civilisation. Hurd analyzes these two conflicting tendencies by applying them to recent interactions between the West and Islam, namely the case of Turkish membership of the European Union, the U.S.-Iran relationship during the Iranian revolution and the Euro-American reactions to so-called political Islam. Hurd includes these case studies because of her belief that in order to understand secularism, it must be studied on a case-by-case basis. Insofar as secularism is defined as a form of political authority that produces conceptions of religion and politics, it operates through the medium of theological-political authorities.

These case studies reveal the untenability of the viewpoint that religion and politics pertain to different spheres, as assumed in secular discourse. In The Politics of Secularism in International Relations, Hurd contends that secularism is to be understood and studied as a form of political strategy where the foundational relationships between religion and politics, the religious and the secular, and the sacred and the profane are constantly contested and negotiated. From this point of view, secularism operates as a theological-political authority that is at times ambiguous and protean in that it assumes various forms in concrete cases. The fundamental question Hurd's book leaves us with is whether the aforementioned two varieties of secularism are sufficient as interpretive tools. Yet if these tools are not sufficient, no supplementary theories are readily evident.

While additional theories might not be applicable, the two interpretive tools provided by Hurd might serve their purpose in being conjoined: the coupling of laicism and British, French, German and American Enlightenments, as well as radical and moderate Enlightenments. These various perspectives represent different conceptions of the role of religion in both political life and the public sphere. They range from an adversarial stance towards religion to the conception of religion's role in politics as rational, minimal and as a precondition for public morality, the latter of which Hurd refers to as "Kantian."

These various Enlightenment traditions in relation to secularism are featured in debates focused on the relationship between religion and politics. Furthermore, the naming of "Enlightenment secularism" as laicism limits the scope of European secularisms to cases consistent with the fundaments of French political history and national identity. Similarly, Judeo-Christian secularism takes a variety of forms depending on the political setting and process. The distinction between a Judeo-Christian secularism of non-establishment, as the case of the United States illustrates, and a Judeo-Christian secularism of establishment, apparent in several European countries, is crucial.

The issue of secularism is not only a discursive disposition that is deeply embedded within national identities, but is also a part of the institutional framework that structures and restricts encounters with religions. In conclusion, The Politics of Secularism in International Relations is extremely rich in its theoretical scope and analytical insights. It is systematic, well-written and convincingly argued, and brings crucial insights from political theory, religious studies and anthropology into play on a topic of current interest. While the interplay between religion and politics is often neglected or cast aside, Hurd has shown that this relationship is a fascinating and insufficiently explored arena.

The surprising thing about international law is that nations ever obey its strictures or carry out its mandates. This observation is made not to register optimism that the half-empty glass is also half full, but to draw attention to a pregnant phenomenon: that most states observe systemic rules much of the time in their relations with other states. That they should do so is much more interesting than, say, the fact that most citizens usually obey their nation's laws, because the international system is organized in a voluntarist fashion, supported by so little coercive authority.

This unenforced rule system can obligate states to profess, if not always to manifest, a significant level of day-to-day compliance even, at times, when that is not in their short-term self-interest. The element or paradox attracts our attention and challenges us to investigate it, perhaps in the hope of discovering a theory that can illuminate more generally the occurrence of voluntary normative compliance and even yield a prescription for enhancing aspects of world order.

Before going further, however, it is necessary to enter a caveat. This chapter attempts a study of why states obey laws in the absence of coercion. That is not the same quest as motivates the more familiar studies that investigate the sources of normative obligation. The latter properly focus on the origins of rules - in treaties, custom, decisions of tribunals, *opinio juris*, state conduct, resolutions of international organisations, and so forth - to determine which sources, qua sources, are to be taken seriously, and how seriously to take them. Our object, on the other hand, is to determine why and under what circumstances a specific rule is obeyed.

To be sure, the source of every rule - its pedigree, in the terminology of this chapter - is one determinant of how strong its pull to compliance is likely to be. Pedigree, however, is far from being the only indicator of how seriously the rule will be taken, particularly if the rule conflicts with a state's perceived self-interest. Thus, other indicators are also a focus of this chapter insofar as they determine the capacity of rules to affect state conduct. This chapter posits that, in a community organized around rules, compliance is secured - to whatever degree it is - at least in part by perception of a rule as legitimate by those to whom it is addressed. Their perception of legitimacy will vary in degree from rule to rule and time to time.

It becomes a crucial factor, however, in the capacity of any rule to secure compliance when, as in the international system, there are no other compliance-inducing mechanisms. Legitimacy is used here to mean that quality of a rule which derives from a perception on the part of those to whom it is addressed that it has come into being in accordance with right process. Right process includes the notion of valid sources but also encompasses literary, socio-anthropological and philosophical insights. The elements of right process that will be discussed below are identified as affecting decisively the degree to which any rule is perceived as legitimate.

Why study the teleology of law? What are laws for? What causes obedience? Such basic questions are the meat and potatoes of jurisprudential inquiry. Any legal system worth taking seriously must address such fundamentals. J. L. Brierly has speculated that jurisprudence, nowadays, regards international law as no more than "an attorney's mantle artfully displayed on the shoulders of arbitrary' power" and "a decorous name for a convenience of the chancelleries." That seductive epigram captures the stilldominant Austinian positivists' widespread cynicism towards the claim that the rules of the international system can be studied jurisprudentially.

International lawyers have not taken this sort of marginalisation lying down. However, their counterattack has been both feeble and misdirected; concentrating primarily on efforts to prove that international law is very similar to the positive law applicable within states. This strategy has not been intellectually convincing, nor can it be empirically sustained once divine and naturalist sources of law are discarded in favour of positivism.

That international "law" is not law in the positivist sense may be irrefutable but is also irrelevant. Whatever label is attached to it, the normative structure of the international system is perfectly capable of being studied with a view to generating a teleological jurisprudence. Indeed, international law is the best place to study some of the fundamental teleological issues that arise not only in the international, but also in national legal systems. This makes it odd that it is not more frequently used as a field for investigation.

Up to a point, the Austinians are empirically right. The international system of states is fundamentally different from any national community of persons and of corporate entities. It is not helpful to ignore those differences or to cling to the reifying notion that states are "persons" analogous to the citizens of a nation. Some of the differences are of great potential interest. In a nation, Machiavelli noted, "there cannot be good laws where there are not good arms." In the international community, however, there are ample signs that rules unenforced by good arms are yet capable of obligating states and quite often even achieve habitual compliance.

The Austinians, beginning with a defensible empirical observation about the difference between national laws and international rules, deduce from the difference that rules governing conduct which are not "law" in the positivist sense cannot usefully be studied as a system of community-based obligations. It is *this* deduction - not the empirical observation - which is wrong. Indeed, it is precisely the curious paradox of obligation in the international rule system that should whet our speculative appetite, provoking the opening, not the closing, of jurisprudential inquiry. Why should rules, unsupported by an effective structure of coercion comparable to a national police force, nevertheless elicit so much compliance, even against perceived self-interest, on the part of sovereign states?

Perhaps finding an answer to this question can help us to find a key to a better, yet realistic, world order. The answer, if there is one, may also incidentally prove useful in designing more widely obeyed, less coerced, laws for ordering the lives of our cities and states. A series of events connected with the role of the U.S. Navy in protecting U.S.-flagged vessels in the Persian Gulf serves to illustrate the paradoxical phenomenon of uncoerced compliance in a situation where the rule conflicts with perceived self-interest. Early in 1988, the Department of Defense became aware of a ship approaching the gulf with a load of Chinese-made Silkworm missiles en route to Iran.

The Department believed the successful delivery of these potent weapons would increase materially the danger to both protected and protecting U.S. ships in the region. It therefore argued for permission to intercept the delivery. The Department of State countered that such a search and seizure on the high seas, under the universally recognized rules of war and neutrality, would constitute aggressive blockade, an act tantamount to a declaration of war against Iran. In the event, the delivery ship and its cargo of missiles were allowed to pass. Deference to systemic rules had won out over tactical advantage in the internal struggle for control of U.S. policy.

Why should this have been so? In the absence of a world government and a global coercive power to enforce its laws, why did the U.S. Government, with its evident power to do as it wished, choose to "play by the rules" despite the considerable short-term strategic advantage to be gained by seizing the Silkworms before they could be delivered? Why did preeminent American power defer to the rules of the sanction less system? At least part of the answer to this question, quietly given by the

State Department to the Department of Defense, is that the international rules of neutrality have attained a high degree of recognized legitimacy and must not be violated lightly.

Specifically, they are well understood, enjoy a long pedigree and are *part of a consistent* framework of rules - the jus in hello - governing and restraining the use of force in conflicts. To violate a set of rules of such widely recognized legitimacy, the State Department argued, would transform the U.S. posture in the gulf from that of a neutral to one of belligerency. That could end Washington's role as an honest broker seeking to promote peace negotiations. It would also undermine the carefully crafted historic "rules of the game" applicable to wars, rules that are widely perceived to be in the interest of all states.

Such explanations for deferring to a rule in preference to taking a short-term advantage are the policymaker's equivalent of the philosopher's quest for a theory of legitimacy. Washington voluntarily chose to obey a rule in the Persian Gulf conflict. Yet it does not always obey all international rules. Some rules are harder to disobey - more persuasive in their pull to compliance-than others. This is known intuitively by the legions of Americans who deliberately underreport the dutiable price of goods purchased abroad, and by the aficionados who smuggle Cuban cigars into the country behind pocket handkerchiefs, but would not otherwise commit criminal fraud. That some rules in themselves seem to exert more pull to compliance than others is the starting point in the search for a theory of legitimacy.

The questions raised by such examples of obedience and disobedience, however, are more interesting when examined in the context of the international than of the national community. It is the voluntariness of international compliance that heightens the mystery and lures us with the possibility of discovery. Thus, while the Austinians are right in pointing to important differences between the place of law in national society and the place of rules in the society of nations, those differences do not justify the closing of the international rule system to jurisprudential inquiry.

Indeed, such inquiry into the international system ought to be aided by the insights developed by the study of national and sub national communities. Research into the teleology of national legal systems has led the way to recognition of the role of legitimacy, as distinct from coercion, as the key to legal order and systematic obedience. While most students of national systems, except perhaps for a few utopians such as Foucault, agree with Machiavelli that governance requires some exercise of power by an elite supported by coercive force, few any longer believe the Austinians' claim that this necessary condition is also a sufficient one.

Having reached this conclusion, most students of law, power and structure in society have sought to identify other characteristics that conduce to the rule of law. Ronald Dworkin identifies three such characteristics: fairness, justice and integrity (the last being a principled, more sensitive variant of consistency). Jórgen Habermas emphasizes the role of discursive validation, following the tradition of Aeschylus and Aristotle. Important scholarship on contract theory has demonstrated that coercion need not be an essential element in ensuring the efficacy of a contract, which is more accurately seen as self-enforcing obligation. In fact, much recent work focusing on the phenomenon of obedience and obligation in national societies concerns itself primarily with non coercive factors conducing to consensual compliance.

While some such studies have emphasized the role of strategic concepts that gain voluntary compliance by mutualizing advantage, others, beginning with the seminal work of Max Weber, have emphasized the role of legitimacy and legitimation. Weber's analysis stressed process legitimacy. He hypothesized that rules tend to achieve compliance when they, themselves, comply with secondary rules about how and by whom rules are to be made and interpreted. In his view, a sovereign's command is more likely to be obeyed if the subject perceives both the rule and the ruler as legitimate. Somewhat different concepts of legitimacy have been developed by Habermas and by neo-Marxist philosophers. Oscar Schachter working in the field of international normativity has elucidated and emphasized the role of "competence and authority" in endowing a rule with capacity to obligate. All have in common, however, their emphasis on non coercive factors as conducing to rule-compliant behaviour.

It thus appears that, despite its residual Austinian propensities, national jurisprudence has quite a bit to say to the international system precisely because there is empirical evidence that, in both systems, non coercive factors play an important part in conducing to rule/law-compliant behaviour. The special value to both national and international jurisprudential inquiry of studying the international system, however, lies in its unalloyed non coercive state. While the dependence of the international system on voluntary compliance is often (and justly) perceived as a weakness, it happens to afford a singular opportunity.

Critics of efforts to study legitimacy as a non coercive factor conducing to compliance in national legal systems have been able to argue that this factor necessarily eludes researchers because it cannot be isolated from other, authoritarian, elements compelling obedience. That critique loses its force, however, in the international context. Thus, the operation of the non coercive element, or, specifically, legitimacy, becomes easier to isolate and study in the interstate system than in societies of persons, where the coercive sovereign always lurks in the background.

Yet there is a stronger motivation for studying legitimacy in the international system than the academic objective of creating a bridge from national to international speculative jurisprudence. A teleology that makes legitimacy its hypothetical center envisages - for purposes of speculative inquiry - the possibility of an orderly community functioning by consent and validated obligation, rather than by coercion. This is surely the realistic approach to an international jurisprudential teleology: one that examines the objective properties of the global rule system so as to study whether and how it may advance or perfect itself in accordance with the propensities of those observable properties. That inquiry begins with the unexplained, yet evident, paradox that autonomous actors systematically engage in rule-determined conduct, not infrequently in the face of a strong countervailing desire to pursue realizable short-term gratification in violation of the rules.

Admittedly, the rule system of the community of states is far from perfected: absence of rules and disobedience continue to be important dissonant features. But it is too readily assumed that these deficiencies are attributable primarily to the lack of an Austinian sovereign with police powers. The weakness of this explanation is its failure to account for significant deviance: that many rules are obeyed much of the time. What if, instead, rule disobedience, or a rule void, were attributable - in whole or in part -not to the absence of coercive power to enforce the rules but to the perceived lack of legitimacy of the actual or proposed rules themselves and of the rule-making and rule-applying institutions of the international system? Put another way, perhaps failure to obey the rules can best be studied through a better understanding of its opposite: voluntary deference to them.

That might be rather good news. Since the world is not about to create a global super sovereign with overriding enforcement powers, it might be encouraging to know that these are not the prerequisites of a developed, functioning international community. It would be even more helpful to know that the global system of rules could be further refined and developed, even in the absence of the Austinian factors, by augmenting the legitimacy of rules and institutions. It would spur the social imagination to realize that the creation of a global regime with enforcement power might only be the final culmination of a process capable of gradually perfecting the community, not the sine qua non for system building.

If such a non coercive, or voluntarist, community were a reasonable goal of the study of legitimation, the resulting society of states would still not resemble the modern nation. In place of coercion, there is only the claim to compliance, based on social entitlement, which a legitimate rule makes on, and on behalf of, all members of the community. In this sense, the international community more closely resembles a membership club with house rules. Membership confers a desirable status, which is manifested when the members have internalized socially functional and status-rooted privileges and duties. Membership is reinforced by valid governance, shared experience, reciprocal gestures of deference and recognition, common rituals, mature common expectations and the successful pursuit of shared goals. Obedience to law, in contrast, at least in part is recognition of the coercive power of the organized state.

In both the state and the voluntarist international system, obedience to commands is evidence of the existence of an organized community. The international community, however, does not closely resemble the modern state, precisely because the activist state exists to issue and enforce sovereign commands, while the more passive international community exists to legitimize, or withhold legitimacy from, institutions, rules and its members and their conduct. The legitimacy of a rule, or of a rule-making or rule-applying institution, is a function of the perception of those in the community concerned that the rule, or the institution, has come into being endowed with legitimacy: that is, in accordance with right process.

What "right process" means in practice is the subject of the remainder of this chapter. Pursuing this line of inquiry, we will focus most of our attention on the legitimacy of *rules*, although attention will also have to be paid to the legitimacy of those institutions and processes through which the rules come into being. In our inquiry we will begin with the rules themselves: their literary structure, origins, internal consistency, reasonableness, utility in achieving stated ends and connection to the overall rule system, and the extent to which their origins and application comport with the international community's "rules about rules." It is the underlying hypothesis of this chapter that rules, to varying degrees, contain the determining elements of their own legitimacy.

If legitimacy can be studied, it can also be deliberately nourished. There lies the practical rationale of this inquiry. Someday, perhaps, the international system will come to have law and legal institutions that mirror their domestic counterparts. But that is not now, and it is not likely to be in the foreseeable future. H. L. A. Hart put it more gently: "though it is consistent with the usage of the last 150 years to use the expression 'law' here, the absence of an international legislature, courts with compulsory jurisdiction, and centrally organized sanctions ha[s] inspired misgivings, at any rate in the breasts of legal theorists." Such misgivings, however, are not a cause for despair, nor should they be the end of the road of theoretical inquiry. On the contrary, the misgivings are valid but, for that very reason, are precisely the right starting point in the search for those elements which conduce to the growth of an orderly voluntarist international community and system of rules.

Four elements - the indicators of rule legitimacy in the community of states - are identified and studied in this chapter. They are determinacy, symbolic validation, coherence and adherence (to a normative hierarchy). To the extent rules exhibit these properties, they appear to exert a strong pull on states to comply with their commands. To the extent these elements are not present, rules seem to be easier to avoid by a state tempted to pursue its short-term self-interest. This is not to say that the legitimacy of a rule can be deduced solely by counting how often it is obeyed or disobeyed. While its legitimacy may exert a powerful pull on state conduct, yet other pulls may be stronger in a particular circumstance.

The chance to take a quick, decisive advantage may overcome the counter pull of even a highly legitimate rule. In such circumstances, legitimacy is indicated not by obedience, but by the discomfort disobedience induces in the violator. The variable to watch is not compliance but the strength of the compliance pull, whether or not the rule achieves actual compliance in any one case. Each rule has an inherent pull power that is independent of the circumstances in which it is exerted, and that varies from rule to rule.

This pull power is its index of legitimacy. For example, the rule that makes it improper for one state to infiltrate spies into another state in the guise of diplomats is formally acknowledged by almost every state, yet it enjoys so low a degree of legitimacy as to exert virtually no pull towards compliance. As Schachter observes, "some 'laws,' though enacted properly, have so low a degree of probable compliance that they are treated as 'dead letters' and ... some treaties, while properly concluded, are considered 'scraps of paper.' "By way of contrast, we have noted, the rules pertaining to belligerency and neutrality actually exerted a very high level of pull on Washington in connection with the Silkworm missile shipment in the Persian Gulf.

The study of legitimacy thus focuses on the inherent capacity of a rule to exert pressure on states to comply. This focus on the properties of rules, of course, is not a self-sufficient account of the socialisation process. How rules are made, interpreted and applied is part of a dynamic, expansive and complex set of social phenomena. That complexity can be approached, however, by beginning with the rules themselves. Those seemingly inert constructs are shaped by other, more dynamic forces and, like tree trunks and seashells, tell their own story about the winds and tides that become an experiential part of their shape and texture.

DETERMINACY AND LEGITIMACY

What determines the degree of legitimacy of any particular rule text or rule-making process? Or, to ask the same question another way: what observable characteristics of a rule or of a rule-making institution raise or lower the probability that its commands will be perceived to obligate? It is to such questions that the remainder of this analysis is addressed. One could approach the social phenomenon of non coerced obedience directly, through such various openings as are afforded by the study of myths, game theory or contractarian notions of social compact. Instead, these and other socializing forces will be approached indirectly, through a unifying notion of rule legitimacy; that is, by approaching dynamic social forces through those rules which the society chooses to obey or to regard as obligatory.

It should be borne in mind, however, that the norm-centered question - what is it about the properties of a rule that conduces to voluntary compliance? - is merely the lawyer's approach to larger sociological, anthropological and political questions: what conduces to the formation of communities and what induces members of a community to live by its rules? Let us begin by examining the literary properties of the text itself that conduce to voluntary compliance or induce a sense of obligation in those to whom the rule is addressed.

Perhaps the most self-evident of all characteristics making for legitimacy is textual determinacy. What is meant by this is the ability of the text to convey a clear message, to appear transparent in the sense that one can see through the language to the meaning. Obviously, rules with a readily ascertainable meaning have a better chance than those that do not to regulate the conduct of those to whom the rule is addressed or exert a compliance pull on their policymaking process. Those addressed will know precisely what is expected of them, which is a necessary first step towards compliance.

To illustrate the point, let us compare two textual formulations defining the boundary of the underwater continental shelf. The 1958 Convention places the shelf at "a depth of 200 meters or, beyond that limit, to where the depth of the superjacent waters admits of the exploitation of the natural resources of the said areas." The 1982 Convention on the Law of the Sea, on the other hand, is far more detailed and specific. It defines the shelf as "the natural prolongation of ... land territory to the outer edge of the continental margin, or to a distance of 200 nautical miles from the baselines from which the breadth of the territorial sea is measured," but takes into account such specific factors as "the thickness of sedimentary rocks" and imposes an outermost limit that "shall not exceed 100 nautical miles from the 2,500 meter isobaths," which, in turn, is a line connecting the points where the waters are 2,500 meters deep.

The 1982 standard, despite its complexity, is far more determinate than the elastic standard in the 1958 Convention, which, in a sense, established no rule at all. Back in 1958, the parties simply covered their differences and uncertainties with a formula, whose content was left in abeyance pending further work by negotiators, courts, and administrators and by the evolution of customary state practice. The vagueness of the rule did permit a flexible response to further advances in technology, a benefit inherent in indeterminacy.

Indeterminacy, however, has costs. Indeterminate normative standards not only make it harder to know what conformity is expected, but also make it easier to justify noncompliance. Put conversely, the more determinate the standard, the more difficult it is to resist the pull of the rule to compliance and to justify noncompliance. Since few persons or states wish to be perceived as acting in obvious violation of a generally recognized rule of conduct, they may try to resolve the conflicts between the demands of a rule and their desire not to be fettered, by "interpreting" the rule permissively. A determinate rule is less elastic and thus less amenable to such evasive strategy than an indeterminate one.

A good example of this consequence of determinacy is afforded by the recent litigation between Nicaragua and the United States before the International Court of Justice. From the moment it became apparent that Nicaragua was preparing to sue the United States, State Department attorneys began to prepare the defense strategy. One option considered was invoking the "Connally reservation," which, as part of the U.S. acceptance of the jurisdiction of the International Court of Justice, specifically barred the Court from entertaining any case that pertains to "domestic" matters as determined by the United States.

Yet the American lawyers chose not to use this absolute defense. Instead, they tried in various other ways to challenge the Court's authority. They argued that the dispute was already before the Organisation of American States and the UN Security Council; that it was not a legal dispute at all, but a political one; that Nicaragua, having failed to perfect its acceptance of the Court's compulsory jurisdiction, had no right to implead the United States. The failure of the lawyers to use the Connally shield is all the more remarkable because, whereas the reservation gave the United States a self-judging escape from the Court's jurisdiction, all the other defenses left the key jurisdictional decision up to the Court, which rejected every one. Had the U.S. Government simply faced the Court with a "finding" that the mining of Nicaragua's harbors was a "domestic" matter for the United States that would have ended the litigation. Instead, the United States went on to lose, not only on the matter of jurisdiction, but also, eventually, on the merits.

Why was the Connally shield rejected? The answer, surely, lies in its determinacy. Anyone reading its language would instantly understand that the reservation, while rather open-ended, nevertheless was not intended to cover such matters as the CIA's alleged mining of the harbors of a nation with which the United States was not at war. Although the term "domestic matter" is not so determinate as to bar all differences of interpretation -that, after all, is why its interpretation was reserved to the U.S. Government and not left to the Court - no reasonable interpretation of the concept could be stretched to cover the events in question. The U.S. legal strategists, anxious to do everything possible to stay out of court, nonetheless were unwilling to subject their client to the obloquy that would have ensued had the Connally shield been deployed. Interest gratification, convenience and advantage were sacrificed so as not to be seen as absurd.

Such foreboding of shame and ridicule is an excellent guide to determinacy. If a party seeking to justify its conduct interprets a rule in such a way as to evoke widespread derision, then the rule has determinacy. The violator's evidently tortured definition of the rule can be seen to exceed its range of plausible meanings. Thus, while it may be true in theory, as Wittgenstein has charged, that no "course of action could be determined by a rule because every course of action can be made out to accord with the rule," some rules are less malleable, less open to manipulation, than others. Although Wittgenstein's point has merit - and has recently been wittily adumbrated by Professor Duncan Kennedy - in practice, determinacy is not an illusion. No verbal formulas are entirely determinate, but some are more so than others.

Bibliography

Abbott, Kenneth W., and Duncan Snidal. 2000. "Hard and Soft Law in International Governance." *International Organization* 54:421-56.

Aslan, Reza. 2009. *Cosmic War: God, Globalization and the End of the War on Terror*. New York: Random House.

Baceviich. 2008. *The Limits of Power*. New York: Metropolitan Books.

Bass, Gary Jonathan. 2000. *Stay the Hand of Vengeance*. Princeton: Princeton University Press.

Benvenisti, Eyal. 1999. "Exit and Voice in the Age of Globalization." *Michigan Law Review* 98:167-213.

Bull, Headley. 1977. *The Anarchical Society*. New York: Columbia University Press.

Dezalay, Yves, and Bryant G. Garth. 1996. Dealing in Virtue. Chicago: University of Chicago Press. Chs. 4-5, pp. 63-114.

Donnelly, Jack. 2002. *Universal Human Rights in Theory and Practice*. rev. ed., Ithaca: Cornell University Press.

Dunne, Tim and Wheeler, Nicholas, eds. 1999. *Human Rights in Global Politics*. Cambridge: Cambridge University Press.

Friedman, Thomas L. 2000. The Lexus and the Olive Tree. New York: Anchor Books. Ch. 4, pp. 44-72.

Friedman, Lawrence M. 2001. "Erewhon: The Coming Global Legal Order." *Stanford Journal of International Law* 37:347-64.

Ginsburg, Tom. 2005. "Bounded Discretion in International Judicial Lawmaking." *Virginia Journal of International Law* 54:631-673.

Halliday, Terence C., and Pavel Osinsky. 2006. "Globalization of Law." *Annual Review of Sociology* 32:447–70.

Harlow, Carol. 2006. "Global Administrative Law: The Quest for Principles and Values." *The European Journal of International Law* 17:187-214.

Headley, John. 2008. *The Europeanization of the World.* Princeton: Princeton University Press.

Held, David, Anthony McGrew, David Goldblatt, and Jonathan Perraton. 1999. *Global Transformations: Politics, Economics and Culture*. Stanford: Stanford University Press.

Helfer, Laurence R., and Anne-Marie Slaughter. 2005. "Why States Create International Tribunals: A Response to Professors Posner and Yoo." *California Law Review* 93:899-956.

Jayasuriya, Kanishka. 1999. "The Rule of Law in the Era of Globalization: Globalization, Law and the Transformation of Sovereignty: The Emergence of Global Regulatory Governance." *Indiana Journal of Global Legal Studies* 6:425-56.

Kagan, Robert. 2003. *Of Paradise and Power: America and Europe in the New World Order.* New York: Knopf.

Keck, Margaret E., and Kathryn Sikkink. 1998. *Activists beyond Borders: Advocacy Networks in International Politics.* Ithaca: Cornell University Press.

Krisch, Nico, and Benedict Kingsbury. 2006. "Introduction: Global Governance and Global Administrative Law in the

International Legal Order." *The European Journal of International Law* 17:1-13.

Merry, Sally Engle. 2006. *Human Rights & Gender Violence: Translating International Law into Local Justice*. Chicago: University of Chicago Press.

Neier, Aryeh. 1991. *Taking Liberties: Four Decades in the Struggle for Rights*. New York: Free Press.

Posner, Eric A., and John C. Yoo. 2005. "Judicial Independence in International Tribunals." *California Law Review* 93:1-74.

Robertson, Geoffrey. 1999. *Crimes Against Humanity: The Struggle for Global Justice*. New York: Penguin Books.

Robertson, Geoffrey. 2006. *Crimes Against Humanity*. New York: The New Press.

Sen, Amartya. 2006. *Identity and Violence*. New York: W.W. Norton.

Slaughter, Anne-Marie. 2003. "A Global Community of Courts." *Harvard International Law Journal* 44:191-219.

Slaughter, Anne-Marie. 2004. *A New World Order*. Princeton: Princeton University Press.

Index

A

Actor and Observer, 55
Analytical Tools and Procedures, 59
Apparent Paradoxes, 241
Art of Guessing in Politics, 2
Assumptions, 59, 64, 65, 67, 78, 79, 85, 86, 141, 218, 224, 250, 265, 266

C

Competing Visions, 131, 133, 137, 235
Conceptual Schemes, 36, 59, 61, 66
Constants and Variables, 70

D

Debate on the Global Compact, 177
Determinacy and Legitimacy, 269

E

Encyclopedic Science, 24
Enthusiasm of the Advocates, 177
Environmental Concepts, 74
Environmental Influences Reconsidered, 83

G

Global Compact, 167, 168, 169, 170, 173, 174, 175, 176, 177, 178, 179, 180, 181, 182, 183, 184, 185, 186, 187, 188

H

Heredity and Environment, 71, 73
Hostility to Partnership, 170
Hypotheses, 40, 46, 59, 62, 65, 66, 67, 69, 70, 82, 102

I

Intellectual Operations, 37, 44, 48, 49, 55, 59, 78, 79
International Political Order, 131, 132, 133, 137, 145, 147, 156, 161, 162, 163, 164, 165
International Politics, 1, 2, 32, 33, 35, 36, 37, 41, 42, 44, 55, 56,

60, 61, 62, 63, 70, 71, 72, 73, 77, 79, 80, 86, 88, 89, 102, 131, 132, 133, 134, 136, 137, 138, 139, 140, 141, 143, 144, 145, 146, 150, 151, 152, 153, 154, 155, 156, 158, 161, 162, 163, 164, 165, 174, 251, 253, 254, 256

International Politics of Exception, 131, 133, 134, 137, 139, 144, 145, 146, 152, 156, 158, 161, 162, 163

International Security Order, 138

Interpreting Innovations in Vocabulary, 236

K

Khalistani Movement, 198, 205, 206, 207, 208, 210

Koselleck, 218, 223, 231

L

Language, 12, 23, 30, 37, 38, 39, 40, 43, 94, 97, 110, 188, 209, 214, 236, 241, 242, 250, 272

League, 1, 2, 24, 30, 35, 209, 219, 220, 225, 226, 227, 228, 233, 234, 243, 244

Local and National Determinants, 114

M

Malawian Economic Policy, 117

Mass Politics in India, 189

Methodological Foundation, 32

Mistrust of the Critics, 182

Mozambican Refugees, 106, 107, 108, 109, 110, 111, 112, 115, 118, 121, 123, 125, 126, 127, 129

N

Natural Conditions, 114

Normalizing Exceptionality, 145

Normative and Skeptical Views, 138

O

One-party Regime, 105

Organisational Rhetoric, 229, 230, 231, 232, 238, 240, 241, 247, 250

P

Periodisation, 218

Political Prophecies, 3

Politicizing Secularism, 253

Politics of International Development, 167

Preliminary Remarks, 233

Premises, 47, 59, 65, 67, 82, 183, 239

R

Refugee Economic Activities, 117

Refugee Policy, 106, 112, 113,114, 119, 121, 124, 125

Regional and International Politics, 123
Religiosity of Nationalist Movements, 205

S

Settlement Policy, 114
Sociology and Institutionalism, 153
Survival of the One-Party System, 121

T

The Basic Tool, 37, 40
The Indian Nation-state, 189, 209, 212, 213
The United Nations, 99, 102, 105, 110, 132, 134, 139, 142, 143, 167, 168, 170, 172, 181, 217, 219, 220, 222, 224, 225, 227, 228, 233, 235, 236, 237, 238, 242, 244, 246, 248, 249, 250
Theories of Social Systems, 99
Theories of Strategy, 88, 107, 112
Time Layers, 217, 218, 221, 228, 251

U

Universal Sovereignty, 145, 147, 148, 150, 151, 153, 156, 162

V

Vishva Hindu Parishad, 191, 211
Vocabulary Innovations, 228, 229, 233, 236, 242

W

World Organisations, 218, 221, 222, 224, 229, 238, 241, 242, 244